Buying a Home
in
Greece

A Survival Handbook

by
Joanna Styles

SURVIVAL BOOKS • LONDON • ENGLAND

First published 2000 (as Buying a Home in Greece & Cyprus)
Second Edition 2001 (as Buying a Home in Greece & Cyprus)
Third Edition 2005

Survival Books Limited, 1st Floor,
60 St James's Street, London SW1A 1ZN, United Kingdom
☎ +44 (0)20-7493 4244, 🖥 +44 (0)20-7491 0605
✉ info@survivalbooks.net
💻 www.survivalbooks.net
To order books, please refer to page 333.

British Library Cataloguing in Publication Data.
A CIP record for this book is available
from the British Library.
ISBN 1 901130 06 1

Printed and bound in Finland by WS Bookwell Ltd.

ACKNOWLEDGEMENTS

M y sincere thanks to all those who contributed to the successful publication of this book, in particular the many people who took the time and trouble to read and comment on the draft versions. I would especially like to thank David Hampshire (editor); Janet Darbey in Corfu (for her invaluable help and advice with research); Sue Harris (proofreading); Joe & Kerry Laredo (layout and desktop publishing); the staff at Corfu Estate Agents, particularly Sarah Wood and Kostas Pouliasis (for their help with taxation figures); Evie Efthimiou (All Greece 4U) and Faris Nejad (Pelion Properties) for providing photographs; countless staff at government offices and private businesses; and everyone else who contributed in any way whom I have omitted to mention. Also a special thank-you to Jim Watson for the superb illustrations, cartoons, maps and cover.

TITLES BY SURVIVAL BOOKS

Alien's Guides
Britain; France

The Best Places To Buy A Home
France; Spain

Buying A Home
Abroad; Cyprus; Florida;
France; Greece; Ireland; Italy;
Portugal; South Africa; Spain;
Buying, Selling & Letting
Property (UK)

**Foreigners Abroad: Triumphs
& Disasters**
France; Spain

Lifeline Regional Guides
Costa Blanca; Costa del Sol;
Dordogne/Lot; Normandy;
Poitou-Charentes

Living And Working
Abroad; America;
Australia; Britain; Canada;
The European Union;
The Far East; France; Germany;
The Gulf States & Saudi Arabia;
Holland, Belgium & Luxembourg;
Ireland; Italy; London;
New Zealand; Spain;
Switzerland

Making A Living
France; Spain

Other Titles
Renovating & Maintaining
Your French Home;
Retiring Abroad

Order forms are on page 333.

WHAT READERS & REVIEWERS

When you buy a model plane for your child, a video recorder, or some new computer gizmo, you get with it a leaflet or booklet pleading 'Read Me First', or bearing large friendly letters or bold type saying 'IMPORTANT – follow the instructions carefully'. This book should be similarly supplied to all those entering France with anything more durable than a 5-day return ticket. It is worth reading even if you are just visiting briefly, or if you have lived here for years and feel totally knowledgeable and secure. But if you need to find out how France works then it is indispensable. Native French people probably have a less thorough understanding of how their country functions. – Where it is most essential, the book is most up to the minute.

LIVING FRANCE

Rarely has a 'survival guide' contained such useful advice. This book dispels doubts for first-time travellers, yet is also useful for seasoned globetrotters – In a word, if you're planning to move to the USA or go there for a long-term stay, then buy this book both for general reading and as a ready-reference.

AMERICAN CITIZENS ABROAD

It is everything you always wanted to ask but didn't for fear of the contemptuous put down – The best English-language guide – Its pages are stuffed with practical information on everyday subjects and are designed to complement the traditional guidebook.

SWISS NEWS

A complete revelation to me – I found it both enlightening and interesting, not to mention amusing.

CAROLE CLARK

Let's say it at once. David Hampshire's *Living and Working in France* is the best handbook ever produced for visitors and foreign residents in this country; indeed, my discussion with locals showed that it has much to teach even those born and bred in l'Hexagone. – It is Hampshire's meticulous detail which lifts his work way beyond the range of other books with similar titles. Often you think of a supplementary question and search for the answer in vain. With Hampshire this is rarely the case. – He writes with great clarity (and gives French equivalents of all key terms), a touch of humour and a ready eye for the odd (and often illuminating) fact. – This book is absolutely indispensable.

THE RIVIERA REPORTER

A mine of information – I may have avoided some embarrassments and frights if I had read it prior to my first Swiss encounters – Deserves an honoured place on any newcomer's bookshelf.

ENGLISH TEACHERS ASSOCIATION, SWITZERLAND

Have Said About Survival Books

What a great work, wealth of useful information, well-balanced wording and accuracy in details. My compliments!

THOMAS MÜLLER

This handbook has all the practical information one needs to set up home in the UK – The sheer volume of information is almost daunting – Highly recommended for anyone moving to the UK.

AMERICAN CITIZENS ABROAD

A very good book which has answered so many questions and even some I hadn't thought of – I would certainly recommend it.

BRIAN FAIRMAN

We would like to congratulate you on this work: it is really super! We hand it out to our expatriates and they read it with great interest and pleasure.

ICI (SWITZERLAND) AG

Covers just about all the things you want to know on the subject – In answer to the desert island question about the one how-to book on France, this book would be it – Almost 500 pages of solid accurate reading – This book is about enjoyment as much as survival.

THE RECORDER

It's so funny – I love it and definitely need a copy of my own – Thanks very much for having written such a humorous and helpful book.

HEIDI GUILIANI

A must for all foreigners coming to Switzerland.

ANTOINETTE O'DONOGHUE

A comprehensive guide to all things French, written in a highly readable and amusing style, for anyone planning to live, work or retire in France.

THE TIMES

A concise, thorough account of the DOs and DON'Ts for a foreigner in Switzerland – Crammed with useful information and lightened with humorous quips which make the facts more readable.

AMERICAN CITIZENS ABROAD

Covers every conceivable question that may be asked concerning everyday life – I know of no other book that could take the place of this one.

FRANCE IN PRINT

Hats off to *Living and Working in Switzerland*!

RONNIE ALMEIDA

CONTENTS

9. LETTING

10. MISCELLANEOUS MATTERS 253

APPENDICES 291

INDEX 319

ORDER FORMS 333

IMPORTANT NOTE

Readers should note that the laws and regulations concerning buying property in Greece aren't the same as in other countries and are liable to change periodically. **I cannot recommend too strongly that you always check with an official and reliable source (not necessarily the same) and take expert legal advice before paying any money or signing any legal documents. Don't, however, believe everything you're told or read – even, dare I say it, herein!**

To help you obtain further information and verify data with official sources, useful addresses and references to other sources of information have been included in all chapters and in Appendices A to C. Important points have been emphasised throughout the book in **bold** print, some of which it would be expensive or foolish to disregard. Ignore them at your peril or cost. Unless specifically stated, the reference to any company, organisation, product or publication in this book doesn't constitute an endorsement or recommendation.

THE AUTHOR

Joanna Styles was born in London but has lived and worked for many years on the Costa del Sol, Spain. She is a freelance writer and the author of several books, including *The Best Places to Buy a Home in Spain, Buying a Home in Greece, Living & Working in the European Union* and *Costa del Sol Lifeline*, all published by Survival Books. She also regularly contributes to and updates many other Survival Books publications. Joanna is married with two daughters.

AUTHOR'S NOTES

- This book was previously published as *Buying a Home in Greece and Cyprus*.

- Various names are often used for a town or region in Greece. This book generally gives the most common name used internationally.

- Prices quoted should be taken as estimates only, although they were mostly correct when going to print and fortunately don't usually change overnight in Greece. Prices in this book include value added tax (unless otherwise indicated), although prices in Greece are sometimes quoted exclusive of tax.

- His/he/him (etc.) also mean her/she/her (no offence ladies!). This is done simply to make life easier for both the reader and, in particular, the author, and **isn't** intended to be sexist.

- Warnings and important points are shown in **bold** type.

- All spelling is (or should be) English and not American.

- All times are shown using am (*ante meridiem*) for before noon and pm (*post meridiem*) for after noon. All times are local, so check the time difference when making international telephone calls.

- The following symbols are used in this book: ☎ (telephone), 🖩 (fax), 🖥 (internet) and ✉ (email).

- Frequent references are made throughout this book to the European Union (EU), which comprises Austria, Belgium, Cyprus, the Czech Republic, Denmark, Estonia, Finland, France, Germany, Greece, Hungary, Ireland, Italy, Latvia, Lithuania, Luxembourg, Malta, the Netherlands, Poland, Portugal, Slovakia, Slovenia, Spain, Sweden and the United Kingdom, and the European Economic Area (EEA), which comprises the EU countries plus Iceland, Liechtenstein and Norway.

- Lists of useful addresses, further reading and useful websites are contained in **Appendices A** to **C** respectively.

- For those who are unfamiliar with the metric system of weights and measures, conversion tables are included in **Appendix D**.

- Maps of Greece showing the regions and transport networks are included in **Appendix E** and a map of the eastern Mediterranean is on page 6.

- Tables showing the scheduled airline services between Greece and the UK and a list of airlines can be found in **Appendix F**.

INTRODUCTION

If you're planning to buy a home in Greece or even just thinking about it, this is **THE BOOK** for you! Whether you want a villa, farmhouse, townhouse or an apartment, a holiday or a permanent home, this book will help make your dreams come true. The purpose of *Buying a Home in Greece* is to provide you with the information necessary to help you choose the most favourable location and the most appropriate home **to satisfy your individual requirements.** Most importantly, it will help you avoid the pitfalls and risks associated with buying a home abroad, which for most people is one of the largest financial transactions they will undertake during their lifetimes.

You may already own property in your home country; however, buying a home in Greece (or in any foreign country) is a different matter altogether. One of the most common mistakes many people make when buying a home abroad is to assume that the laws and purchase procedures are the same as in their home country. **This is almost certainly not the case!** Buying property in Greece is generally safe, although if you don't obtain legal advice and follow the rules provided for your protection, a purchase can result in a serious financial loss – as many people have discovered to their cost.

Before buying a home in Greece you need to ask yourself *exactly* why you want to buy a home there? Do you 'simply' want a holiday home, is your primary concern a long-term investment, or do you wish to work or retire there? Where and what can you afford to buy? Do you plan to let your home to offset the running costs? How will local taxes affect your investment? *Buying a Home in Greece* will help you answer these and many other questions. It won't, however, tell you where to live, what to buy, or, having made your decision, whether you will be happy – that part is up to you!

For many people, buying a home in Greece was previously a case of pot luck. However, with a copy of *Buying a Home in Greece* to hand you'll have a wealth of priceless information at your fingertips – information derived from a variety of sources, both official and unofficial, not least the hard won personal experiences of the author, her friends, colleagues and acquaintances. Furthermore, this book will reduce the risk of making an expensive mistake that you may bitterly regret later and will help you make informed decisions and calculated judgements instead of uneducated guesses (forewarned is forearmed!). **Most important of all, it will help you save money and will repay your investment many times over.**

The world-wide recession in the early '90s caused an upheaval in world property markets, during which many so-called 'gilt-edged' property investments went to the wall. However, property remains one of the best long-term investments and it's certainly one of the most pleasurable. Buying a home in Greece is a wonderful way to make new friends, broaden your horizons and revitalise your life – and it provides a welcome bolt-hole to recuperate from the stresses and strains of modern life. I trust this book will help you avoid pitfalls and smooth your way to many happy years in your new home, secure in the knowledge that you have made the right decision.

Good luck!   **Joanna Styles**
                                                                     March 2005

1.

MAJOR CONSIDERATIONS

Buying a home in Greece is not only a major financial commitment, but also a decision that can have a huge influence on other aspects of your life, including your health, security and safety, your family relationships and friendships, your lifestyle, your opinions and your outlook. You also need to take into consideration any restrictions that might affect your choice of location and type of property, such as whether you will need (or be able) to learn Greek, whether you will be able (or permitted) to find work, whether you can adapt to and enjoy the climate, whether you will able to take your pets with you, and not least, whether you will be able to afford the kind of home (and lifestyle) that you want. In order to ensure that you're making the right move, it's advisable to face these and other major considerations before making any irrevocable decisions.

WHY GREECE?

Greece – land of the Gods and the ancient cradle of modern civilisation – is a country rich in culture, history and tradition. The country evokes images of glorious summer sunshine and cobalt blue skies, endless white sandy beaches, picturesque whitewashed villages and deserted islands, sleepy harbours and colourful fishing boats, friendly people (the Greek work for 'foreigner' is the same as 'guest'), and a simple, relaxed way of life. Greece is largely unspoilt with little industry and few high-rise buildings outside the major cities – the islands in particular have escaped the scourge of indiscriminate development common in many other Mediterranean countries. The country also enjoys one of the healthiest diets in Europe, consisting largely of fish, fresh fruit and vegetables, olive oil and wine. Greece is one of the most beautiful countries in the world and a holiday paradise with more than 1,400 islands (relatively few of which are inhabited), over 15,000km (9,320mi) of coastline and some of the finest beaches in the world. It's also one of Europe's last 'undiscovered' paradises for holiday homeowners and retirees.

As a location for a holiday, retirement or permanent home, Greece has much to offer, and in addition to a wide choice of properties and good value for money, it enjoys a mild climate with over 300 days of sunshine a year. There are many excellent reasons for buying a home in Greece, although it's important not to be under any illusions about what you can expect from a home there. The first and most important question you need to ask yourself is **exactly** why you want to buy a home in Greece. For example, are you seeking a holiday or a retirement home? If you're seeking a second home, will it be mainly used for short holidays, e.g. one or two weeks, or for lengthier stays? Do you plan to let it to offset the mortgage and running costs? If so, how important is the property income? Are you primarily looking for a sound investment or do you plan to work or start a business?

Often buyers have a variety of reasons for buying a home abroad; for example, many people buy a holiday home with a view to living abroad permanently or semi-permanently when they retire. If this is the case, there are many more factors to take into account than if you're 'simply' buying a holiday home that you will occupy for just a few weeks a year, when it's usually wiser not to buy at all! If, on the other hand, you plan to work or start a business in Greece, you will be faced with a completely different set of criteria.

Can you really afford to buy a home in Greece? What of the future? Is your income secure and protected against inflation and currency fluctuations? In the '80s, many foreigners purchased holiday homes abroad by taking out second mortgages on their principal homes and stretching their financial resources to the limit. Not surprisingly, when the recession struck in the early '90s many people lost their homes or were forced to sell at a loss when they were unable to keep up their mortgage payments. Buying a home abroad can be a good, long-term investment, although it's possible to get your fingers burnt in the occasionally volatile property market in many countries, including Greece. For an overview of the cost of living and the cost of property in Greece see pages 25 and 23 respectively.

Advantages & Disadvantages

There are both advantages and disadvantages to buying a home in Greece, although for most people the benefits far outweigh any drawbacks. Among the many advantages are:

- guaranteed sunshine and high temperatures (year round in some areas);
- one of the least polluted regions in the world;
- good value for money;
- easy and relatively inexpensive to get to (particularly for most Europeans);
- good rental possibilities in many areas;
- good local tradesmen and services (particularly in resort areas);
- a healthy diet and good food and wine at reasonable prices;
- relatively low cost of living (25 to 50 per cent lower than in many northern European and North American cities);
- a slow, relaxed pace of life typified by *avro* – it can wait until tomorrow;

- the friendliness and hospitality of the local people;
- the dramatic beauty of the Mediterranean on your doorstep;
- an unsurpassed quality of life.

Naturally, there are also a few disadvantages, including:

- the relatively high purchase costs associated with buying property in Greece;
- unexpected renovation and restoration costs if you don't do your homework;
- the dangers of buying a property with debts and other problems if you don't take legal advice;
- overcrowding in popular tourist areas during the peak summer season;
- traffic congestion and pollution in many towns and cities;
- severe water shortages in some regions, particularly during the summer;
- homes can be difficult to sell;
- the expense of getting to and from Greece if you own a home there and don't live in a nearby country (or a country with good air connections).

Before deciding to buy a home in Greece, you should do extensive research and read a number of books especially written for those planning to live or work there. It also helps to study specialist property magazines such as *Homes Overseas*, *Homes Worldwide*, *International Property* and *World of Property* (see **Appendix B** for a list), and to visit property exhibitions such as those organised by Outbound Publishing (1 Commercial Road, Eastbourne, East Sussex BN21 3XQ, UK, (☎ 01323-726040; 🖳 www.outboundpublishing.com).

> **SURVIVAL TIP**
> Bear in mind that the cost of investing
> in a few books or magazines (and other research) is
> tiny compared with the expense of making a big
> mistake – however, don't believe everything
> you read or are told!

This chapter addresses the most serious concerns of anyone planning to buy a home and live in Greece, including the climate, economy, cost of property, cost of living, permits and visas, language, health and pets.

Restrictions

EU Nationals

There are no property ownership restrictions for EU nationals, although if you wish to buy in a border area you must obtain a permit from the local authorities. This is usually issued automatically.

Non-EU Nationals

Non-EU nationals (unless they are of Greek descent) aren't permitted to purchase property in certain areas of Greece for security reasons. The areas are usually border areas on the mainland such as Ioannina in Epirus; Florina, Pella and Thessaloniki in Macedonia; Halkidiki in northern Greece; some islands including Lesbos in the Dodecanese; and Chios and Samos in the North-eastern Aegean islands. Waivers can be obtained and usually involve forming a Greek company, but the procedure is long and expensive.

BUYING FOR INVESTMENT

In recent years, Greek property has been an excellent investment, particularly on popular islands such as Crete, Corfu and Rhodes, and in the Peloponnese. There are various kinds of property investment. Your principal home is an investment in that it provides you with rent-free accommodation. It may also yield a return in terms of increased value (a capital gain), although that gain may be difficult to realise unless you trade down or move to another region or country where property is cheaper. Of course, if you buy property other than for your own regular use, e.g. a holiday home, you will be in a position to benefit from a more tangible return on your investment. There are essentially four main categories of investment property:

- **A holiday home**, which can provide a return in many ways. It can provide your family and friends with rent-free accommodation while (hopefully) maintaining its value, and you may be able to let it to generate supplementary income. It may also produce a capital gain if property values rise faster than inflation (as in recent years).

- **A home for your children or relatives**, which may realise a capital gain. This could also be let when not in use to provide an income.

- **A business property**, which could be anything from a private home with bed and breakfast or guest accommodation, to a shop or office.

- **A property purchased purely for investment**, which could be a capital investment or provide a regular income, or both. Many people have invested in property to provide an income on their retirement.

A property investment should be considered over the medium to long term, say a minimum of five and preferably 10 to 15 years. Bear in mind that property isn't always 'as safe as houses' and investments can be risky over the short to medium term. You also need to take into account income tax if the property is let (see **Chapter 7**). You also need to recoup the high purchase costs (see **Fees** on page 121) of up to 15 per cent when you sell.

CLIMATE

In general, Greece enjoys a typical Mediterranean climate with hot, dry summers and cool, wet winters. However, the Greek climate varies considerably depending on the location, elevation and distance from the coast, and it isn't possible to generalise. Many regions and areas are influenced by the surrounding mountains, islands and other geographical features, and some even have their own micro-climates. If you're planning to live in Greece and don't know whether the climate in a particular region will suit you, you should rent accommodation until you're sure, as the extremes of hot and cold in some areas are too much for some people. Winter can also be harsh and/or extremely wet in many areas. However, you can be sure of sunshine throughout most of the country from spring to autumn and Greece boasts over 3,000 hours of sunshine a year.

Greece can be divided into several main climatic regions:

Northern Macedonia and **northern Epiros** have a climate similar to the Balkans, with freezing winters and very hot, humid summers. In the mountains in this part of Greece, summers can also be very short and during the winter the mountains are covered in snow from November to May. Temperatures in Thessaloniki average 5°C (40°F) in winter and 25°C (70°F) in summer, although high humidity can make it appear much hotter. The area experiences rain most of the year and the average rainfall is around 50mm (2in) per month.

The Attica peninsula, the Cyclades, the Dodecanese, Crete, and the central and eastern Peloponnese enjoy a typically Mediterranean climate. Winters are generally mild (particularly by northern European standards) with daytime temperatures averaging around 14°C (58°F). Snow is extremely rare in the Cyclades but the high mountains of Crete and the Peloponnese are snow-covered throughout the winter and it has been known to snow in Athens. Summers are very hot with average daytime temperatures of 32°C (94°F), although some respite is provided by the northern *meltémi* winds in July and August. However, although the *meltémi* lowers the temperature and reduces humidity, the strong wind often causes havoc with ferry schedules and sends everything flying. Summer evenings are usually pleasantly cool on the islands.

The western Peloponnese, Stereá Ellhada, Epiros and the Ionian islands escape the *meltémi* winds and have less severe winters than northern Greece, but have the highest rainfall, with an average of around 270mm (11in) a month during the winter in Crete. Crete is, however, the warmest place in Greece and you can swim in the warm waters off its southern coast from mid-April to November.

The north-eastern Aegean islands, Halkidiki and the Pelion peninsula have a climate that's mid-way between that of the harsher Balkans to the north and the southern Mediterranean.

The best time to make a house-hunting visit to Greece is in the spring (or autumn), when it's pleasantly warm but not usually too hot, the countryside is a mass of flowers and the hordes of tourists have yet to arrive. However, note that outside the high season not all services will be operating or offering the quality of service they provide in the summer, and some islands may be virtually at a standstill.

Winters can be harsh in most of Greece, but the most dependable winter weather can be found in the Dodecanese (especially Rhodes) and in southern Crete, although winters in most islands are generally mild and a blessed relief from frozen northern Europe. However, you should not underestimate a Greek winter, which can be cold and very damp! In summer, hot and dry conditions are common everywhere except for some higher altitudes, which should be borne in mind when buying a home in Greece. The average sea-level temperature in July is around 27°C (81°F). Most islands have little rainfall in summer and parts of the country frequently suffer drought conditions.

Earthquakes

Greece is situated in one of the most earthquake-prone areas of the world and seismic activity is almost a daily occurrence (there have been over 20,000 tremors over the last four decades). Fortunately most of this is limited to minor or imperceptible tremors, but occasionally the country suffers a major earthquake. In 1953 most of the towns and villages on the Ionian islands of Ithaki and Kefallonia were destroyed by an earthquake. More recently in 1999 an earthquake in Athens killed 139 and left thousands homeless, and in 2003 the island of Lefkada suffered an earthquake measuring 6.4 on the Richter scale.

There's strict legislation regarding construction and all new properties must be built to withstand earth tremors. Older properties, particularly village houses and farmhouses, tend to have thick stone walls strong enough to hold up against earthquakes.

Information about recent seismic activity and which areas are most prone can be found on the Athen's Institute of Geodynamics website (🖥 www.gein.noa.gr) or at 🖥 http://lemnos.geo.auth.gr/the_seisnet/en/greekquakes.htm.

Temperatures

Approximate average maximum/minimum temperatures for selected towns are shown below in Centigrade and Fahrenheit (in brackets):

Location	Spring	Summer	Autumn	Winter
Athens	20/11 (70/52)	33 /23 (96/76)	24/15 (78/60)	13/6 (56/42)
Corfu	22/14 (74/58)	29/20 (88/70)	26/17 (82/64)	13/7 (56/44)
Halkidiki	24/14 (77/58)	30/20 (90/70)	26/17 (82/64)	10/3 (50/36)
Heráklion	20/12 (70/54)	29/22 (88/72)	24/17 (78/64)	16/9 (61/48)
Rhodes	22/14 (74/58)	28/20 (86/70)	26/22 (82/72)	14/10 (58/50)

Frequent weather forecasts are broadcast on television and radio, and published in daily newspapers. A quick way to make a **rough** conversion from Centigrade to Fahrenheit is to multiply by two and add 30.

ECONOMY

When considering buying a property in Greece, the financial implications are usually one of the major factors influencing your decision. This includes the state of not only the Greek economy, but also that of your **home country** (or the country where you earn your income). The state of the economy in your home country (and your assets and job security there) may dictate how much you can afford to spend on a property, whether you can maintain your mortgage payments and the upkeep of the property, and how often you can afford to visit Greece each year. For example, the prolonged German recession from 2002 onwards meant that many prospective German property owners could no longer afford to buy in Greece and many property owners were unable to travel as often as they wished. Your home country's economy is also important if you plan to retire to Greece and will be primarily living on a pension. If you intend to live and work in Greece, or more importantly, run a business, then the state of the Greek economy will be a major consideration.

Greece currently has one of the fastest growing economies in Europe and has been transformed in the last few decades from a rural, backward agricultural country into a nation with a diversified economy largely dependent on industry and its highly successful tourism sector. Nevertheless, although Athens is a dynamic cosmopolitan city and was a superb host to the 2004 Olympic Games, there are parts of Greece where life has hardly changed. Numerous pockets of poverty also exist. Despite having the highest GDP growth figures among EU member states over the last few years, Greece remains the poorest member of the 'original' 15 members (prior to the entry of 10 new members in 2004).

Problems facing the Greek economy include its huge underground or submerged (black) economy, which analysts claim is around 30 per cent of economic activity – the highest in OECD countries; reform of the under-funded public pension and welfare system; and the demise of the shipping industry, traditionally the country's economic backbone. However, the outlook is bright and growth in 2004 was 3.7 per cent (4 per cent in 2003), and forecasts for 2005 and 2006 are 3.2 and 3.1 per cent respectively (figures from the Economist Intelligence Unit (🖳 www. eiu.com). Inflation, however, was 3.7 per cent in 2004 (3.5 per cent in 2003) and remains consistently higher than most other western European countries. Unemployment is also a problem (over 11 per cent in 2004) and is one of the highest in the EU, despite government attempts to reduce it.

Greece adopted the euro and the European Central Bank (ECB) interest rates along with 11 other EU countries in January 2002. Three years later prices have generally risen across the board (in common with most other Euro-zone countries). To compensate, interest rates are among the lowest ever (under 3 per cent in December 2004). Economists predict that Greece will have considerably higher GDP growth between 2005 and 2008 than the UK, France, Germany and Italy, and the positive economic benefits from the Olympic Games are expected to last until 2010.

COST OF PROPERTY

One of the major considerations (or the major consideration) for anyone contemplating buying a home in Greece is whether you can afford to buy a home there and if so, what kind of home can you afford and where? Because foreigners couldn't own property in Greece until 1990 the property market for foreigners is relatively young, and although Greece is now gaining in popularity, it isn't on a par with other Mediterranean countries such as Spain, France and Italy. However, the foreign property market is on the increase (some 3,000 properties were sold to foreigners in 2003) and as a consequence prices are rising. Note that Greeks don't generally buy property as an investment (most live in the same house for years) and you shouldn't expect to make a quick profit when buying property in Greece. **You also need to take into account the fees (see page 121), which are usually up to 15 per cent of the purchase price.**

If you're seeking a holiday home and cannot afford to buy one outright, you may wish to investigate a scheme that provides sole occupancy of a property for a number of weeks each year, rather than buying a property. Schemes available include part-ownership, leaseback and timesharing (see **Timeshare & Part-ownership Schemes** on page 133 for information).

 Don't rush into any of these schemes without fully researching the market and before you're absolutely clear what you want and what you can realistically expect to get for your money.

Property values generally increase at an average of less than 5 per cent a year or in line with inflation (with no increase in real terms), although in fashionable areas and on popular islands prices rise much faster than average, which is usually reflected in much higher purchase prices. For example, prices have increased by 8 per cent a year in Crete and 20 per cent a year in the Man' peninsula in the Peloponnese. Athens is also an exception and prices in some areas of the capital, e.g. Glyfada, Plaka and Voula, have risen nearly 50 per cent since 1997.

With the exception of Athens, there's a stable property market in most of Greece (barring recessions), which acts as a discouragement to speculators wishing to make a fast buck, particularly when you consider the high cost of fees and taxes associated with buying a home.

> **You shouldn't expect to make a quick profit when buying property in Greece, but should look upon it as an investment in your family's future happiness, rather than merely in financial terms.**

Foreign property buyers in Greece are concentrated on the most popular holiday islands, e.g. Corfu, Crete and Rhodes, and the Peloponnese. A slice of the good life in Greece needn't cost the earth, with 'old' apartments and village homes available from as little as €40,000, modern apartments from €60,000 and detached villas from

€150,000, although prices in popular areas are considerably higher. However, if you're looking for a substantial home with a sizeable plot of land and swimming pool, you will usually need to spend over €200,000 (depending on the area). For those with the financial resources the sky's the limit, with luxury apartments and villas costing over a million euros!

COST OF LIVING

It's virtually impossible to calculate an average cost of living in Greece, as it depends on each individual's circumstances and lifestyle. For example, the difference in your food bill will depend on what you eat and where you lived before arriving in Greece. Nevertheless, the following information gives an indication of how far your euros will stretch and how much (if any) you will have left after paying your bills.

Greece has enjoyed a stable and strong economy in recent years, reflected in the strong drachma before 2002 and the entry of the country into the single European currency, the euro. Salaries are generally low compared to the EU average, but Greeks enjoy a high standard of living, although social security costs are very high, particularly for the self-employed, and the combined burden of social security, income tax and indirect taxes make Greek taxes among the highest in Europe. Anyone planning to live in Greece, particularly retirees, should take care not to underestimate the cost of living, which has increased considerably in the last decade. However, Greece is still a relatively inexpensive country by American and northern European standards. You should be wary of published cost of living comparisons with other countries, which are often wildly inaccurate (and usually include non-essential items which distort the results).

With the exception of Athens, other major cities and some islands such as Hydra and Mykonos, the cost of living in Greece is around 30 per cent below the average of northern European countries. In the *Mercer Cost of Living Survey 2004*, Athens ranked 50th in Europe (London was 2nd and Dublin 14th) and 71st internationally. Food costs less than in many other European countries and around the same as in the USA, although you may have to modify your diet. In fact, it's possible to live very frugally in Greece if you're willing to forego luxuries and live largely 'off the land'. Shopping for 'luxury' items such as cars, stereo equipment, household apparatus, electrical and electronic goods, computers and photographic equipment abroad, e.g. via the internet, can also result in significant savings, as well as offering a wider choice.

PERMITS & VISAS

Before making any plans to buy a home in Greece, you must check whether you will need a visa or residence permit and ensure that you will be permitted to use a property when you wish and for whatever purpose you have in mind. If there's a possibility that you or a family member will wish to live or work permanently in Greece, you should enquire whether it will be possible before making any plans to buy a home there.

European Economic Area (EEA) nationals are free to buy property in Greece and those who plan to remain longer than three months a year and work, must apply for a residence permit (*Adeia Diamonez*). Application for permits must be made to the local police (*Astynomia*) or at the Aliens' Bureau (*Grafio Tmimatos Allodapon*) in larger cities such as Athens, Patra, Rhodes and Thessaloniki. Note that offices aren't common in small towns and in many areas you will need to travel to a regional capital or large city to apply. Allow plenty of time when making applications, as Greek bureaucracy grinds slowly. EEA residence permits are valid for five years, while residence and work permits for non-EEA nationals are valid for one year and may be renewed for up to five years, after which an application to extend a permit is necessary.

Citizens of certain European Economic Area (EEA) countries, including Belgium, Germany, Italy, Luxembourg, the Netherlands and Spain can visit Greece with a national identity card, while others require a full passport. A non-EEA national usually requires a visa to work, study or live in Greece.

When in Greece you must always carry your passport or residence permit (if you have one), which serves as an identity card, which all local nationals must carry by law. You can be asked to produce your identification papers at any time by the police and other officials, and if you don't have them you can be taken to a police station and interrogated. **Permit infringements are taken very seriously by the authorities and there are penalties for breaches of regulations, including fines and even deportation for flagrant abuses.**

Visits of Under 90 Days

Visitors can remain in Greece for a maximum of 90 days at a time. Visitors to Greece from EEA countries plus Andorra, Argentina, Australia, Bolivia, Brazil, Canada, Chile, Costa Rica, Croatia, El Salvador, Guatemala, Israel, Japan, Malaysia, Mexico, Monaco, New Zealand, Nicaragua, Panama, Paraguay, Singapore, South Korea,

Switzerland, Uruguay, the USA and Venezuela **don't** require a visa for stays of up to 90 days. All other nationalities require a visa to visit Greece, although the list of countries requiring visas is liable to change at short notice and therefore you should check with the Greek embassy in your home country.

A three-month tourist visa costs around US$20. Greek immigration authorities usually require non-EEA visitors to produce a return ticket and proof of accommodation, health insurance and financial resources. **Note that Greece will refuse entry to any foreigners, whatever their nationality, whose passport indicates that they've visited Northern Cyprus since November 1993.** If you plan to travel to Greece overland via Bulgaria, Croatia, FYR Macedonia, Romania or Serbia and Montenegro, you should check visa regulations for these countries (some require transit visas, usually obtainable at the border).

 If you're a non-EEA national you must ensure that you have your passport stamped upon entering Greece (this may not be automatic if you arrive from another Schengen state) so that when you leave it's clear that you haven't overstayed the 90-day limit. If you remain in Greece for longer than 90 days without extending your visa (see Visa Extensions below) you're liable for a fine (€450) and may be temporarily banned from re-entering Greece. Note that Greek immigration authorities are very strict with regard to visas and the 90-day limit.

Visa Extensions

A three-month extension to a tourist visa is available for non-EEA nationals, although this can be difficult to obtain. Applications should be made to a local police station at least two weeks before your tourist visa or 90-day stay expires.

Changing Status

If you're a non-EEA national, it isn't possible to enter Greece as a tourist and change your status to that of an employee, student or resident. You must return to your country of residence and apply for a long-stay visa.

Non-EEA nationals should make sure their passport is valid for at least three months _after_ they plan to leave Greece.

Visits Over 90 Days

EEA Nationals

Non-working: If you're an EEA national and plan to stay in Greece for longer than 90 days but not work, you require a residence permit and should apply for this as soon as possible at the nearest police station or Aliens' Bureau. You need to present your passport, four photographs, proof of accommodation (e.g. a rental contract or title deeds), proof you have sufficient income (e.g. bank statements) and proof of health insurance cover (EU Health Card – which has replaced Form E-111 and E-121 – or a private health insurance policy). **The government is expected to abolish residence permit regulations for EEA retirees sometime during 2005, therefore you should check with the local police after your arrival.**

Working: EEA nationals with employment in Greece must apply for a residence permit after 90 days at the nearest police station or Aliens' Bureau. You need to present your passport plus two photocopies, four photographs, and, if you're employed, a completed employment application and employer's declaration (offer of employment), both of which are obtainable from the nearest Department of Employment. If you're self-employed, you need to present confirmation from the tax authorities that you plan to set up in business and provide a certificate from the local court stating that your business has been legally recognised and declared. If your employment involves food preparation or working with children, you must also present a health certificate (see below). Applications for residence permits, valid for five years, currently takes at least one month, although the current government (as part of its campaign to reduce bureaucracy) has pledged to simplify the procedure and process residence permits for EEA nationals within ten days by June 2005.

Non-EEA Nationals

Residence permits for non-EEA nationals are difficult to obtain unless you're married to a Greek or someone of Greek origin. You should obtain a residence visa from the Greek embassy or consulate in your country of origin and when you arrive in Greece apply for a residence permit at the nearest Aliens' Bureau within two months. Immigration lawyers recommend that you apply as soon as you arrive so that if the permit is delayed you don't have to leave the country because your visa has expired. You need to present your visa, passport plus a copy, two photographs, a certificate of medical insurance, a health certificate from a state hospital (see below), proof of a local address (title deeds or rental contract) and proof that you can support yourself financially. The initial residence permit is valid for one year, after which it may be renewed for five to ten years.

Health Certificate: EEA nationals in certain jobs (e.g. food preparation or childcare) and all non-EEA nationals applying for a residence permit must obtain a health certificate from a state hospital. The certificate is issued after you have passed several medical examinations including a chest x-ray (TB), blood tests (hepatitis B and C, and HIV), a psychiatric evaluation and drug tracing. Note that you must pay for all examinations.

WORKING

If there's a possibility that you or any family members will wish to work in Greece, you must ensure that it will be possible before buying a home there. If you don't qualify to live and work in Greece by birthright, family relationship or as an EEA national, obtaining a work permit may be difficult or impossible. Greek employers must apply for a work permit on behalf of a non-EEA national whom they wish to employ. If you're a national of an EEA country you don't require official approval to live or work in Greece, although you still require a residence permit. If you visit Greece to look for a job, you have three months to find employment or set up in business and once employment has been found you must apply for a residence permit within one week (see **EEA Nationals** above).

Greece has a virtual freeze on the employment of non-EEA nationals, which has been strengthened in recent years by the high unemployment rate and the fact that Greece has been forced to accept numerous EEA nationals looking for work. Before granting or renewing work permits certain factors are taken into account, including the level of unemployment in the relevant profession or activity and the number of vacancies in the profession or trade. Certain non-EEA nationals are given preference, particularly those of Greek origin or those married to a Greek citizen.

The Greek equivalent of an Employment or Job Centre is the OAED (*Organismos Apasholisseos Ergatikou Dynamikou*), which has a special department for European jobseekers. The main areas where foreigners find work in Greece are in the tourism sector (employment may be limited to the tourist season) and teaching English, although some positions in language schools can only be filled by Greek nationals. Note that salaries are generally low, particularly on the islands where a qualified teacher can expect to earn only around €10 an hour, a labourer around €30 a day and a waiter from €3 an hour.

Before moving to Greece to work, you should dispassionately examine your motives and credentials.

- What kind of work can you realistically expect to do there?
- What are your qualifications and experience?
- Are they recognised in Greece?
- How good is your Greek? Unless your Greek is fluent, you won't be competing on equal terms with the Greeks. Most Greek employers aren't interested in employing anyone without, at the very least, a working knowledge of Greek, unless it's in the tourist industry dealing exclusively with foreigners.
- Are there any jobs in your profession or trade in the area where you plan to live?

The answers to these and many other questions can be quite disheartening, but it's better to ask them **before** moving to Greece, rather than afterwards.

Many people turn to self-employment or start a business to make a living, although this path is strewn with pitfalls for the newcomer. **Many foreigners don't do sufficient homework before moving to Greece.** While hoping for the best, you should plan for the 'worst-case scenario' and have a contingency plan and sufficient funds to last until you're established (this also applies to employees). If you're planning to start a business in Greece, you must also do battle with the notoriously obstructive and slow local bureaucracy. It's difficult for non-EEA nationals to obtain a residence permit to be self-employed in Greece.

> Greek immigration authorities are strict with illegal immigrants irrespective of their nationality and non-EEA nationals discovered working illegally in Greece face the risk of deportation.

RETIREMENT

Retired and non-active EEA nationals don't require a long-stay visa before moving to Greece, but a residence permit is necessary and an application should be made within one week of your arrival. This requirement may be abolished in 2005, therefore you should check with the local police after your arrival. Non-EEA nationals require a visa to live in Greece for longer than three months and should make an application to their local Greek consulate well before their planned departure date. Non-employed residents must provide proof (on request) that they have an adequate income or financial resources to live in Greece without working.

LANGUAGE

The Greek language is probably the oldest in Europe and has been spoken for some 4,000 years. It was once the *lingua franca* in the Middle East during its colonisation under Alexander the Great and, along with Latin, forms the basis of many modern European languages. Modern Greek is actually a southern dialect now spoken by most Greeks, although in some parts of the country dialects and languages such as Turkish and Albanian are spoken.

English is widely spoken in resorts and major cities in Greece; many Greeks have lived and worked in English-speaking countries (particularly Australia), English is widely taught in schools and many people live off the fruits of tourism. However, it isn't so easy to find someone who speaks English in remote areas, particularly on the mainland, and outside the holiday season many locals in resort areas revert to speaking Greek only! Unfortunately, many residents (particularly the British) make very little effort to learn more than a few words of Greek and live life as if they were on a brief holiday. **For anyone living in Greece, learning Greek shouldn't be seen as an option, but as a necessity, particularly if you're going to run a business.**

If you're a retiree, it's important to make an effort to learn at least the rudiments of Greek so that you can understand your bills, use the telephone, deal with servicemen and communicate with your local town hall (plus performing a myriad of other 'daily' chores). If you don't learn Greek, you'll often be frustrated in your communications and will be constantly calling on friends and acquaintances to assist you, or even paying people to do jobs you could easily do yourself. **The most important reason to learn Greek is that in an emergency it could save your life or that of a loved one!** Learning Greek also helps you appreciate the Greek way of life and make the most of your time in the country, and opens many doors that remain firmly closed to resident 'tourists'.

Greek is a difficult language to learn, added to which is the problem of an entirely different alphabet, although in practice this can be mastered 'relatively easily'. The alphabet has 24 letters as well as 12 combinations and diphthongs, and if you can master it you'll find speaking the language easier as well as being able to understand signs and notices. The key to speaking and understanding Greek is the stress placed on particular letters, which, when put in the wrong place, can change the meaning completely! Greek grammar also has its difficulties, particularly verbs, but it's easy to acquire a rudimentary understanding of how the language works. 'All' that's required is a little hard work and some help and perseverance, particularly if you only have English-speaking friends and colleagues. You won't just 'pick it up' (only young children are blessed with that advantage), but must make a real effort to learn. Fortunately the Greeks are tolerant of foreigners' tortured attempts to speak their language and any effort is appreciated, although you may find that they reply in English. **Note that your business and social enjoyment and success in Greece may be directly related to the degree to which you master Greek.**

Learning Greek

Methods

Most people can teach themselves a great deal through the use of books, tapes, videos and even CD-ROM computer-based courses. However, even the best students require some help. Classes are offered by language schools, local and foreign colleges and universities, private and international schools, foreign and international organisations, local associations and clubs, and private teachers. Tuition ranges from courses for complete beginners, through specialised business or cultural courses, to university-level seminars leading to recognised diplomas. Many Greek universities offer language courses and many organisations run residential holiday courses in the summer months, particularly for children and young adults (it's best to stay with a local Greek family).

Language Schools

There are many language schools in Greece, although the majority are located in Athens and other large towns, and on the islands during the summer. Most schools run various classes depending on your language ability, how many hours you wish to study a week, how much money you want to spend and how quickly you wish to learn. Courses are usually open to anyone over the age of 18 and some also accept students aged from 14. Courses are graded according to ability, e.g. beginner, intermediate or advanced, and usually last from 2 to 16 weeks. Most schools offer free tests to help you find your appropriate level and a free introductory lesson.

Don't expect to become fluent in a short time unless you have a particular flair for languages or already have a good command of Greek. Unless you desperately need to learn quickly, it's best to schedule your lessons over a long period. However, don't commit yourself to a long course of study, particularly an expensive one, before ensuring that it's the right course for you. Language classes generally fall into the following categories:

Category	Hours per Week
Extensive	4-10
Intensive	15-20
Total immersion	20-40+

Some schools offer combined courses where language study is linked with optional subjects, including business Greek, Greek art and culture, reading and commentary of a daily newspaper, conversation, Greek history, and traditions and folklore. Some schools also combine language courses with a range of cultural and sports activities such as visits to monuments, tennis or water sports.

The most common language courses in Greece are intensive courses, providing four hours tuition a day from Mondays to Fridays (20 hours per week). The cost of an intensive course is usually quite reasonable, e.g. a four-week intensive course costs around €200. The highest fees are charged in the summer months, particularly during July and August. Commercial courses are generally more intensive and expensive, e.g. around €400 for three weeks and a total of 60 hours tuition. Courses that include accommodation are usually good value and some schools arrange home stays with a Greek family (full or half board) or provide apartment or hotel accommodation. Those for whom money is no object, can take total immersion courses where study is for eight hours a day, five days a week. Whichever course you choose, you should shop around as tuition fees vary considerably. For more information contact the Greek national tourist office or embassy in your home country.

Private Lessons

You may prefer to have private lessons, which are a quicker, although more expensive way of learning a language. The main advantage of private lessons is that you learn at your own speed and aren't held back by slow learners or left floundering in the wake of the class genius. You can advertise for a teacher in local newspapers, on shopping centre/supermarket bulletin boards, on university notice boards, and through your or your spouse's employer. Don't forget to ask your friends, neighbours and colleagues if they can recommend a private teacher.

HEALTH

One of the most important aspects of living in Greece (or anywhere else for that matter) is maintaining good health. The quality of health care and health care facilities in Greece leaves much to be desired, although they are improving. In 1983, a national health-service (IKA) was introduced in common with many other countries of southern Europe. However, although medical training is of a high standard, the health service is one of the worst in Europe, largely because of under-funding. Public hospitals are inundated with patients, although standards of hygiene are high and hospital viruses are almost non-existent.

Not surprisingly, health care costs per head in Greece are the lowest in the European Union and the country spends a relatively small percentage of its GDP on health. Public and private medicine operate alongside each other in Greece and complement one another, although public health facilities are limited in some areas, particularly on the islands. Transfers from provincial and island hospitals to hospitals in Athens or other major hospitals (e.g. the University Hospital at Ionnina) are common.

The government is currently improving the health system and a substantial investment (much of which comes from EU funding) is being made on upgrading the country's existing hospitals, building new facilities (e.g. a large hospital on Corfu is scheduled to open in 2005), developing mobile medical units, installing high-tech equipment, and improving accident and emergency facilities.

Greece's public health system (IKA) provides free or low cost health care for those who contribute to Greek social security, plus their families and retirees (including those from other EU countries). Members are charged 25 per cent of the actual cost of prescriptions, although there are higher charges for non-essential medicines plus substantial contributions for many services, including spectacles, dentures and other treatment. Essential dental treatment is largely free.

You aren't required to register with a doctor in Greece and may choose a doctor, dentist or specialist from the approved IKA list. If you need to see a specialist you don't need a referral from your doctor. Specialists generally have waiting lists, but if it's urgent you can usually pay to see a private specialist and claim up to 85 per cent of the cost from IKA afterwards. Free home visits by doctors are uncommon, although you can arrange one for a small fee.

If you don't qualify for health care under the public health system, it's essential to have private health insurance. This is recommended in any case if you can afford it, owing to the inadequacy of public health services and long waiting lists for specialist appointments and non-urgent operations in some areas. Visitors to Greece should have holiday health insurance (see page 221) if they aren't covered by a reciprocal arrangement. Note that the EU Health Card (old Form E-111) covers basic medical care only and it's advisable to have extra holiday insurance to cover eventualities such as repatriation.

Emergency treatment is free to all nationalities in public hospitals and there are outpatient clinics (*yatr'a*) attached to hospitals in rural areas. They're typically open from 8am to noon and treat minor health problems and it's often easier to obtain prompt emergency treatment here than at a public hospital. There are 24-hour emergency hospitals in major towns and on the large islands, and private hospitals and clinics in major towns and resort areas. English-speaking Greek doctors and foreign doctors practise in resort areas and major cities, and advertise in the local expatriate press. **In a medical emergency you should phone 166 for an ambulance.**

Pharmacists are highly qualified in Greece and you can obtain treatment for minor ailments at chemists (*farmak'o*) as well as medical advice. In larger towns and resort areas, pharmacists often speak English. Pharmacies aren't usually open in the afternoon or at weekends, but a duty roster is posted in pharmacy windows and published in the local press indicating the nearest pharmacy that's open outside normal business hours. Homeopathic remedies are widespread and there are homeopathic pharmacies in most large towns.

Greeks are among the world's healthiest people and have one of the highest life expectancies in the EU. The incidence of heart disease is among the lowest in the world, which is attributed in large part to their diet (which includes lots of garlic, olive oil and red wine), as is that of cancers. However, the country has a high rate of smoking-related health problems and the proportion of smokers is one of the highest in the EU.

General

Among expatriates, common health problems include sunburn and sunstroke, stomach and bowel problems (due to the change of diet and more often, water, but also poor hygiene), and various problems caused by excess alcohol. Other health problems are caused by the high level of airborne pollen in spring (note that spring comes earlier to Greece than northern European countries), which particularly affects asthma and hay fever sufferers. If you aren't used to the very hot sun, you should limit your exposure and avoid it altogether during the hottest part of the day, wear protective clothing (including a hat) and use a sun block. Too much sun and too little protection will dry your skin and cause premature ageing, to say nothing of the risks of skin cancer. Care should also be taken to replace the natural oils lost from too many hours in the sun and the elderly should take particular care not to exert themselves during hot weather.

The mild Greek climate is therapeutic, especially for sufferers of rheumatism and arthritis and those who are prone to bronchitis, colds and pneumonia. The slower pace of life is also beneficial for those who are prone to stress (it's difficult to remain up-tight while napping in the sun), although it takes some foreigners time to adjust. The climate and lifestyle in any country has a noticeable affect on mental health and people who live in hot climates are generally happier and more relaxed than those who live in cold, wet climates (such as northern Europe).

Health (and health insurance) is an important issue for anyone retiring abroad. Many people are ill-prepared for old age and the possibility of health problems, and foreigners who can no longer care for themselves are often forced to return to their home countries. There are few state residential nursing homes in Greece or hospices for the terminally ill. Provision for handicapped travellers is also poor and wheelchair access to buildings and public transport is well below the average for Western Europe, although efforts are being made to change this.

There are no immunisation requirements for Greece, although you may be advised to consider having certain vaccinations as a precaution if you're going to live there permanently (e.g. diphtheria, tetanus, measles, mumps, rubella and polio). Domestic tap water is safe to drink, but you should be wary of drinking from public fountains, as not all of them provide drinking water (some have signs). Many people prefer the taste of bottled water, particularly in periods of drought when the quality of tap water sometimes deteriorates.

PETS

If you plan to take a pet to Greece, it's important to check the latest regulations. Make sure that you have the correct papers, not only for Greece, but for all the countries you will pass through to reach your destination. Particular consideration must be given before exporting a pet from a country with strict quarantine regulations. If you need to return, even after just a few days abroad, your pet may have to go into quarantine, which, apart from the expense, is distressing for both pets and owners.

UK Regulations

The UK has particularly strict quarantine laws, which were originally introduced to avoid importing rabies from continental Europe. However, in 2000, the UK introduced a pilot 'Pet Travel Scheme (PETS)', which replaced quarantine for qualifying cats and dogs. Under the scheme, now included under the European Union (EU) Pet Passport scheme, pets must be micro-chipped (they have a microchip inserted in their neck), vaccinated against rabies, undergo a blood test and are issued with an EU Pet Passport. **Note, however, that the EU Pet Passport isn't issued until six months <u>after</u> all the above have been carried out!** In the UK EU Pet Passports are issued only by Local Veterinary Inspectors (LVIs). In other EU countries passports are issued by registered vets.

The scheme is restricted to animals imported from rabies-free countries and countries where rabies is under control, including EU countries. However, the current quarantine laws will remain in place for pets coming from Eastern Europe, Africa, Asia and South America. The new regulations cost pet owners around GB£200 (for a microchip, rabies vaccination and blood test), plus GB£60 per year for annual booster vaccinations and around GB£20 for a border check. Shop around and compare the fees levied by a number of veterinary surgeons. To qualify, pets must travel by sea via Dover, Newhaven, Plymouth, Poole or Portsmouth, by train via the Channel Tunnel or via Gatwick, Heathrow or Manchester airports. Only certain carriers are licensed to carry animals and these are listed on the Department of Environment, Food and Rural Affairs (DEFRA) website (🖳 www.defra.gov.uk/animalh/quarantine). Additional information is available from DEFRA, (☎ UK 0870-241 1710, ✉ pets.helpline@defra.gsi.gov.uk.

Greek Regulations

You may bring a pet into Greece from another EU country, but on entering the country you must present a valid EU Pet Passport or a bi-lingual export health certificate and a rabies certificate. The export health certificate is obtainable from the Ministry of Agriculture in your home country. A form must be completed and approved by a local veterinary inspector, who will inspect your pet within 48 hours of your departure. Obtaining a rabies certificate entails a visit to a vet and paying a fee. The rabies vaccine must be administered not less than 20 days or more than 11 months before leaving your home country. On arrival in Greece you may be required to have your pet inspected by a Greek veterinary officer.

Looking After Your Pet

If you intend to live permanently in Greece, most veterinary surgeons recommend that dogs and cats be vaccinated against certain diseases, and in some cases you'll need a veterinary certificate confirming that your pet has been vaccinated before it can enter the country. Note also that there are a number of diseases and dangers for pets in Greece that aren't found in many other European countries. You should obtain advice from a vet on arrival in Greece about the best way to protect your pets.

Veterinary surgeons are well trained in Greece, and emergency veterinary care is also provided in animal clinics, some of which provide a 24-hour emergency service. Note that some Greek islands may not have a resident veterinary surgeon, therefore if your pet requires any treatment you may have to travel to the mainland or another island. You may also find it difficult to obtain pet supplies in Greece.

Veterinary surgeons (including many English-speaking vets), animal clinics, kennels and catteries advertise in English-language publications in Greece. If you plan to leave your pet at a kennel or cattery, ensure that it's a registered and bona fide establishment and book well in advance, particularly for school holiday periods. There are also foreign residents in resort areas who will look after your pets in their own homes for a reasonable fee while you're away, which many believe is preferable to leaving it at a kennel or cattery. Bear in mind that there may be discrimination against pets when renting accommodation, particularly when it's furnished (the statutes of community properties can legally prohibit pets).

2.

THE BEST PLACE TO LIVE

After having decided to buy a home in Greece, your first tasks will be to choose the region and what sort of home to buy. If you're unsure about where and what to buy, the best decision is usually to rent for a period. The secret of successfully buying a home is research, research and more research. You may be fortunate and buy the first property you see without doing any homework and live happily ever after. However, a successful purchase is much more likely if you thoroughly investigate the towns and communities in your chosen area, compare the range and prices of properties and their relative values, and study the procedure for buying property. It's a wise or lucky person who gets his choice absolutely right first time, although there's a much better chance if you do your homework thoroughly.

When choosing a location, take into account its popularity, which hugely influences prices. Instead of the resort areas in Crete, the Maní peninsula in the Peloponnese or Halkidiki, for example, where prices are rising, you may wish to consider a 'quieter' island such as Ithaki or the south-east coast of Crete. Bear in mind also the typical buyers in each area: for example, property in resorts that are popular with German owners may be cheaper than resorts where British, Irish or Dutch buyers are prominent, as there have been fewer German buyers in recent years due to the relatively weak German economy.

This chapter is principally designed to help you decide where to buy a home in Greece, as location is the most important aspect of buying a home. It also includes useful information on getting to Greece (a vital consideration when choosing where to buy) and on getting around once you're there.

GEOGRAPHY

Greece is situated at the southern tip of the Balkan peninsula and is the only continental member of the European Union (EU) without a land frontier with another member. To the north, Greece borders Albania, the former Yugoslav Republic of Macedonia, and Bulgaria, while to the east lies Turkey and the south of the country is surrounded by the Ionian and Aegean seas. Greece consists of a peninsula and more than 1,400 islands, around 150 of which are inhabited.

Around 80 per cent of the mainland is mountainous, with ranges extending into the sea as peninsulas or chains of islands. Greece is a mountainous country with a highly indented and rugged coast, dotted with ancient fortifications. According to Greek mythology, when making the world the gods distributed the available soil to each country after sieving it and tossed the rejected stones over their shoulders – to make Greece! The Pindos range of mountains almost divides the country in two from north-west to south-east.

The capital of Greece is Athens, the country's largest city with a population of 4.5 million and home to its principal port, Piraeus. The second-largest city is Thessaloniki, the capital of Macedonia, which has a population of around 800,000 and is itself an important seaport, providing a gateway to the Balkans. Greece is divided into ten regions or prefectures of which Macedonia is the largest. The mainland regions are Central Greece, Epiros, Macedonia, Peloponnese, Thessaly and Thrace, while the island groups are the Cyclades, Dodecanese, Ionian, North-Eastern Aegean, Saronic Gulf and Sporades. Crete and Evia don't belong to any group and for administrative purposes are divided into prefectures or nomes (*nomoi*). The regions of Greece are shown on the map in **Appendix E** and a map of the eastern Mediterranean showing Greece is on page 6.

REGIONS

For the purpose of this book, Greece has been divided into the following 12 regions: Attica, central Greece, Crete, the Cyclades Islands, the Dodecanese Islands, Epirus and the west, Evia and the Sporades, the Ionian Islands, the North-Eastern Aegean Islands, northern Greece, Peloponnese and the Saronic Gulf Islands, all of which are shown on the maps on page 6 and in **Appendix E**.

Attica

- **Nearest Airport** – Athens (international).

The region of Attica lies at the south-eastern end of mainland Greece and includes the capital city of Athens. The Apollo coast is home to a number of crowded and overdeveloped resorts such as Glyfádha and Vouliagméni, which are popular with both visitors and Athenians at weekends, and home to a sizeable expatriate population. The famous historical sites of the Temple of Poseidon and Marathon are situated in Attica, while Mount Párnitha in the

north has spectacular forests and rock scenery. The region is also noted for its extensive olive and grape production. The climate in Attica is temperate with hot summers, mild winters and low rainfall, although it can snow in Athens.

Athens (pop. 4.5m) is the oldest city in Europe and the birthplace of western civilisation and democracy, with a history dating back some 7,000 years. Many cultures have passed through Athens (named after the Greek goddess Athena), which in 1834 – soon after the end of Ottoman rule – was declared the capital of Greece. It remained a relatively small city until 1923, when a huge influx of refugees from Turkey forced a rapid expansion, and the city now covers some 450km^2 (174mi^2). In the intervening years Athens has grown from a population of less than 500,000 to 4.5 million, which has created considerable urban and environmental problems, although these have been reduced greatly in recent years. The city is largely a vast sprawl of virtually identical six-storey, cement apartment blocks known as 'multiple dwellings', hurriedly constructed to house the influx of immigrants, and is home to over two-thirds of the country's cars.

The improvements made to the city for the 2004 Olympic Games transformed it into a 'new' Athens with vastly improved traffic systems (the nightmare traffic jams are almost a thing of the past), a cleaner environment, and new improved museums and cultural centres. Some Athenians claim the city is almost unrecognisable! Traffic jams have been reduced drastically by the new road network as has the thick, acrid smog (called *néfos*), a combination of traffic fumes and oppressive heat, which used to envelop Athens for days at a time during summer. The city is still extremely busy, however, and the cradle of Greek civilisation is visited by over 4 million tourists annually.

Athens has the best medical and education facilities in the country. The standard of living is also higher than in the rest of Greece and job opportunities are plentiful, as over half of the country's industry is concentrated around the capital, which is the political, commercial and cultural hub of Greece. Athens is a fascinating amalgamation of cultures where east meets west in a vibrant, exciting ambience, with traditional coffee-houses and donkey carts vying for space with modern office blocks, deluxe hotels and the ubiquitous motor vehicles. Despite its rapid expansion, Athens is really a conglomeration of small villages, its people friendly and gregarious, with suburbs that are relatively calm and peaceful with beautiful restored 19th century mansions. You can also marvel at the Acropolis, which dominates the skyline from practically every street corner. When the hustle and bustle of Athens becomes too much to bear, an escape to the tranquillity of the surrounding mountains and countryside is never far away.

Communications are excellent in Athens and the city has comprehensive bus and metro services (three lines with connections to Piraeus and the airport), and a new and modern international airport at Spata, opened in 2001. Trains and buses leave the capital at regular intervals for the rest of the country. Piraeus, Athens' port and one of the Mediterranean's busiest, is also Greece's ferry hub from where ferries and hydrofoils service most of the islands. Athens is connected by road to western and northern Greece by the E75 motorway.

In keeping with the high standard of living, house prices in Athens and the surrounding beach resorts are the highest in the country, where property is in high demand. Prices have risen nearly 50 per cent in most areas of the capital since 1997. Property in the leafy suburbs (e.g. Kifissia, Kolonaki and Plaka) with their spacious villas is highly sought-after and houses generally sell quickly. Expect to pay from €80,000 for a small one-bedroom flat in a less desirable area to over €400,000 for a new apartment in a good area. Houses range from €400,000 to over €5 million.

Central Greece

- **Nearest Airports** – Athens and Vólos (international), Kythira (domestic).

The land of the mythical centaur, central Greece is home to flourishing fruit orchards and dense oak and beech forests. The region is dotted with some of the prettiest villages in Greece, including Makrinítsa with its stunning churches and monasteries. Local architecture is a unique blend of whitewashed, half-timbered houses, which are often decorated with intricate frescoes. The Aegean-facing east coast has some excellent beaches and popular resorts such as Platanías and Áfissos. The area is much cooler  in summer than the rest of mainland Greece, which, when added to its natural charm, makes it extremely popular in summer and more expensive than many other areas.

Communications are quite good between the main towns, most of which are served by trains and buses and have reasonable roads. Outside the main areas, however, there are narrow mountain roads and infrequent bus services, particularly outside the summer season, when private transport is a must. Kythira has a domestic airport serving a limited number of routes.

Central Greece comprises two large regions: Stereá Ellhada and Thessaly, and offer some of the country's most varied scenery.

Stereá Ellhada, situated north-west of Athens, was the only independent Greek territory during the 19th century and encompasses a vast expanse of wild, mountainous countryside punctuated by small towns (the region was largely depopulated in the 20th century). Its most famous sights are at Delphi, Greece's most ancient oracle with its unique amphitheatre and Temple of Apollo, and Mount Parnassós, site of two ski resorts. Seismic activity in this area is among the highest in the country.

Thessaly lies to the north of Stereá Ellhada and consists of a vast, rich agricultural plain surrounded on three sides by mountain ranges, including Mount Olympus to the north. The region's main towns include Larissa, a busy market centre, Vólos (see below), and Kalambáka, a modern town which is the base for visitors to the nearby spectacular Metéora rock monasteries. The earliest Orthodox religious communities made their homes on the black pinnacles of the naturally sculptured rock, which is one of the most spectacular sights on the Greek mainland.

Vólos, situated just west of the Pelion peninsula, is a rapidly expanding industrial area and home to Greece's third-largest port, which has excellent hydrofoil and ferry connections to the nearby Sporades. The airport (Nea Aghialos) has some charter flights from the UK. The town has been largely rebuilt since 1957 when it was ruined by an earthquake and it now has an attractive new marina. Vólos is nationally famous for its potent *tsipouro*, the local version of *ouzo* (an acquired taste!).

The Pelion peninsula, crowned by Mount Pliassidi (1,650m/5,445ft) in the north, has lush fruit orchards, picturesque mountain villages, dense forests and fine beaches, and is popular with both Greeks and foreigners. Resorts such as Aghios Ioannis, Kala Nera and Mikro are busy for much of the year, and the Pelion peninsula offers excellent bird watching and trekking possibilities, as well as ski-ing in the winter. Local buses run services throughout the area, although services are infrequent on some routes and therefore private transport is essential. Road conditions vary greatly and some roads are extremely windy. The property market has taken off in this area and prices are high. Two-bedroom apartments are available from €150,000, villas from €200,000 and typical stone mansions from €250,000. In the Pagastic Gulf, unique island bungalows can be purchased from €72,000 for one bedroom and from €117,000 for two bedrooms. The rental market is buoyant, therefore property is potentially a good investment.

In the north of Thessaly, near Larissa, is the Vale of Témbi, one of the country's most famous and popular beauty spots, which meanders 10km (6mi) through a spectacular mountain gorge carved by the River Pinio. The coastline beyond Témbi has been heavily developed and is popular with Greek tourists. North of Larissa is Mount Olympus National Park containing the country's highest peak, Mount Olympus (2,972m/9,751ft), legendary home of the gods. It's snow-capped for much of the year and offers spectacular hiking in a unique terrain carpeted with wild flowers.

Crete

- **Nearest Airports** – Heráklion and Chania (international), Sitia (domestic).

Crete (pop. 578,250) is the largest Greek island (almost a country on its own) and the fifth-largest in the Mediterranean; for many it's the quintessential Greek island. It's noted for its mild winter climate, beautiful beaches, hospitable people, and as a botanical and ornithological paradise (it's a great place for walkers). These attractions have made Crete the destination of a quarter of all tourists visiting Greece and the most popular region for holiday homes – consequently it has a large number of
resident expatriates. It was home to Europe's first civilisation, the Minoans, and their ancient sites are scattered throughout the island. Crete has a flourishing agricultural economy and is one of the few places in Greece that could survive without the tourist trade, although much of the coast has been developed as resort areas. Crete is an island of contrasts – inland and away from the packed resort areas are small villages almost completely untouched by modernity. The island is divided into four administrative prefectures: Chania, Heráklion, Lassithi and Rethimnon.

Heráklion, the capital, lies on the north coast of the island and is the fifth-largest city in Greece and home to nearly half the island's population. It has the highest per capita income in the country, although its wealth isn't reflected in the infrastructure. The city has a glorious past, particularly during the Middle Ages, a splendour that's reflected in its Venetian architecture and city walls. Heráklion is a busy city with a vibrant night-life. Knossos, the main Minoan site and largest palace, is situated close to the city.

To the east of the capital is the area known as the 'Cretan Riviera', packed with popular resorts such as Hersonissos, Malia and Stalidha, and bustling beaches. Aghios Nikolaos (known as 'Ag Nik') was once the 'St. Tropez of Crete' and has the best and most expensive hotels on the island. Inland is the rich agricultural plain of Lasithi, famous for its windmills that are used for irrigation.

On the east coast, **Sitia** has a busy port and is the site of a number of new residential developments, although this part of the island is relatively unspoilt. Europe's only palm tree forest is at Vái on the east coast. In the south, the numerous gorges and cliffs mean there are few towns, although Mátala has a well-known beach and Arvi's microclimate permits the cultivation of bananas and pineapples. Samariá Gorge in the White Mountains (Lefka Ori) is the longest ravine in Europe and one of Greece's most visited natural spots (open from May to October).

The west of the island is the least inhabited and although there are a number of resorts, they're less developed than those in the east. **Rethimnon**, a town of many contrasts, is the smallest of Crete's four major towns and the least visited. It has an attractive Venetian harbour surrounded by fish restaurants and a handsome old town with a wealth of Venetian buildings from the 13th to 17th centuries. Crete's second-largest city **Chania** – like Rethimnon a former Venetian town – was the island's capital until 1971 and the old city around the Venetian harbour has retained its unique charm. It's a bustling harbour town with many attractive townhouse properties (home to many expatriates) and offers good amenities and services. Around 15,000 Britons live on Crete, most of whom are concentrated around the areas of Apokoranos in the west and Elounda in the east.

Communications in the north of the island are excellent, with international airports at Heráklion and Chania (Haniá), and a small domestic airport at Sitia, where a new runway is currently under construction. There are six ferry ports with frequent, fast services in summer and a reduced service during the winter months. The north of the island has good communications, including a dual carriageway running along the north coast linking the main cities and resorts, and there's a good bus service. In the south, however, there are few roads and infrequent buses (private transport is usually essential here). Note also that it takes around five hours to drive from the east side of the island to the west, and many towns in the south-east are easier to reach by boat from one of the ports.

Crete's climate is mild in winter with almost guaranteed sunshine, although there's often snow on the highest peaks. Summers are hot, with the highest temperatures in Greece (which is very hot!). In general, property on the island is more expensive than other parts of Greece, but there's an abundance of cheaper, secluded rural properties available, although many require complete restoration. The south-east corner of the island currently offers particularly good value for money. Property is generally a good investment and prices are currently rising at around 8 per cent a year.

In general, apartments start at €70,000 and villas from €100,000, although you can expect to pay at least twice as much in or near resort areas. Exclusive new developments are even more expensive, e.g. from €350,000 for a two-bedroom apartment. Remote village houses start at €75,000. There are several companies on Crete specialising in property restoration packages. Experts generally agree that the best time to look for property is in the winter, when prices are generally lower.

The Cyclades Islands

● **Nearest Airports** – Mykonos and Santorini (international), Naxos and Paros (domestic).

The Cyclades (pop. 113,000), a group of 56 islands (of which 24 are inhabited), are one of the most popular locations for holiday homes in Greece. Their name derives from the circle they form around the island of Delos, the birthplace of Apollo and once the centre of religion and commerce in the central Mediterranean. The islands form a disparate group and are mostly different in character, yet small and close enough to allow easy 'island hopping'. They all share the characteristic Greek whitewashed houses, blue domed churches and the warm hospitality of the inhabitants.

The Cyclades enjoy mild winters, although they experience strong winds virtually all year round. The summer *meltémi* can sometimes disrupt ferry schedules, although it reduces the heat, and in winter strong north winds often make ferry travel impossible. Rainfall can be scarce and water shortages are commonplace.

Communications with mainland Greece and between the islands is mainly by ferry, where Paros is the main port of call for most inter-island services. During the summer there are frequent ferry services linking the islands, although services are severely curtailed in winter and can be suspended altogether when the weather is bad. Six islands have airports, although only two, Mykonos and Santorini, cater for international flights (charter only). Bus services are provided on most islands, although the quality of buses and frequency of services varies considerably, and the inaccessibility of some areas means private transport is often essential.

There's a good choice of resale and new property on the islands, particularly Mykonos, Naxos and Paros. Small village houses can be bought from €60,000, farmhouses requiring restoration from €70,000, restored farmhouses from €160,000 and new maisonettes (100m²) from €170,000. Land typically costs from €18 to €50 per m² depending on the location. Typical Cyclades windmill properties are also available, e.g. €300,000 for windmill, house and an 8,000m² plot.

The most popular islands include the following:

Ios (pop. 1,800) is especially popular with the younger generation and has a reputation as the 'party capital' of the Cyclades, although there's more to the island than nightclubs and bars. Ios is attempting to attract more upmarket tourism and boasts several excellent beaches and the supposed site of Homer's tomb. Ios is quiet out of season.

Mykonos (pop. 9,360) receives around a million visitors a year, who come to enjoy a hedonistic lifestyle, and is the most expensive of all the Greek islands. Its capital, Mykonos Town, is one of the most attractive, with 'sugar-cube' architecture and numerous churches and shrines, although it's extremely busy and commercial with a lively nightlife. Beaches are generally excellent and resort areas are concentrated on the south side – the north side is windy and therefore less developed. Property is expensive here, but there's good rental potential.

Naxos (pop. 18,100) is the largest and most fertile of the Cyclades and is largely self-sufficient. It's also the most scenic of the islands and has their highest mountain, Mount Zas, and excellent beaches.

Paros (pop. 12,800) is the third-largest of the Clyclades islands and the hub of its ferry services. Its main resorts include Naoussa and Parikia, with excellent beaches and a hectic nightlife. Paros attracts many foreign homebuyers, particularly the British.

Santorini (pop. 13,400), the most spectacular of all Greek islands, is a partly submerged volcanic crater thought to be the legendary city of Atlantis. It's an important port of call for cruise ships and is famous for its black sand beaches and capital Fira, situated on top of a steep cliff reached via 500 steps cut into it. Property here is very expensive.

Tinos (pop. 8,500), with its charming traditional villages and famous 'lacework' dovecotes, is the Greek Lourdes with its church of Panayia Evangelistria and its miraculous icon attracting thousands of Greek Orthodox pilgrims each year. Tinos offers excellent hiking.

Syros (pop. 16,800), the most densely populated of the Cyclades Islands, also contains its administrative centre, the attractive town of Ermoúpolis. Syros, **Andros**, **Kéa** and **Kythnos** are popular with Athenians for weekend breaks and summer holidays.

The islands of **Anafi**, **Folégandros**, **Milos** and **Sikinos** are barely populated and practically untouched by tourism, and therefore good places to experience the 'real' Greece.

The Dodecanese Islands

● **Nearest Airports** – Kos and Rhodes (international), Leros (domestic).

The Dodecanese (pop. 162,000) form an archipelago of 12 main islands off the west coast of Turkey and are Greece's southernmost and most recent territorial acquisition. The islands' history and architecture reflect their previous occupants who range from the Knights of St John and the Ottomans to the Italians, although each island has a distinctive landscape. Many are popular with tourists, particularly Rhodes and Kos, while others are barely touched by modern life and many of the local women still wear traditional dress. The islands are a paradise for water-sport lovers and divers, although scuba diving is strictly controlled in some areas.

As with all Greek islands, transportation is mainly by boat, and services are frequent in summer but few and far between in winter, or cancelled altogether when the weather is bad. Rhodes is the hub of the inter-island ferries, which also serve the mainland. The islands have three international airports, on Rhodes, Karpathos and Kos, which also have domestic connections. The larger islands have good bus services, but these are limited on the smaller islands. Private transport can be useful, although some of the islands have poor to non-existent roads.

Rhodes (pop. 68,000) is an alluring mixture of sun, sea and beautiful landscapes, and is the best known of the islands and the most popular with tourists and holiday homebuyers. Rhodes is less popular as a package tour destination nowadays and has done much to shake off its 'lager lout' image. It enjoys a unique climate with over 300 days of sunshine annually (it's the sunniest spot in Greece) and excellent beaches on the east coast. Most of the island has been heavily developed for the flourishing tourist trade, although Rhodes Town, a World Heritage Site, remains one of

the architectural treasures of the Mediterranean with its medieval walls and monuments, and blend of churches, mosques and synagogues. It also has an exciting nightlife. The city of Lindos – with its stunning Acropolis – in the south-east is an attractive car-free resort. Rhodes has strict building regulations and there's little apartment-type property available. Prices start at €140,000 for a two-bedroom townhouse and from €90,000 for a village house. Property here is a good investment and there's excellent rental potential.

Kos (pop. 21,500), birthplace of Hippocrates the father of medicine, has the second-largest population in the Dodacanese islands. It's one of Greece's most beautiful islands, essentially flat and fertile with some of the country's best beaches. It's popular with tourists and has many resorts, although it isn't as developed as Rhodes. Property prices on Kos are higher than on the other Dodecanese islands, although it's a good investment.

Other islands of note in the group include **Karpathos** with its excellent beaches; **Kálymnos** (reached by boat from Kos), a centre of sponge fishing with its attractive port of Póthia and increasingly popular with foreign property buyers; **Symi**, known as the 'jewel of the Dodecanese' due to its well-preserved, 19th century, neo-classical architecture and good beaches; **Tílos** with fine beaches and excellent hiking; and **Níssyros**, one of the most fertile islands thanks to its dormant volcano.

Epirus & the West

● **Nearest Airport** – Ioannina (domestic).

The regions of Epirus and Western Macedonia share their borders with Albania and the former Yugoslav Republic of Macedonia, and their scenery provides a stark contrast to 'tourist' Greece. This is a land of rocky peaks, deep river gorges (including Vikos Gorge, the world's deepest), lakes and forests, where poor roads and transportation links mean that much of the area is barely inhabited. However, extensive government investment in recent years has improved communications  and many villages and towns have been restored and offer quality tourism for hikers and nature lovers. There are several national parks in the area with unique wildlife, including bears, wolves and lynx, and excellent hiking. Communications away from the coast remain limited and private transport is essential. The west is the wettest region of the country and the winters are very cold with heavy snowfalls. The coastal area in the north-west around Parga is heavily developed with many hotels and several villages are popular tourist and hiking centres. However, the region isn't popular with holiday homebuyers and unless you're looking for a remote rural dwelling to restore, it's of little interest.

Evia & the Sporades

● **Nearest Airports** – Athens, Skiathos and Skyros (international).

The island of **Evia** (pop. 165,000), the second-largest in Greece after Crete, lies just off the coast of mainland Greece – to which it's joined by a suspension bridge – north of Athens. The main town, Halkída, is a big industrial centre and port and is of little interest to visitors. There are some beautiful villages in the centre and north of the island, including Stení, the starting point for the climb to the top of Mount Dirfys (1,743m/5,718ft), Evia's highest mountain. The south of the island has

a number of resorts, although they're generally more popular with Greeks than foreigners. There are some good beaches to the north and east. Property prices vary hugely from €30,000 for a village ruin to over €1 million for a luxury villa. Rental potential is good, particularly if you cater for the Greek market.

The **Sporades** lie to the north and east of Evia and are a collection of 11 islands, of which four are inhabited: Alonnisos, Skiathos, Skopelos and Skyros.

Alonnisos (pop 2,700) is a green island and the least developed of the four, with many natural harbours (no mooring fees). The surrounding waters are a 'marine conservation park' with some of the cleanest waters in the Aegean – a paradise for divers. This is a quiet, peaceful island with little nightlife and a reputation for excellent food. The island isn't easy to get to and only has one road. There's a shortage of building land, but available plots range from €60,000 to over €100,000 and a new two-bedroom house costs from €150,000.

Skiathos (pop 6,160) is one of Greece's most attractive islands with an abundance of dense woods, rugged mountains, golden-sand beaches, azure seas and enchanting villages – many believe it's the most beautiful island in the Aegean. Koukounaries Bay in the south-west lays claim to one of the best beaches. It's a popular (and busy) tourist destination and home to a relatively large expatriate population, although it's also one of Greece's most expensive islands. The property market is somewhat limited and prices start at €160,000 for apartments, €250,000 for townhouses and €280,000 for small villas.

Skopelos (pop 4,700) is extensively cultivated and less developed due to its pebbly beaches, although the island is popular with hikers. The capital, Skopelos Town, is one of the prettiest towns in the Aegean and the island is more of a retreat than a resort – not for nothing are there more than 125 churches! There's a good choice of property on the island, with prices starting at €70,000 for a traditional house and €50,000 for a 100m² plot in town with permission to build up to 160m².

Skyros (pop 2,600) is different from the other Sporades islands and more reminiscent of the Cyclades in its architecture. Its capital, Skyros Town, boasts some extremely attractive traditional architecture. The north of the island is green and fertile, while the south is generally barren. Skyros is home to many artists and offers numerous holiday courses ranging from cooking to Reiki. This creative island isn't easy to get to and the airport has no flights from the UK.

Communications in the region vary considerably, although as would be expected, Evia has good road and rail connections with the mainland, and regular local bus and ferry services. Skiathos and Skyros both have international airports, although flights are infrequent outside the summer tourist season. There's a regular ferry service between the islands and the mainland in summer, but this is much reduced in winter. Although there are bus services on the islands, private transport is often essential.

The Ionian Islands

- **Nearest Airports** – Corfu, Kefallonia and Zakynthos (international), and Kythira (domestic).

The Ionian Islands (pop. 214,900) consist of seven main islands – Corfu, Ithaki, Kefallonia, Kythira, Lefkas, Paxos and Zakynthos – situated off the west coast of mainland Greece. Thanks to the abundant rainfall, they are the greenest and most verdant of all Greek islands, and among the most beautiful, with superb beaches. Their culture and cuisine are quite different from other parts of Greece, with a distinct Venetian character.

The Ionian climate is the wettest in Greece, particularly Corfu, and outside the summer season the weather is often unsettled with heavy rainfall. Winters can be very damp and cool, and shouldn't be underestimated, while summers can be extremely hot, as unlike many other islands they don't benefit from cooling winds. However, in late spring and early autumn the weather is usually perfect.

Communications are generally excellent and Corfu, Kefallonia and Zakynthos all have international airports and good connections with Athens. In the summer there are frequent ferry services between

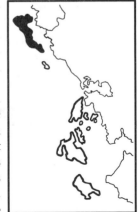

the islands and the mainland, which, although severely curtailed in winter, remain reasonable. Bus services on Corfu and Zakynthos are good, but poor on Kefallonia (although improving), and private transport is advantageous on all the islands.

Corfu (pop. 110,000) is the most popular of all the Greek islands and synonymous with package holidays; it's over-developed in parts, although due to its size it's easy to escape the tourist hordes. It's the greenest of the Greek islands (dubbed the 'emerald isle') thanks to its abundance of ancient olive groves and fir trees, with tiny fishing villages in sheltered coves on the east coast and sandy beaches on the west. The capital, Corfu Town, is one of the country's most charming and sophisticated island capitals, with an elegant blend of Venetian, French and Greek architecture.

Paleokastrítsa on the west coast is a picturesque, unspoilt resort, while the main family resorts tend to be on the north side. Further to the east between Kassiopi and Barbati are some favourite hideaways (the gem is San Stefano) of the expatriate population (around 11,000), mainly British, where there's an abundance of villas. There are beautiful sandy beaches on the west coast and the Korísson Lagoon in the south is a large nature reserve and a paradise for ornithologists. Corfu also has several attractive satellite islands. It has been called 'the bridge connecting Greece with the rest of Europe' and is served by both international and domestic flights, plus ferries from Ancona, Brindisi and Trieste (Italy), and Patra and Igoumenitsa on the mainland.

The property market is buoyant in Corfu and has grown steadily over the last few years, helped by publicity generated from British property and relocation television programmes. Prices are reasonable by Greek standards and are currently increasing at around 5 per cent a year. Popular areas with expatriate buyers (the majority are British) include Corfu Town, San Stefano and Agios Ionnes in the north, and the villages of Gardelelades near Palaiokastritsa and Nyfes situated in the mountains in the north. Prices for a two-bedroom apartment in a resort area start at €95,000 (from €140,000 in town), €90,000 for a small renovated townhouse, €45,000 for a village house needing restoration and €30,000 for a ruin.

Ithaki (pop. 3,100) off the north-east of Kefallonia, was Odysseus' long lost home (ancient Ithaca) and is one of the least spoilt islands in Greece. Most boats dock at the main town of Vathi, situated at the end of a deep bay, which was badly damaged in an earthquake in 1953 but has since been rebuilt in the old style.

Kefallonia (pop. 35,600) is increasingly popular as a tourist destination (mainly thanks to its Captain Corelli fame) and is the largest and most mountainous of the group, where Mount Enos is the highest peak on the islands. Much of the island's towns and villages were destroyed in an earthquake in 1953, but have since been rebuilt. Its capital, Argostóli, is a large thriving town and Sami is its main port. The north and west coasts have excellent sandy beaches and there are several expatriate developments, particularly around Argostóli. Property is currently a good investment on the island where prices are rising because of increased foreign

interest. Prices start at €75,000 for a one-bedroom apartment (€105,000 for two bedrooms) and €250,000 for a luxury villa. There's currently plenty of new development on the island.

Kythira (pop. 3,000), around 30km (19mi) long and 18km (11mi) wide, is an island of some 600 churches. It's essentially a bleak plateau crossed by well-watered ravines and forms part of a sunken land bridge between the Peloponnese and Crete. Geographically it's an extension of the Peloponnese, but historically it's part of the Ionian archipelago. Kythira Town is one of the best preserved capital towns of the Ionian, with fine medieval mansions and Venetian fortifications. Until recently Kythira was little visited by tourists and is consequently unspoilt, but is becoming more popular and property is a good investment.

Lefkas (pop. 22,500) is connected to the mainland by a long causeway through lagoons and hardly feels like an island at all. It's reached from mainland Greece via a floating drawbridge over a canal that was dug by the Corinthians in the seventh century (historically it has always been an important strategic site). It's a fertile island and the main industry is agriculture rather than tourism, although the resort of Vassilikí in the south is reputedly Europe's largest windsurfing centre and Nidrhí in the east has good beaches. Property here is a good investment and has good rental potential if you cater for the Greek market.

Paxos (pop. 2,000) is the smallest of the main Ionian islands and the least developed. It has no sandy beaches or historical sites, few hotels and a serious water shortage, despite which it's extremely popular in summer. Paxos is also a favourite stopping-off point for visiting yachts, which has helped make it one of the most expensive islands in the group.

Zakynthos (pop. 39,000), also called Zante, like Corfu, features heavily on the package tour circuit, although the island is less developed. It's exceptionally beautiful – the Venetians called it 'the flower of the east' – with some of the best beaches in Greece. Main resort areas are Alykes, Argasi and Laganas.

The North-eastern Aegean Islands

● **Nearest Airports** – Samos (international), Chios, Ikaria, Lesbos, Limnos and Thassos (domestic).

The North-Eastern Aegean islands are a collection of seven major islands that are grouped together for convenience rather than any administrative or historical reason. Nearly all the islands are closer to Turkey than Greece and are less visited than the Cyclades and Dodecanese islands. The scenery on the islands is mountainous and forested, and hiking is a popular pastime.

All the North-Eastern Aegean islands except Samothraki have airports, with good domestic and international connections, although the latter are infrequent in winter. Samos is the ferry hub of the north-eastern Aegean, with frequent services during the summer. There are also boats to mainland Greece, and several islands have (relatively expensive) connections with Turkey. Road transport varies considerably on the islands, and public transport is limited in the more remote parts.

The property market on the islands varies from buoyant, with a good choice on some islands, to limited on others. Two-bedroom apartments are available from €100,000, typical village houses from €50,000 and land can be bought from €20 per m².

Chios (pop. 50,800) is a relatively large island (reputedly the birthplace of Homer and Christopher Columbus) that has traditionally been the home of Greek ship-owners, and therefore less dependent on tourism. In the south is the Mastihohoria area, noted for its mastic gum production and characteristic architecture of white lime and black sand decoration, which is particularly vibrant at Pyrgi, one of the most extraordinary villages in Greece. Off the north-east coast lie nine tiny islets, the Inousses, home to many wealthy ship-owners who have built luxury villas there. Chios is more expensive than other islands in the group.

Ikaria (pop. 8,200) is a fertile, mainly agricultural island, famous for its spa resort, Therma, with its therapeutic radioactive springs. It's mainly mountainous and little developed. Tourism on this very traditional island is low-key and as a consequence the property market is limited, although properties are cheap, e.g. from €50,000 for a traditional village house.

Lesbos (pop. 110,000) is largely influenced by its proximity to Turkey and is known as the 'Garden of the Aegean' thanks to its fertile soil that produces the best olive oil in Greece (it also claims to make the finest *ouzo*). Trekking and bird-watching are popular activities on Greece's third-largest island, which has one of only two fossilised forests in the world (on the west side). Lesbos is popular with Greek holidaymakers, who particularly favour Molivos, a beautiful resort in the north of the island.

Limnos (pop. 18,100) is one of the Aegean's best kept secrets and is largely unspoilt with many fine beaches, despite having a large military air base. (Limnos is close to Turkey.) The capital, Myrina, is the main port, with an impressive Byzantine fortress. One of the drawbacks is that Limnos regularly suffers water shortages.

Samos (pop. 33,800) is situated just 3km from the Turkish mainland and is the closest Greek island to Turkey. It's the most visited island in the group and the east coast is particularly well developed with many resorts. Its verdant landscape is famous for its vines and orchids, which give it an exotic flavour, and makes the island a popular destination for ramblers and hikers. Samos was devastated by a forest fire in July 2000, which destroyed a vast area of woodland. The property market is buoyant and rental potential good.

Samothraki (pop. 3,000) is a small island but scenically one of the most dramatic, with dense forests dominated by Mount Fengari, the highest peak in the Aegean. The island is mainly agricultural and one of the most ecologically conscious in Greece. The island only caters for visitors during July and August, outside of which it's *very* quiet. It's also difficult to get to.

Thassos (pop. 16,000), 175km (110mi) from Thessaloniki, is a relatively unknown island outside Greece, although it has plenty to offer in terms of wild, wooded countryside and fine beaches. The climate is milder than the other islands in the group, cooler in summer and warmer in winter. There are strict building regulations on the island and new properties must conform to traditional styles and proportions. A wide range of new and old property is available on the island and prices are generally low, e.g. from €100,000 for a new villa on a small plot. This island only really caters for visitors during July and August and is quiet for the remainder of the year.

Northern Greece

- **Nearest Airports** – Kavala, Preveza and Thessaloniki (international), Alexandroupolis (domestic).

Northern Greece comprises two regions, Macedonia and Thrace, and is the least visited part of the country. The region's climate is quite different from the rest of Greece: the short summers are hot and humid, the winters very cold, and there's less rainfall than in most other areas. Communications between Macedonia and the rest of mainland Greece are excellent, with well-maintained, fast roads and frequent bus and coach services linking the major towns. Thessaloniki has an international  airport and there are smaller airports at Kavala and Preveza with limited international services. There's also a regular train service between most towns, although journeys are slower than by bus. In the more remote areas, private transport is essential.

Macedonia is the largest prefecture in Greece and its capital is **Thessaloniki** (pop. 796,175), a lively, sophisticated Byzantine city set on the edge of the Thermaic Gulf, whose port is the natural gateway to the Balkans. The area's three highlights are Pella, the birthplace of Alexander the Great, Vergina, site of the royal tombs of several Macedonian monarchs, and Dion, Macedonia's sacred city. In the north-west are the attractive Prespa lakes and in the south Mount Olympus (see **Thessaly** above), surrounded by a large national park with excellent hiking.

To the south of Thessaloniki and separated by two large lakes lies the region of **Halkidiki**, whose south coast consists of three peninsulas: Cassandra, Sithonia and Athos. The peninsulas have a coastline of over 500km (312mi) and superb sandy beaches, making them a popular resort area, but note that the area all but shuts down outside July and August. Cassandra is the favourite among package tourists and includes Greece's largest resort, Sani Beach. Sithonia is greener and less developed, although it has an abundance of villas and its resorts of Neos Marmatas and Porto Karrás are two of Greece's largest holiday complexes. The third peninsula, Athos, is where the Virgin Mary is said to have landed and declared it her garden, and Mount Athos is the holiest of places for the Orthodox religion. Nowadays it's a semi-autonomous, 'theocratic republic' run by Orthodox monks, who live in some 20 monasteries with access strictly controlled and restricted to men.

The property market on Halkidiki is growing fast and foreign buyers are on the increase. Infrastructure in the area is improving and property prices are expected to rise significantly in the near future. Prices start at €75,000 for an apartment or small house. Land is available from €15 per m² in a rural location to €300 per m² in a front line beach position.

Thrace is Greece's most recent acquisition (1923) and is something of a backwater, being tucked away in the north-east corner of the country. The architecture and culture of the region are largely Turkish. The area's main towns are Kavala, the principal port for northern Greece and one of the most attractive Greek cities; Komotini, where the population is half Greek and half Turkish; and Alexandroupolis, an important military garrison. The country's vast tobacco industry is centred in Thrace, where sunflower oil and cotton are also produced. Close to the border with Turkey, the Evros Delta is one of Europe's most important wetlands, and Dhadhiá Forest is an important nature reserve.

The Peloponnese

● **Nearest Airports** – Athens and Kalamata (international).

The Peloponnese peninsula (pop. 1.17 million) is the southernmost part of the Greek mainland, lying south-east of Athens. The Peloponnese is practically an island, joined to the Greek mainland by the man-made Corinth canal crossing the narrow isthmus in the north-west. The peninsula takes its name from the legendary Greek hero, Pelops, and is reputed to have the best of everything Greek. It's an area of outstanding natural beauty with high, snow-capped mountains and some of the  most famous archaeological sites in Greece, notably the ancient citadel of Mycenae, the sanctuary of Zeus at Olympia (where the first recorded games were held in 776BC), and the theatre at Epidaurus. Parts of the east and north coasts are fast developing into resort areas, although the peninsula as a whole remains more popular with Greeks than with foreigners. The beaches on the relatively undeveloped west coast are among the best in the country.

The climate in the Peloponnese varies considerably. The west has hot and dry summers, but rainfall is among the highest in the country and its winters are less severe than other parts of mainland Greece. The mountains in the central Peloponnese are snow-covered for much of the winter, and the nights can be cold even in summer. The east experiences very hot summers and is influenced by the strong north wind, the *meltémi*.

Communications in the northern Peloponnese are among the best in Greece. The north and west coasts as far as Olympia and south to the city of Tripoli (soon to be extended to Kalamata) are served by motorways and there are frequent bus and train services to most destinations in the north of the peninsula and to the rest of the mainland. The world's longest cable suspension bridge, the Rio-Antirrio (road and rail) with a length of 2.3km (1.4mi), has recently been completed joining the Peloponnese with the mainland.

Getting around in the southern part of the Peloponnese is more difficult, and private transport is essential if you wish to travel at a reasonable speed. Kalamata in the south-west has an international airport with limited connections – charter flights from the UK are usually only available during the summer, although budget airlines have recently shown an interest in the route and may include it in their schedule in the near future. The journey from Athens airport to the popular Maní peninsula in the south takes around two and a half hours.

There's a buoyant property market on the Peloponnese where prices have increased sharply over the last few years (by up to 20 per cent) and interest from foreign buyers is strong. There's plenty of property for sale and you can choose between rural dwellings requiring total restoration from around €50,000, modern apartments from around €100,000 and villas in resort areas starting from around €150,000. Traditional stone houses are also available from €150,000. Areas popular with property buyers are the resorts around the Gulf of Corinth, where prices are among the highest in Greece, and the Maní peninsula in the south (one of the most popular areas in Greece with expatriate residents).

The Peloponnese is divided into seven prefectures and there are several important cities in the region. **Corinth**, at the canal entrance to the Peloponnese, is a busy city famous world-wide for its currents. South of Corinth is the vast plain of **Argos**, where much of the Peloponnese's agricultural production of citrus fruits, grapes and olives is concentrated. On the Argos coast are some of the most popular resorts on the peninsula, including **Killini** and **Porto Heli**, which have some of the most expensive property in Greece. Nearby are **Náfplio**, one of the most beautiful towns in the Peloponnese, **Epidauros** with its spectacular Greek theatre, and the ancient town of **Mycenae**. Further south is the prefecture of **Lakonia** with its dramatic, harsh landscape. The famous town of **Sparta** is also located here as well as the remote region of **Maní**, noted for its fierce opposition to both foreign and home rule. Off the southern tip of Lakonia is the island of **Kythira**, a relatively expensive island with excellent beaches and developing resorts.

In the south-west is **Messinia**, one of the least-known and least developed regions of Greece, although this is changing and new development is taking place including a large golf course-complex near Finikounda. Kalamata, the capital town of Messinia, is essentially a military town and has the Peloponnese's main airport. On the west coast are some of the best beaches in Greece, although their remoteness and the general lack of development in the area make them rather inaccessible. Inland at **Arcadia**, as the name suggests, is the best agricultural land in Greece, surrounded by mountains and medieval villages. In the north-west lies the city of **Patra** (pop. 150,000), Greece's third-largest city and a major port serving the western Mediterranean, particularly Italy.

The Saronic Gulf Islands

● **Nearest Airport** – Athens (international).

The Saronic Gulf Islands form a rocky, volcanic chain, known as the 'Athenian Riviera', running south of the mainland and east of the Peloponnese peninsula. They're the closest islands to the capital and popular with wealthy Greeks, particularly Athenians, many of whom own second homes there. The Saronic Gulf Islands have good communications with the mainland and with each other through frequent ferry and hydrofoil services. The climate is temperate with hot summers and mild winters. The five main islands in the group are:

Aegina (pop. 11,000) is the largest island in the Saronic Gulf group and lies close enough to the mainland to be a popular commuter base and to be packed with Athenians at weekends. Due to its ideal strategic position, the island has a glorious past and was briefly the capital of Greece – Aegina is the site of the Temple of Aphaia, one of the most complete ancient buildings in Greece. It's a verdant and beautiful island blessed with magnificent mountain scenery and many secluded rocky coves. Property here tends to consist mainly of luxury villas.

Hydra (pop. 3,000), a popular venue with artists and writers during the '60s, is a national monument and one of the most popular and expensive resorts in Greece. Hydra Town has an attractive waterfront and gracious stone mansions, a legacy of its wealthy shipbuilding past, and has a sizeable expatriate population. Motorised vehicles are banned on the island, where the only means of transport is the donkey. Property here is expensive, but has the advantage of holding its value.

Poros (pop. 4,000) is a forested island close to the Peloponnese peninsula, separated from the mainland at Galatas by a narrow channel of water. Most inhabitants live in Poros Town, the only settlement apart from the many tourist hotels around the island. It's a popular holiday destination, particularly with the British and its population swells to over 15,000 in the summer months. Around 300 expatriates live here.

Salamis (pop. 23,000), birthplace of one of the great Greek playwrights, Euripedes, is barely 1km from Piraeus and consequently is almost an extension of Athens. As a result the island is heavily developed and industrialised.

Spétses (pop. 3,750) is a pine covered island with small coves and the best beaches in the Saronic Gulf islands, and is popular with foreign holidaymakers and Athenians. It's less spoilt than its neighbours and, like Hydra, is car-free. Only certain vehicles are allowed on the island (buses, motorbikes and horse-drawn carriages), so there's little traffic. Spétses is one of the more expensive islands in Greece, with prices starting at around €150,000 for a three-bedroom property.

Property in the Saronic Gulf islands is generally more expensive than in other parts of Greece but rental potential is good, particularly if you cater for the Greek market.

LOCATION

The most important consideration when buying a home in Greece is usually its location – or, as the old adage goes, the **three** most important points are location, location and location! **This is particularly important if you're buying for investment or plan to let a property.** A property in a reasonable condition in a popular area is likely to be a better investment than an exceptional property in a less attractive location. There's usually no point in buying a dream property in a terrible location. Greece offers a wide choice of homes to suit practically everybody, but you must choose the right property in the right spot **to suit your purposes.**

 The wrong decision regarding location is one of the main causes of disenchantment among foreigners who have purchased property in Greece.

Where you buy a property in Greece will depend on a range of factors, including your personal preferences, your financial resources and, not least, whether you plan to work or not. If you've got a job abroad, the location of your home will probably be determined by the proximity to your place of employment. However, if you intend to look for employment or start a business, you must live in an area that allows you the maximum scope. Unless you've good reason to believe otherwise, it would be foolish to rely on finding employment in a particular area. If, on the other hand, you're looking for a holiday or retirement home, the whole of Greece is your oyster.

A large number of regions and islands attract foreign property buyers in Greece. The most popular islands include Crete; the Cyclades, e.g. Ios, Mykonos, Naxos, Paros; the Dodecanese, e.g. Rhodes, Kos, Kalymnos; the Ionian Islands, e.g. Corfu, Kefallonia, Paxos and Zakynthos; the

Sporades, e.g. Skiathos, Skopelos, Alonissos and Skyros; and the Saronic Gulf Islands. Crete is the most favourable location if you're seeking winter sunshine, while the most popular mainland area among foreigners is the Peloponnese.

When seeking a permanent home, don't be too influenced by where you've spent an enjoyable holiday or two. A town or area that was adequate for a few weeks holiday may be totally unsuitable for a permanent home, particularly regarding the proximity to shops, medical services, and sports and leisure facilities. If you're looking for a holiday home that you also plan to let, you will need to look in an area attractive to holiday markets and the property should have a pool and be within easy reach of an airport (see **Chapter 9**).

If you've little idea about where you wish to live, read as much as you can about the different regions (see **Regions** on page 43) and spend some time looking around your areas of interest. Note that the climate, lifestyle and cost of living can vary considerably from region to region (and even within a particular region). Before looking at properties, it's important to have a good idea of the type of property you want and the price you wish to pay, and to draw up a shortlist of the areas and towns of interest. Most importantly, make a list of what you want and don't want in a property – if you don't do this you're likely to be overwhelmed by the number of properties to be viewed.

The 'best' area in which to live depends on a range of considerations, including proximity to your place of work, schools, coast or town, shops, public transport, entertainment and sports facilities, swimming pool, restaurants, bars, etc. There are beautiful areas to choose from throughout Greece, most within easy travelling distance of a town or city. Don't, however, accept at face value the travelling times and distances stated in adverts and quoted by estate agents. According to many developers and agents, everywhere in the Greek islands is close to an international airport.

When looking for a home, bear in mind the travelling times and costs to your place of work, shops and schools (and the local bar/restaurant). If you buy a remote country property, the distance to local amenities and services could become a problem, particularly if you plan to retire abroad. If you live in a remote rural area you will need to be much more self-sufficient than if you live in a town and you will also need to use the car for everything, which will increase your cost of living.

If possible, you should visit an area a number of times over a period of a few weeks, both on weekdays and at weekends, in order to get a feel for the neighbourhood (it's better to walk rather than drive around). A property seen on a balmy summer's day after a delicious lunch and a few glasses of wine may not be nearly so attractive on a subsequent visit without sunshine and the warm inner glow. If possible, you should also visit an area at different times of the year, e.g. in both summer and winter, as somewhere that's wonderful in summer can be forbidding and inhospitable in winter (or vice versa if you don't like extreme heat). In any case, you should view a property a number of times before deciding to buy it.

 If you're unfamiliar with an area, most experts recommend that you rent for a period before deciding to buy (see Renting Before Buying on page 109).

This is particularly important if you're planning to buy a permanent or retirement home in an unfamiliar area. Many people change their minds after a period and it isn't unusual for buyers to move once or twice before settling down permanently.

If you will be working in Greece, obtain a map of the area where you will be based and decide the maximum distance that you'll consider travelling to work, e.g. by drawing a circle with your work place in the middle. Obtain a large-scale map of the area and mark the places that you've seen, at the same time making a list of the plus and minus points of each property. If you use an estate agent, he will usually drive you around and you can then return later to the properties that you like best at your leisure – provided that you've marked them on your map and the estate agent agrees to give you the keys. The best maps of Greece are produced by Road Editions (🖳 www.road.gr) and widely available in Greece at bookshops, petrol stations and some tourist offices.

There are many points to consider regarding the location of a home, which can roughly be divided into the local vicinity, i.e. the immediate surroundings and neighbourhood, and the general area or region. Take into account the present and future needs of all members of your family.

Accessibility

Is the proximity to public transport, e.g. an international airport, port or railway station, or access to a motorway, important? Don't believe all you're told about the distance or travelling times to the nearest airport, port, railway station, motorway junction, beach or town, but check for yourself. If you choose an island with no airport, bear in mind that ferry services are much reduced outside high season and may be cancelled altogether in bad weather.

Although it isn't so important if you're buying a permanent home in Greece and planning to stay put, one of the major considerations when buying a holiday home is communications (e.g. air links) with your home country. Most flights from the UK and Ireland to airports other than Athens operate from April or May to October only.

If you're buying a home with a view to retiring, check the local public transport as you may not always be able (or wish) to drive. There's little point in choosing an isolated spot or somewhere with limited public transport, when in a few year's time you may have to rely on local bus, taxi or train services to get about. You should also consider the terrain of your chosen home, as a location with lots of hills or steps could become an insurmountable problem if you have mobility problems or become disabled. A home in a town is usually a much better proposition for retirees than a country home. See also **Location** on page 64.

Amenities

What local health and social services are provided? How far is the nearest hospital with an emergency department? Are there any English-speaking doctors and dentists, and private clinics or hospitals in the area?

What shopping facilities are provided in the neighbourhood? How far is it to the nearest sizeable town with good shopping facilities, e.g. a supermarket or hypermarket? How would you get there if your car was out of order? Note that many rural villages are dying and have few shops or facilities, so they aren't usually a good choice for a retirement home.

> **Many islands and resort areas in Greece practically 'close down' out of high season offering few or no amenities at all.**

Climate

Do you want or need winter **and** summer sunshine? If you want a relatively warm winter climate, then the best choice is Crete or Rhodes. Note, however, that although the days are mild and pleasant in winter with daytime maximum temperatures in the southernmost Greek islands around 15 to 20°C (60 to 68°F), this will seem quite cool if you're accustomed to the blazing heat of high summer (when air-conditioning is a blessed relief). In winter, it's too cold for sea bathing anywhere in Greece. Bear in mind both the winter and summer climate, position of the sun, average daily sunshine, plus the rainfall and wind conditions (see **Climate** on page 20). The orientation or aspect of a building is vital and if you want morning or afternoon sun (or both) you must ensure that balconies, terraces and gardens are facing the right direction (take a compass when house hunting!).

Community

Do you wish to live in an area with many other expatriates from your home country or as far away from them as possible? If you wish to integrate with the local community you should avoid the foreign 'ghettos' and choose a village, area or development with mainly local inhabitants. However, unless you speak good Greek or intend to learn it, you should think twice before buying a property in a Greek village, although residents in rural areas who take the time and trouble to integrate into the local community are invariably warmly welcomed. Many Greeks in resort areas speak English.

If you're buying a permanent home, it's important to check your prospective neighbours, particularly when buying an apartment. For example, are they noisy, sociable or absent for long periods? Do you think you will get on with them? **Good neighbours are invaluable, particularly when buying a second home in a village.**

On the other hand, if you wish to mix only with your compatriots and don't plan to learn Greek, then living in a predominantly foreign community may be ideal. Note, however, that some developments and areas are inhabited largely by second homeowners and are like ghost towns for much of the year. In these areas many facilities, businesses and shops are closed outside the main tourist season, when even local services such as public transport may be severely curtailed.

Crime

What is the local crime rate? The crime rate in Greece is generally very low, but in some resort areas the incidence of housebreaking and burglary is high, which also results in more expensive home insurance. Check the crime rate in the local area, e.g. burglaries, housebreaking, stolen cars and crimes of violence. Is crime increasing or decreasing? Note that crooks love isolated houses, particularly those full of expensive furniture and other belongings that they can strip bare at their leisure. You're much less likely to be the victim of thieves if you live in a village, where crime is virtually unknown – strangers stand out like sore thumbs in villages, where their every move is monitored by the local populous.

Employment

How secure is your job or business and are you likely to move to another area in the near future? Can you find other work in the same area, if necessary? If there's a possibility that you may need to move in a few years' time, you should rent or at least buy a property that will be relatively easy to sell and recoup the cost. Consider also your partner's job and children's job prospects.

If necessary, ensure that a property has a telephone line installed (or that you can get one installed quickly) and that you can get access to the internet and broadband (ADSL) if required (see page 273). This is particularly important if you will be working from home or running a business. You may also wish to check whether mobile phone reception is possible in the local area (reception is poor in some areas).

Garden

If you're planning to buy a country property with a large garden or plot of land, bear in mind the high cost and amount of work involved in its upkeep. If it's to be a second home, who will look after the house and garden when you're away? Do you want to spend your holidays gardening and cutting back the undergrowth? It's best to choose low-maintenance gardens with little lawn, plenty of paved areas and drought-loving plants. If you buy a plot with fruit and/or olive trees, bear in mind that they require a lot of work – pruning, tending and picking fruit, etc.

Do you want a home with a lot of outbuildings? What are you going to do with them? Can you afford to convert them into extra rooms or guest accommodation?

Local Council

Is the local council well run? What are the views of other residents? If the municipality is efficiently run you can usually rely on good local social and sports services and other facilities.

Natural Disasters

Check whether an area is liable to natural disasters such as earthquakes, floods, forest fires or severe storms. If a property is located near a waterway, it may be expensive to insure against floods (or flash floods) which are a threat in some areas. Note that in areas with little rainfall there may be frequent droughts, severe water restrictions and high water bills.

Earthquakes are common in many parts of Greece, therefore you should check that a property has been built to withstand tremors.

Noise

Noise can be a problem in some areas, particularly in summer. Although you cannot choose your neighbours, you can at least ensure that a property isn't located next to a busy road, industrial plant, commercial area, building site, discotheque, night club, bar or restaurant (where revelries may continue into the early hours).

Look out for objectionable neighbouring properties that may be too close to the one you're considering and check whether nearby vacant land has been zoned for commercial activities. In community developments, e.g. apartment blocks, many properties are second homes and are let short-term, which means you may have to tolerate boisterous holiday-makers as neighbours throughout the year (or at least during the summer months). In towns, traffic noise, particularly from motorcycles, can continue all night!

Outside the summer season, Greek islands are blissfully quiet and a haven of tranquillity.

Parking

If you're planning to buy in a town or city, is there adequate private or free on-street parking for your family and visitors? Is it safe to park in the street? Note that in cities it's important to have secure off-street parking if you value your car.

Parking is a problem in cities and most large towns, where private garages or parking spaces are unobtainable or expensive. It's also increasingly difficult to find parking in villages, so it's advisable to ensure that you have a private garage or reserved parking space close to your home.

Traffic congestion is also a problem in many towns and tourist resorts, particularly during the high season. Bear in mind that an apartment or townhouse in a town or community development may be some distance from the nearest road or car park. How do you feel about carrying heavy shopping hundreds of metres to your home and possibly up several flights of stairs? If you're planning to buy an apartment above the ground floor, you may wish to ensure that the building has a lift.

Property Market

If you're planning to buy a property mainly for investment (see page 19), you should base your decision regarding the location and type of property on the investment potential, rather than your own preferences. If you plan to let a property (see **Chapter 9**) you will need to ensure that it's in a popular area, preferably with maximum letting potential, with good access to a beach and other facilities. It should have, or have access to, a pool and be within easy travelling distance of an airport (most holidaymakers don't want to travel for more than 30 minutes by car from an airport).

Schools

What about your children's present and future schooling? What is the quality of local schools? Note that even if your family has no need, or plans to use local schools, the value of a home may be influenced by the quality and location of schools. Most international schools are situated in Athens or Thessaloniki.

Sports & Leisure Facilities

What is the range and quality of local leisure, sports, community and cultural facilities? What is the proximity to sports facilities such as beaches, golf courses, ski resorts or waterways? Bear in mind that properties in or close to coastal or ski resorts are generally more expensive, although they also have the best letting potential.

Tourists

Bear in mind that if you live in a popular tourist area, i.e. almost anywhere on the coast or the islands, you will be inundated with tourists in the summer. They won't only jam the roads and pack the beaches and shops, but will also occupy your favourite table at your local bar or restaurant! Bear in mind that while a 'front-line' property on a beach sounds attractive and may be ideal for short holidays, it isn't always the best solution for permanent residents. Many beaches are hopelessly crowded in the peak season, streets may be smelly from restaurants and fast food joints, parking may be impossible, services stretched to breaking point and the incessant noise may drive you crazy. You may also have to tolerate water shortages, power cuts and sewage problems.

Some people prefer to move inland or to higher ground, where it's less humid, you're isolated from the noise and can also enjoy excellent views. Note, however, that getting to and from hillside properties is often precarious and the often poorly-maintained roads (usually narrow and unguarded) are for sober, confident drivers only.

Town or Country?

Do you wish to be in a town or do you prefer the country? Inland or by the sea? How about living on an island? Life on a Greek island is more restricted and remote, e.g. you cannot jump into your car and drive to Athens or another large town or 'pop' over the border into a neighbouring country. You should also bear in mind that many Greek islands have only a restricted ferry service in winter and are often cut off for days at a time due to rough seas.

If you buy a property in the country you will have to tolerate poor public transport, long travelling distances to a town of any size, solitude and remoteness, and the high cost and amount of work involved in the upkeep of a country house and garden. You won't be able to nip to the local shop for fresh bread, drop into the local taverna for a glass of your favourite tipple with the locals, or have a choice of restaurants on your doorstep. In a town or large village, the weekly market will be just around the corner, the doctor and pharmacy close at hand, and if you need help or run into any problems, your neighbours will be nearby.

On the other hand, in the country you will be closer to nature, have more freedom, e.g. to make as much noise as you wish, and possibly complete privacy, e.g. to sunbathe or swim *au naturel*. Living in a remote area in the country will suit those looking for peace and quiet who don't want to involve themselves in the 'hustle and bustle' of town life (not that there's a lot of this in Greek rural towns). If you're after peace and quiet, make sure that there isn't a busy road or railway line nearby or a local church within 'donging' distance.

Note, however, that many people who buy a remote country home find that the peace of the countryside palls after a time and they yearn for the more exciting city or coastal night-life. If you've never lived in the country, it's advisable to rent before buying. Note also that while it's cheaper to buy in a remote or unpopular location, it's usually much more difficult to find a buyer when you want to sell.

GETTING THERE

Although it isn't so important if you're planning to live permanently in Greece and will be spending most of your time there, one of the major considerations when buying a holiday home is the cost of getting to Greece from your home abroad. How long will it take to get to a home in Greece, taking into account journeys to and from airports, ports and railway stations? How frequent are flights, ferries or trains at the time(s) of year when you plan to travel? Are direct flights available? What is the cost of travel from your home country to the region where you're planning to buy a home? Are off-season discounts or inexpensive charter flights available? If a long journey is involved, you should bear in mind that it may take you a day or two to recover, e.g. from jet lag after a long flight. Obviously the travelling time and cost of travel to a home abroad will be more critical if you're planning to spend frequent weekends there, rather than a few longer stays.

Flight times to Greece from the UK are from three and a half to four and a half hours, depending on your starting point and destination. Travel by train or road takes at least three days, so is really only an option if you wish to visit other countries on the way or take a car with you. Bear in mind that outside the high season flights and ferries are reduced or suspended. Often the only flight option is to fly to Athens or Thessaloniki and then take a connecting domestic flight. Note that the last connecting flights (and ferries) generally leave before 6pm so you need to arrive at least two hours before this to ensure you make the connection.

Airline Services

Most European international airlines provide scheduled services to Athens and many also operate scheduled services to Thessaloniki and Heráklion (Crete). Currently only two carriers fly direct to Greece from North America and the best option is often to fly to London and get a flight to Greece from there. Other international airports in Greece with charter and/or budget flights only are Corfu, Hania (Crete), Kavala, Kefallonia, Kos, Mykonos, Prevesa, Rhodes, Samos, Santorini, Skiathos, Skyros, Thessaloniki, Vólos and Zakynthos.

The Greek national airline, Olympic Air, is Greece's principal international carrier, which shares major routes to the UK with British Airways. Olympic Air has a poor reputation for punctuality and is one of Europe's least profitable airlines. Government attempts to privatise the airline have so far been unsuccessful and the authorities continue to inject vast sums of public money into Olympic Air, a practice forbidden by the EU who have instigated an investigation.

Nowadays there's a reasonable choice of flights from airports in the UK to airports in Greece, and the number is increasing all the time. However, some regions are less well-served than others (see **Appendix**

F) and charter flights are generally available only from May to October. In recent years budget airlines have introduced much needed competition into the market and there's an excellent choice of charter flights in the summer months. Note, however, that the instability of the airline business means that airlines can (and do) merge or go bankrupt, which often results in a cut-back of services or the disappearance of a route. Budget airlines also frequently change their routes and prices. You therefore shouldn't invest in a property if you need to rely on cheap flights to a local airport. Bear in mind that it's relatively easy to reach regional airports in Greece via Athens, but domestic flights (see page 82) are invariably expensive and time-consuming.

Note that flights advertised in the press or on the internet often don't include the following:

- Airport taxes;
- Credit or debit card fee (e.g. 2.5 per cent of the price or a fixed amount – €5 to €7);
- Fuel supplement (in January 2005 some airlines were charging from GB£5 to GB£20 per flight);
- Security charge.

When all of the above are included, they may total more than the basic flight cost!

Scheduled Flights

Scheduled flights from the UK are provided by British Airways and Olympic Air, from Ireland by Aer Lingus and British Airways, and from North America by Delta Airlines and Olympic Air. All transatlantic flights from North America are via Athens. Fares on scheduled flights have fallen in recent years due to increased competition, although they're still high compared with charter and budget fares. Scheduled flights can usually be booked well in advance and offer flexibility on return dates.

Budget Flights

The introduction of 'no-frills' flights into the Greek holiday market has provided a welcome breath of fresh air and some much needed competition and choice. Budget airlines generally offer lower fares, although they are high in the summer and may not be cheaper than a scheduled flight (particularly if you're able to take advantage of a special offer from British Airways or Olympic Air). Food and drinks on budget airlines are expensive. The main budget airlines currently operating between the UK and Greece are Easyjet and Hellas Jet.

Charter Flights

Inexpensive charter flights to Greece are common from many European countries, particularly the UK and Germany. The vast majority of Greece's summer visitors from the UK arrive on charter aircraft. Charter flights generally run from mid-April or May to the end of October and aren't necessarily the cheapest options, particularly in high season when it may be cheaper to fly to Athens and get a connecting domestic flight. Charter flights often leave and arrive at 'unsociable' hours, i.e. late night or very early morning.

The main charter companies operating to Greece from the UK are:

* Air2000 (First Choice, ☎ 0870-850 3999, 💻 www.firstchoice.co.uk);
* Avro (☎ 0870-458 2841, 💻 www.avro.com);
* Excel Airways (☎ 0870-169 0169, 💻 www.excelairways.co.uk);
* Monarch (charter flights can only be booked through tour operators);
* Thomas Cook (☎ 0870-752 0918, 💻 www.flythomascook.com).

Flights are available from numerous regional airports in the UK to destinations in Greece (see **Appendix F: Airline Services**). Other European charter airlines, e.g. Azura and Scandik, also offer flights to Greece from the UK during the summer only.

Flying via Italy

An alternative way of reaching Greece is to fly to Italy and take the ferry (see **International Ferry Services** on page 80) to Corfu, Igoumenitsa or Patra. Ryanair (☎ 0871-246 0000, 💻 www.ryanair.com) operates flights to the Italian ports of Ancona, Bari, Brindisi and Trieste from London Stansted, and to Venice from Liverpool, London Luton and London Stansted.

Airports

This section contains a survey of Greece's main airports and lists the UK airports serving them. (A table showing Greek airports with flights from the UK and Ireland is shown in **Appendix F**.) There are naturally flights from many other European and world-wide destinations, but to list them all is beyond the scope of this book.

Limited information in English about Greek airports is available from the Hellenic Civil Aviation Authority website (🖳 www.hcaa-eleng.gr). Note that Athens airport is the main international airport for Attica, Evia and the Sporades, the Peloponnese and the Saronic Gulf Islands.

Athens

Greece's main airport is Athens' Eleftherios Venizelos (☎ 2103-530 000, 🖳 www.aia.gr), a much needed new international airport which opened in 2001, situated 26km (16mi) east of the city. It's the country's air transport hub serving 12 million passengers a year and handling the vast majority of international flights. Scheduled flights from most European destinations operate throughout the year, plus charter and budget flights. The airport is large (allow plenty of time between connecting flights – see below) and spacious, and provides a wide range of services (24-hour) including a transit hotel. It has excellent road and public transport links to Athens including metro, express bus and taxi, and there's also a regular bus service to Pireas.

Athens airport is served by regular flights from the UK and Ireland from Belfast, Dublin, Glasgow, London Gatwick, London Heathrow, London Luton and Manchester (see **Appendix F**).

Connecting Flights at Athens: Athens international airport is one of the world's largest, therefore if you need to take a connecting flight to your final destination you should allow at least 90 minutes between flights. If possible, check your luggage through to your final destination at your first departure point, so that you don't need to collect your luggage at Athens and check it in again on the domestic flight.

Central Greece

Vólos: Nea Aghialos airport (☎ 2428-076 886), situated 19km/12mi south-west of the city, is very small and served by charter flights only. Buses connect the airport with Vólos and the Pelion peninsula, but services can be erratic and taxis are scarce.

Crete

Chania (☎ 2821-063 224): This airport (situated 15km/10mi to the east of the city) is a small international airport served only by charter flights from the UK airports of London Gatwick and Manchester. Domestic flights connect with Athens and Thessaloniki. Taxis are the main means of getting to the airport from the city; buses are infrequent.

Heraklion (☎ 2810 397 136): Crete's main international airport (situated 4km/2.5mi east of Heraklion) is served by regular flights from the UK from London Gatwick (GB Airways as from May 2005) and Belfast (Excel Airways). Domestic flights run from Athens, Rhodes, Santorini and Thessaloniki. Buses operate from the airport to the city centre and taxis are also available.

Cyclades

Mykonos: Mykonos airport (☎ 2289-079 000), situated 3km south-east of the capital, has recently been expanded and charter flights are available from London Gatwick and Manchester, and domestic flights to Athens, Santorini, Rhodes and Thessaloniki. Taxis are the only means of public transport to the airport.

Naxos: Naxos airport (☎ 2285-023 969), 3km south of Hora, is small and has domestic flights to Athens.

Paros: The airport (☎ 2284-021 878), situated in the south-east of the island, has domestic flights to Athens. Buses operate from Aliki and Parikia to the airport and taxis are also available.

Santorini: Charter flights from Santorini airport (☎ 2286-028 400), situated in the east of the island, are available from London Gatwick, Manchester and Newcastle. Regular buses connect the airport with Fira in the summer and taxis are also available.

Dodecanese Islands

Kos: Kos airport (☎ 2242-056 000) is situated at the southern end of the island, some 26km (16mi) from Kos Town. Charter flights to Kos are available from Birmingham, Bristol, East Midlands, Glasgow, London Gatwick and Manchester. Domestic flights are also available to Athens and Thessaloniki. Buses and taxis provide transport from the airport to points throughout the island.

Leros: The airport (☎ 2247-022 275) is situated in the north of the island near the town of Partheni. Taxis are the only means of public transport to and from the airport, which operates domestic flights only to Athens, Kos and Rhodes (via Kos).

Rhodes: Rhodes airport (☎ 2241-083 222) in the north of the island near Paradisi has charter flights from Birmingham, Bristol, Cardiff, East Midlands, Exeter, Glasgow, London Gatwick, Manchester and Newcastle. Domestic flights are also available to most main airports.

There's a scheduled bus service between the airport and Rhodes Town, some 16km (10mi) away.

Epirus & the West

Ioannina: This small airport (☎ 2651-027 058) offers only domestic flights to Athens and Thessaloniki.

Evia & the Sporades

Skiathos: The island's airport (☎ 2427-022 376) is situated in the north-east and has charter flights from London Gatwick and Manchester, and a daily flight to Athens.

   Skyros: The airport (☎ 2222-091 607) is situated in the far north of the island and has charter flights to several northern European countries (but not the UK) and domestic flights. The only transport to/from the airport is by taxi.

Ionian Islands

Corfu: Corfu airport (☎ 2661-039 040) is situated south of Corfu Town and handles charter flights from Birmingham, Bristol, Cardiff, East Midlands, Glasgow, Leeds Bradford, Liverpool, London Gatwick, London Luton, London Stansted, Manchester and Norwich. Corfu also offers domestic flights to many Greek airports. There are no buses from the airport to the capital and taxi or private transport are the only options.

   Kefallonia: The island's airport (☎ 2671-029 900) is situated 9km (5mi) south of Argostoli and has charter flights from Birmingham, Cardiff, London Gatwick, London Luton and Manchester. Domestic flights connect the island with Athens, Corfu and Zakynthos. There's no airport bus service.

   Zakynthos: The airport (☎ 2695-029 500) is situated 6km (4mi) to the south-west of the capital and has charter flights from Birmingham, Bristol, East Midlands, Glasgow, London Gatwick, London Stansted, Manchester and Newcastle. Domestic flights are available to Athens, Corfu and Kefallonia. There's no bus service at the airport.

North-eastern Aegean Islands

Lesbos: The island's airport (☎ 2251-038 700) is some 8km (5mi) south of Mytilini and offers domestic flights to Athens, Chios, Limnos and Thessaloniki. **Note that airlines refer to Lesbos as Mytilene.**

Samos: The airport (☎ 2273-087 800) is situated to the south-east of the island, just west of Pythagorio. Charter flights are available from London Gatwick and Manchester, and domestic flights connect the island with Athens and Thessaloniki. There's no airport bus service.

Northern Greece

Kavala: The airport (☎ 2591-053 271), located 29km (18mi) east of the town, currently has no charter flights to the UK. Domestic flights connect Kavala with Athens.

Preveza: Domestic flights connect Preveza with Athens, Kefallonia, Thessaloniki and Zakynthos. The airport (☎ 2682-026 113) is sometimes referred to as Lefkada or Aktion.

Thessaloniki: The airport (☎ 2310-473 700) is situated 16km (10mi) south-east of the city and offers both bus and taxi connections to the city. Charter flights are available from Birmingham, Bristol, East Midlands, Glasgow, London Gatwick, London Stansted, Manchester and Newcastle. Thessaloniki is Greece's second largest airport and has domestic flights to most Greek destinations.

Peloponnese

Kalamata: The airport (☎ 2721-063 805) is situated 11km (7mi) west of Kalamata near Messini. Charter flights are available from London Gatwick, Manchester and Newcastle (Air2000).

International Rail Services

It's possible to travel to Greece by rail from northern Europe via Italy, although the journey is long (over a day) and expensive — flights are considerably cheaper unless you have an Inter-Rail or Eurail pass. You can't buy a ticket from Ireland or the UK to Greece, but must buy tickets as you travel. The most practical route is London to Paris, Paris to Brindisi, a ferry from Brindisi to Patra in the Peloponnese and then on to your final destination. Athens, Thessaloniki and Larissa are connected by rail to some major cities in Eastern Europe (e.g. Belgrade, Istanbul and Skopje).

International Bus Services

There are no direct bus services to Greece from the UK or Northern Europe. If you wish to travel to Greece by bus you will need to change buses a number of times – a time-consuming and expensive option.

International Ferry Services

The only country that has regular passenger and car ferries to Greece is Italy. Note, however, that schedules can be erratic and are much reduced from December to April, and they may be cancelled altogether in bad weather. Reservations are essential in high season – discounts of around 30 per cent are available for return tickets.

Ferries operate from the following Italian ports:

- **Ancona** – Several companies operate services to Igoumenitsa (15 hours) and Patra (19 to 21 hours). One-way deck class to Patra costs from €50 and a car from €65.

- **Bari** – Several companies run services to Corfu (summer only, ten hours), Igoumenitsa (from eight hours) and Patra (14 hours). One-way deck class to Patra costs from €35 and a car from €35.

- **Brindisi** – Several companies run services to Corfu (summer only, four hours high-speed, seven hours regular service), Igoumenitsa (eight hours), Kefallonia (eight hours) and Patra (10 hours direct service). One-way deck class to Patra costs from €40 and a car from €35.

- **Trieste** – ANEK ferries run services to Corfu (27 hours), Igoumenitsa (27 hours) and Patra (32 hours). One-way deck class to Patra costs from €50 and a car from €75.

- **Venice** – Minoan runs services to Igoumenitsa (21 hours) and Patra (29 hours). One-way deck class to Patra costs from €45 and a car from €50.

Always allow plenty of time to get to and from airports, ports and railway stations, particularly when travelling during peak hours when traffic congestion can be dreadful.

Strikes in the public transport sector are commonplace. Most are announced well in advance and don't usually last very long. Check the situation in advance (the Greek embassy in your home country should have the latest details) and reconfirm all travel arrangements.

Driving to Greece

The drive to Greece from the UK or northern Europe takes at least two to three days and is really only a feasible option if you need your car while you're there, are taking lots of luggage or wish to visit places on the way. It can be an expensive way of getting there if you take into account petrol and toll costs (toll costs are high in France and Italy), overnight stays and ferry tickets if you travel via Italy. The most popular route from the UK is via France to Italy where you can get a ferry to Greece (see **International Ferry Services** above or page 80). A less popular and longer option is via Hungary, Romania and Bulgaria – **but make sure you have valid visas for these countries.** The more direct route through the former Yugoslavian countries is currently considered unsafe and therefore isn't recommended.

Crossing the Channel

There's a wide choice of routes for travellers between France and Britain, depending on where you live and your planned route, but only one for Irish travellers. These are (from east to west):

- Dover/Dunkerque (Norfolk Line, 💻 www.norfolkline.com);

- Dover/Calais (Hoverspeed, 💻 www.hoverspeed.co.uk, P&O Ferries, 💻 www.poferries.com, and Sea France, 💻 www.seafrance.co.uk);

- Dover/Boulogne (Speed Ferries, 💻 www.speedferries.com) – a five-times daily fast ferry service with a crossing time of 50 minutes; **note that this is one of the cheapest ways to cross the Channel.**

- Newhaven/Dieppe (Hoverspeed and Transmanche Ferries, 💻 www.transmancheferries.com);

- Portsmouth/Le Havre (P&O Ferries, 💻 www.poferries.com);

- Portsmouth/Caen (P&O Ferries, 💻 www.poferries.com and Brittany Ferries, 💻 www.brittany-ferries.co.uk);

- Portsmouth/Cherbourg (P&O Ferries, 💻 www.poferries.com);

- Portsmouth/Saint-Malo (Brittany Ferries, 💻 www.brittany-ferries.co.uk);

- Poole/Cherbourg (Brittany Ferries, 💻 www.brittany-ferries.co.uk, Condor Ferries, 💻 www.condorferries.co.uk);

- Poole/Saint-Malo via Guernsey and Jersey (Condor Ferries, 💻 www.condorferries.co.uk);

- Weymouth/Saint-Malo via Guernsey and Jersey (Condor Ferries, 💻 www.condorferries.co.uk);

- Plymouth/Roscoff (Brittany Ferries, 💻 www.brittany-ferries.co.uk);

Channel fares have risen in recent years and except for special deals or last minute fares, they're no longer cheap on any routes and it's **much** cheaper to fly and rent a car on your arrival. If you're travelling to Greece, you won't be able to take advantage of economy returns, which are usually valid for only five days. Fares vary greatly depending on the time of day and when you travel, with peak fares during July and August. Ferry companies offer different deals and discounts for advance bookings and most have loyalty schemes, usually based on points-allocation.

Shop around for the best deal, which is probably best done by a travel agent who has access to fares from all companies or a company specialising in discount Channel crossings, e.g. Cross-Channel Ferry Tickets (☎ 0870 442 8957, 🖥 www.cross-channel-ferry-tickets.co.uk) whose search engine provides a listing of the cheapest crossing for the dates and times you choose. It's difficult to check fares online as you don't have access to the full range and can only find the price by using the (time-consuming) booking form or quote facility. Brochures rarely include fares.

GETTING AROUND

Public transport services in Greece vary considerably depending on where you live, although there have been improvements in recent years. Public transport is good (if chaotic) in Athens where there's a metro system with three lines that connect with Piraeus and the airport. However, outside the main towns and cities public transport can be sparse, and most people find it necessary to have their own transport. Many Greek island airports are served only by taxis. Information about public transport can be obtained from local tourist offices in Greece and from national tourist offices abroad.

> **Strikes in the public transport sector are commonplace, although most are announced well in advance and don't usually last very long. Check the situation in advance (strikes are publicised in the press) and reconfirm all domestic flights.**

Domestic Flights

Air travel is by far the most expensive way of getting around Greece, but it is also the quickest. Greece's main domestic airline is Olympic

Airways, which, although it lost the domestic market monopoly in 1993, currently has only one competitor, Aegean Airlines. Olympic Airways' sister company, Olympic Aviation, also operates some domestic flights. Both companies offer flights between most islands and the larger mainland towns, but most routes involve travelling to or from Athens or Thessaloniki. Air Sea Planes is a new arrival on the domestic flight scene operating seaplanes.

The domestic network is adequate and useful, particularly for inter-island travel, and especially for islands poorly served by ferries. Tickets can be purchased from travel agents, by telephone or online, and last-minute flights can sometimes be bought from airline offices at airports. Domestic fares aren't refundable and at peak times (especially to the islands) flights must be booked well in advance.

Flights may be cancelled in bad weather or strong winds, particularly if the aircraft is small (e.g. an 18-seater). Baggage allowances are limited to 15kg per person or 20kg when the flight is part of an international journey. Airport tax on domestic flights is levied at €12 per passenger aged over 5 and Athens airport also levies a tax of around €11 per passenger aged over 2 on international flights (tax is usually included in the ticket price).

The following airlines provide domestic flight services:

- **Aegean Airlines** (☎ Greece only 8011-120 000, 🖥 www.aegean air.com) — Aegean Airlines, voted Airline of the Year 2004/5 by the European Regions Airline Association, offers fewer and less frequent flights than Olympic Airways, but the service is better and fares are occasionally lower. Discounts are available for those aged under 26 or over 60. Year-round flights are available from Athens and Thessaloniki to several destinations including Alexandroupolis, Crete, Kavala, Mykonos, Rhodes and Santorini, with tickets costing from €40 to €100 one-way.

- **Olympic Airways** (☎ UK only – 0780-606 0460, ☎ Greece only – 8011-144 444, 🖥 www.olympic-airways.gr) — Olympic Airways operates frequent year-round flights to Alexandroupolis, Kastoria, Kavala, Preveza and Thessaloniki from Athens (there are around 70 flights a week to Thessaloniki). Olympic Airways offers no discounts. Journey times average an hour and ticket prices are from €70 to €100 one-way. In high season there are frequent flights from Athens to many islands, although some (e.g. Skyros and Syros) are less well-served than others (e.g. Heráklion, Mykonos and Santorini). Flight times range from 40 to 80 minutes and one-way tickets cost from €50 to €120. Olympic Airways have representatives in most large towns and islands.

- **Air Sea Lines** (☎ 210-940 2880, 💻 www.airsealines.com) — This new company chartering seaplanes and based at Gouvia Marina on Corfu, offers an efficient and time-saving alternative to island-hopping by plane or boat. Services currently operate between Corfu and Paxos (journey time 14 minutes, €33 one-way) and the following services are planned for summer 2005: Corfu to Argostoli, Brindisi (Italy), Ioannina, Lefkada, Patras and Zakinthos, and Patras to Argostoli, Ithaki and Zakinthos. Journey times will be from 20 to 55 minutes and single fares from €70 to €110. Check-in time is 20 minutes and the maximum baggage allowance is 13kg per passenger.

Domestic Rail Services

The Greek railway organisation, *Organismos Sidirodromon Ellados* (OSE, 💻 www.ose.gr, available in English), operates a generally efficient train service, but rail travel isn't the best way of getting around Greece (although it can be pleasant) and there are few lines. The main routes are Athens to Alexandroupolis via Thessaloniki, and the narrow gauge railway from Athens to the Peloponnese. The train service from Athens to Thessaloniki has recently been electrified and there are two types of train: slow, stopping at every station but with very low fares (around half the standard bus fare), and intercity with fast, modern trains stopping at the main cities only. The journey takes six hours and costs around €30 second-class. On the Peloponnese service, a new high-speed train links Athens with Corinth in 48 minutes, but the pace of travel is slower beyond Corinth. Athens has two mainline stations situated within close proximity of one another: Larissa for northern Greece and Peloponessos for the Peloponnese.

Trains usually leave on time, although they aren't so punctual in arriving, and in high season it's advisable to book your ticket and seat well in advance. An excellent book for rail buffs is *Greece by Rail* by Zane Katsikis (BRADT Travel Guides).

Domestic Bus Services

The standard method of public transport in Greece is the bus. There's an extensive network of routes covering nearly every part of the Greek mainland and buses also provide connections between ports and major towns on the islands. Services on major routes, both on the mainland and on the islands, are frequent and efficient. Buses are generally punctual, particularly on the major routes, and prices reasonable, e.g. Athens to Thessaloniki costs around €30 one way. Services are less frequent off the major routes, although even the remotest villages are connected by bus to the provincial capital at least once a week. On the Greek islands there are usually buses connecting the main towns and ports, but bear in mind that they may not run to/from the airport.

The bus network throughout Greece is run by *Kratikó Tamío Ellinikón Leoforión* (KTEL, 🖳 www.ktel.org, with information in English), an association of regional bus companies whose fares are fixed by the government. KTEL provides an extensive service and all main towns on the mainland have frequent connections with Athens. Most islands also have bus services, although remote villages may be served by only one or two buses a week. On many islands, boats are met by the bus service. Buses operating between major towns and cities are usually air-conditioned and can be booked through travel agents. For other bus routes, tickets can be purchased at bus stations or the local coffee house (*kafeneio*) or bar if there's no bus station; all bus tickets have a seat number on them. You can also buy tickets on board buses, although you may not get a seat!

It's advisable to arrive at least 15 minutes before the scheduled departure time, as buses are known to leave early! Note that in some remote areas, bus timetables are in Greek only. The KTEL website provides comprehensive information about timetables and bus companies, but you cannot book tickets online. The State Railway Organisation (OSE) also operates express buses on a few long-distance routes, which depart from train stations.

Domestic Ferry Services

Island-hopping is one of the delights of Greece for the independent traveller and one of the last public transport 'adventures' in western Europe. However, it isn't the most reliable form of transport as ferry services can be erratic with sailings greatly reduced out of season and often cancelled altogether in bad weather. It's worth noting that outside the summer season most Greek ferries operate primarily for the benefit of Greeks, most of whom travel from their island to the mainland (Athens) and back, and not between islands.

Ports

The main ports in Greece include:

● **Lavrio** – Situated in southern Attica, Lavrio is the main departure point for Kea and Kythnos, and catamaran services to the western Cyclades. Buses run from central Athens to the port (journey time 75 minutes). Port Police: ☎ 2292-025 249.

- **Patra** – Situated on the north coast of the Peloponnese, Patra is the main departure point for ferries to the Ionian islands and Italy. Patra can be reached by bus and train from Athens. Port Police: ☎ 2610-321 002.

- **Piraeus** – Situated in Athens, Piraeus is the principal gateway to most islands, although some island groups (such as the Ionian and Sporades) aren't served. Piraeus is one of the most confusing ports in the world and becomes a 'circus' in summer, when it's virtually impossible to make sense of the timetables. Piraeus can be reached by bus, train and metro from central Athens, and by bus from the airport (journey time 90 minutes). Port Police: ☎ 2104-511 310.

- **Rafina** – Situated on the east coast of Attica, Rafina is Athens' back door to Andros, Mykonos, Paros, Naxos and Tinos, and is much closer to the new international airport than Piraeus (journey time is 20 minutes). Rafina is also smaller and much less chaotic than Piraeus. Port Police: ☎ 2294-022 300.

Tickets

Fares are reasonable for long journeys, although shorter inter-island hops are more expensive. Catamarans and hydrofoils are twice as fast and expensive as conventional ferries. On most services, fares for cars are high – bear this in mind when travelling by car as it may be cheaper to rent a car at your destination. Tariffs are set by the government, therefore all ferry companies (should) charge the same fare for the same route. It's best to buy your ticket on the day of departure (arrive early in high season) unless you need to reserve a cabin or a car space. Most companies provide Internet and/or telephone booking services.

Note that on most services you can't buy a ticket on board ferries.

It's usually best to buy single tickets, as you may wish to return by a different route or with a different ferry company, although return tickets are usually cheaper. Children under four travel free and children aged 4 to 10 or 12 (depending on the company) pay half fare. If a journey is cancelled because of bad weather, you receive a refund or the option to travel on the next available service.

Timetables

Correct, up-to-date information about sailings is notoriously difficult to come by and even schedules issued by the ferry companies are subject to changes. The most reliable information is available from the local port police (*limenarkhío*) who have offices at most harbours. Smaller islands may have only a marine post, but the officer will have a list of schedules posted outside.

Advance information (but subject to change) can be obtained from ferry companies and travel agents; the Athens tourist office also publishes weekly schedules. The Greek National Tourist Office (GNTO) publishes a comprehensive annual ferry schedule, *Greek Travel Routes, Domestic Sea Schedules*, and the annually-updated *Greek Island Hopping* (Thomas Cook) is invaluable for inveterate sailors. A number of websites publish ferry schedules, including 💻 www.gnto.gr, 💻 www.greece ferries.gr and 💻 www.gtp.gr.

Types of Boats

There are four different kinds of boat: ordinary ferries that operate on the main routes, hydrofoils, catamarans and local boats (*kaïkia*), which do short trips and excursions during the summer.

Catamarans: Catamarans are relatively new on the island-hopping scene and offer a similar fast service to hydrofoils, but also take cars. They are also more likely to operate during bad weather and are very popular, therefore it's advisable to book in advance. Two companies operate the main catamaran routes:

● Blue Star Ferries (☎ 2108-919 800, 💻 www.bluestarferries.com) operate from Rafina to Mykonos, Paros and Tinos.

● Hellas Flying Dolphins (☎ 2104-199 100, 💻 www.dolphins.gr) operate from Piraeus to the Cyclades and the Saronic Gulf, and from Rafina to the central and northern Cyclades.

Ferries: Ferries provide the main transportation and all islands have a ferry service, although this may be much reduced in winter. The larger ferries have four classes: deck (or third class), the cheapest and most popular; first class, very expensive with air-conditioned cabin accommodation; second class cabin accommodation; and tourist class with shared berth accommodation. Routes and journey times on ferries vary enormously and before you purchase a ticket it's advisable to check the exact route (find out how many stops there are) and the estimated duration. The main ferry companies are:

- ANEK (☎ 2104-197 420, 💻 www.anek.gr) operates mainly from Piraeus to Crete.

- Blue Star Ferries (☎ 2108-919 800, 💻 www.bluestarferries.com) operate from Piraeus to Rhodes, Chania (Crete) and most of the Cyclades.

- GA Ferries (☎ 2104-199 100, 💻 www.gaferries.com) operate from Piraeus to the Cyclades and Dodecanese, and from Alexandroupolis to Nikaria via several islands, including Chios and Lesvos.

- Hellas Flying Dolphins (☎ 2104-199 100, 💻 www.dolphins.gr) ferry services operate mainly in the Cyclades and the East Aegean Islands.

- LANE Lines (☎ 1427-400 910, 💻 www.lane.gr) operate from Crete to Kasos, Karpathos, Piraeus and Rhodes.

- Minoan Lines (☎ 2104-145 700, 💻 www.minoan.gr) operate from Heraklion to Piraeus and Thessaloniki, and from Patras to Corfu via Igoumenitsa.

- NEL Lines (☎ 2251-026 299, 💻 www.nel.gr) operate from Piraeus to (Syros, Tinos, Mykonos), Chios, Thessaloniki and Limnos. NEL Lines operate high-speed ferries on some routes.

Hydrofoils: Hydrofoils (*dhelfínia* or flying dolphins) are twice as fast and expensive as conventional ferries, but they don't take cars or motorbikes. They operate mainly during the high season and services are likely to be cancelled when the sea is rough. Hydrofoils increasingly serve more routes, although they operate mainly between the Cyclades, Dodecanese and Sporades island groups. The main hydrofoil operators are:

- Hellas Flying Dolphins (☎ 2104-199 100, 💻 www.dolphins.gr) is the largest company and runs services from Piraeus to the Saronic Gulf and around the Cyclades on four high-speed vessels.

- Kyriacoulis Hydrofoils (☎ 2241-024 000) operates services around the North-Eastern Aegean and the Dodecanese islands, connecting Kalymnos, Rhodes and Samos.

- Saronic Dolphins (☎ 2104-224 777, 💻 www.saronicdolphins.gr – only available in Greek at the time of writing) operate from Piraeus to the Saronic Gulf Islands.

Kaïkia & **Small Ferries:** *Kaïkia* (local boats) and small ferries mostly operate during the summer on short trips between islands within the same group. Tickets are more expensive than conventional (larger) ferries.

Taxi Boats: Taxi boats (small speedboats) offer a useful and quick way of getting to more remote or inaccessible parts of islands. Prices are reasonable and are charged per person or per boat, when the cost is divided between passengers.

Safety

Some 18 million passengers use Greek ferries annually – a fleet consisting of around 200 different vessels – and travel by sea is usually quite safe. There's room for improvement, however, highlighted by the *Express Samina* ferry disaster in 2000, which left 82 dead and numerous injured. Safety has never been the high priority it is in some other countries and there has been a lack of enforcement regarding safety practices and the seaworthiness of boats. Despite new legislation regarding safety, including a 30-year limit on the life of passenger boats, comprehensive safety measures still aren't entirely in place. Older boats are best avoided (it's easy to tell which they are – the new boats are always very crowded!) and when boarding a ferry or hydrofoil it's advisable to locate the nearest exits and where the life jackets are stored. When travelling on new vessels you will probably need to book at least 24 hours in advance, even in the low season.

Taxis

Taxis are widely available in most parts of Greece except on the smallest islands. Prices are reasonable compared to many other EU countries, particularly if there are several people sharing the cost. Taxis in cities and towns (usually yellow) have meters and must charge Tariff 1 or Tariff 2 (double Tariff 1 between midnight and 5am). Taxis in rural areas (usually dark blue or black with white tops) rarely have meters and you should agree the fare before starting your journey. There are supplements for airport and port journeys, luggage and when booking a taxi by phone. Taxi drivers in Greece (with the exception of Athens — see below) are generally honest and helpful.

Taxis in Athens

Taxi drivers in Athens have a poor reputation and often overcharge (both tourists **and** locals), particularly for journeys to and from the airport at night.

If you get a driver who refuses to use the meter, you should either take another taxi or agree the fare before commencing your journey (as you should do in a taxi without a meter in any country).

Picking up other passengers along the way is also common practice, but although you share the taxi you don't share the price! Take a note of the meter reading when you get and check that the correct fare is calculated. You may find, however, that because you're a foreigner the taxi driver overcharges you, in which case it's best to pay up and leave quickly!

Driving

Greek Roads

Greece has some of the worst traffic problems in Europe. Traffic jams and pollution are part of daily life in Athens, where some 1.5 million cars pack the streets, and the country has one of the highest accident rates in Europe. In an attempt to reduce pollution in central Athens, petrol-driven cars can only enter the city on alternate days (depending on whether their number plate is odd or even) and Greek-registered diesel cars are banned altogether.

 Rental cars and cars with foreign number plates are allowed access, but it's best to use public transport in Athens and leave your car at home.

Road conditions are often perilous, road surfaces changing dramatically without warning and rights of way are (apparently) decided on a whim by drivers. Petrol and diesel in Greece cost around the EU average, although cheaper than in the UK. The average cost per litre in January 2005 was €0.77 for lead-free, €0.89 for lead-free premium, €0.80 for diesel and €0.88 for diesel-premium. You should also bear in mind that some islands, such as Hydra, are completely car-free.

Like motorists in all countries, Greeks have their own idiosyncrasies and customs, many of which are peculiar to a particular city or region. The personalities of most Greeks change the moment they get behind the wheel of a car, when even the most placid person can become an aggressive, impatient and intolerant homicidal maniac with a unshakeable conviction in his own immortality. The average Greek driver aspires to be a racing driver, as is evident on most country roads where many accidents are due to dangerous overtaking – stricter controls, that were introduced in 1992, haven't had much impact on the death toll.

When driving in Greece you should regard all drivers as totally unpredictable and **drive defensively**. On motorways and main roads you must keep a safe distance from the vehicle in front and can be fined for not doing so. **As a general rule, the closer the car is behind you, the further you should be from the vehicle in front.** Greeks have little respect for traffic rules and many believe that many rules are merely recommendations, particularly those regarding parking (in Athens, a car is a device used to create parking spaces).

Greece's major road network covers around 40,000km (25,000mi), 9,000km (5,600mi) of which are national roads. Road improvements are one of the government's priorities and there's a major programme under way to convert many national roads into motorways. The most ambitious project (Europe's largest road construction project) is the Egnatia Motorway running 680km (425mi) across the north of the country, connecting the west coast at Igoumenitsa with Thrace in the east. In early 2005 the road was mostly completed with the remaining section to be finished by 2006. A north-south axis motorway (1,000km/620mi) is complete and there are other fast roads between Patra, Athens, Corinth, Vólos and Thessaloniki, although these are toll roads costing between €1.50 and €2.50 per section. However, tolls are more than compensated for by the speed and safety of these roads. Note that some toll booths are unmanned and are equipped only with a net into which you deposit the correct change.

Greek motorways are generally good, although the quality of other roads is extremely variable and in some areas even fairly major roads are full of potholes and in a dreadful state. You should therefore exercise extreme caution when driving, as an apparently good road can rapidly turn into a bumpy track without warning. Speed limits for cars in Greece are 50kph (31mph) in built up areas (e.g. towns), 90kph (56mph) or 110kph (68mph) on main roads outside built up areas, and 120kph (75mph) on motorways. Speed limits for motorcycles are 40kph (24mph), 70kph (43mph) and 90kph (56mph) respectively.

If you exceed the speed limit in Greece, you're liable to a large fine depending on your speed and the prevailing speed limit. Police are empowered to issue traffic fines, but cannot collect them on-the-spot. If you receive a fine, it should be paid within ten days at a Public Treasury Office. Railway crossings often don't have protective barriers and caution must be used when approaching them.

Importing a Car

Before planning to import a car into Greece you should check the latest regulations and consider whether the cost, time and paperwork involved is worthwhile – expatriate residents generally agree that it's much easier and less stressful to buy a vehicle in Greece than import your own! In Greece, EU nationals can import and use an EU-registered car for up to six months, after which you have one of the following options:

1. Re-export the car. Note that the car cannot be brought back into Greece until a further six months have passed or a new calendar year starts.

2. Seal the car with customs for at least six months but no more than 12. You can re-claim your car after six months as long as you can prove you have been out of Greece during these six months. You can then drive the car in Greece for another six-month period. **The car must have valid road tax and insurance.** This can be a problem as Greek insurance companies are reluctant to insure foreign-registered cars and British companies will only insure vehicles with a valid MOT certificate, which is impossible to obtain unless the car is in the UK.

3. Officially import the car and pay Greek road tax and customs duties (or remove it from the country).

 If you take your car to Greece, you must be able to prove when it was imported and therefore you should have your papers stamped at customs when entering the country. If you enter with a non-EU registered car, your passport is stamped on entry so you cannot leave without your car!

There are heavy fines for unregistered cars and those without their papers stamped. Further information regarding imported cars can be obtained from the Directorate for the Supervision and Control of Cars (DIPEAK), 32 Akti Kondyli, 18510 Piraeus (☎ 2104-627 325).

If you wish to import an EU-registered vehicle, you are exempt from VAT and Special Consumption Tax/SCT provided:

● You've owned the vehicle for at least six months and VAT and taxes were paid when it was purchased;

● You've been resident in Greece for less than two years and resident in an EU country for at least a year prior to the import application;

● You have a change of residence certificate (issued by a Greek consulate or embassy in your previous EU country of residence);

● You have a five-year residence permit. EU nationals without one are usually required to pay a tax directly to the Customs Authorities or as a bank guarantee, which is returned once you have obtained the permit.

The paperwork associated with the above can be completed by a customs agent and is well worth the fee, although you must go in person to the nearest Customs Authority a month after you've imported your vehicle to request exemption from VAT and SCT. Further information on importing a vehicle is available from the Director of Customs, Ministry of Finance, 10 Karageorgi Servias Street, 10562 Athens (☎ 21033-75250 or 75725).

The above procedure follows EU directives and should in theory be what happens.

 In practice, however, owners of EU-registered cars are made to pay VAT at 18 per cent and high SCT taxes, which often total more than a vehicle's market value! SCT, supposedly based on the market value of the car, is levied at seemingly arbitrary rates that are often far higher than a vehicle's real value.

Greece repeatedly ignores EU law (like some other EU countries) and has been taken to court (and lost all cases) over levying illegal import taxes, but expatriate forums are full of complaints from British car owners who have had to pay small fortunes (several thousand euros) to import their cars.

Once you obtain a Greek residence card you aren't permitted to drive a vehicle with foreign registration, although a period of grace is allowed (six months) while awaiting your Greek registration papers. Full information regarding the importation of vehicles is available from the Ministry of Transport and Communications, Directorate General for Transport, Xenofondos 13, TK 101 91 Athens (☎ 01-325 4515, 🖳 www.yme.gov.gr).

An alternative to importing your car legally is to continue to drive your foreign-registered car and many foreigners apparently do this with no problems. If you live (and drive) on a small island or in a remote area and are well-known by the locals, the chances of your car being stopped are small. However, as soon as you leave your local area (e.g. drive onto the ferry) you risk being stopped by customs officers who will probably (literally) seize the car on the spot.

Driving Licences

EU Residents: If you have a pink EU licence you don't need to exchange it for a Greek licence.

Non-EU Residents: You must apply for a Greek driving licence as soon as you become a resident and you may have to take the Greek driving test (practical and/or theoretical) if your original driving licence isn't recognised by the Greek authorities. (All EU licences are recognised.)

Non-residents: You don't require a Greek driving licence to buy or operate a Greek-registered car and may drive in Greece for a maximum of six months a year with a foreign or international driving permit (IDP).

Note that for your licence to be recognised by the Greek authorities it must have been valid for at least six months. Your licence must be carried when driving in Greece, along with your vehicle's registration papers (proof of ownership) and insurance certificate. The minimum age for driving in Greece is 18 for a motor car or a motorcycle over 125cc, 16 for a motorcycle between 50 and 125cc, and 14 for a motorcycle (moped) up to 50cc.

Car Insurance

Under Greek law, motor vehicles, trailers and semi-trailers must be insured when entering the country. However, it isn't mandatory for cars insured in most European countries to have an international insurance 'green' card. Motorists insured in an EU country, Liechtenstein, Norway and Switzerland are automatically covered for third party liability in Greece.

 Note that car insurance issued in a country other than Greece is only valid if your road tax payments and vehicle inspections (e.g. MOT in the UK) are valid and up-to-date.

Numerous companies offer car insurance and the categories available in Greece include third party, which is the minimum required by law, third party fire and theft (called part comprehensive in some countries) and fully comprehensive (total loss). Policies are now much more user-friendly and companies generally settle claims promptly. When a claim involves more than one party, your insurance company will usually pay your claim first and then settle with the other company, rather than waiting for the other company to pay first.

Car Crime

Most European countries have a problem with car crime, i.e. thefts of and from cars, and Greece is no exception. Foreign registered vehicles are popular targets. If you drive anything other than a worthless heap you should have theft insurance, which includes your car stereo and your personal belongings. If you drive a new or valuable car, it's wise to have it fitted with an alarm, an engine immobiliser (the best system) or another anti-theft device, plus a visible deterrent, such as a steering or gear stick lock. It's particularly important to protect your car if you own a model that's desirable to car thieves, e.g. most new sports and executive cars, which are often stolen by professional crooks to order and spirited abroad.

A good security system won't stop someone breaking into your car (which usually takes most thieves a matter of seconds) and may not prevent your car being stolen, but it will at least make it more difficult and may persuade a thief to look for an easier target. Radios and CD players attract a lot of the wrong attention in some towns and coastal resorts. If you buy an expensive stereo system, you should buy one with a removable unit or with a removable (face-off) control panel that you can pop in a pocket or bag. However, never forget to remove it, even when stopping for a few minutes. Some manufacturers provide stereo systems that won't work when they're removed from their original vehicle or are inoperable without a security code.

When leaving your car unattended, store any valuables (including clothes) in the boot or out of sight. If you leave your car papers in your car, make sure that you have a copy. If possible, avoid parking in long-term car parks as they are favourite hunting grounds for car thieves. Foreign-registered cars, particularly camper vans and mobile homes, are popular targets in Greece. When parking overnight or when it's dark, parking in a well-lit area may help deter car thieves. If your car is stolen or anything is stolen from it, report it to the police in the area where it was stolen. You can report it by telephone, but must go to the police station to complete a report. Don't, however, expect the police to find it or even take any interest in your loss. Report a theft to your insurance company as soon as possible.

General Road Rules

The following general road rules may help you adjust to driving in Greece. Don't, however, expect other motorists to adhere to them (many local drivers invent their own 'rules').

● Greeks drive on the right-hand side of the road so if you aren't used to driving on the right, take it easy until you're accustomed to it. Be particularly alert when leaving lay-bys, T-junctions, one-way streets, petrol stations and car parks, as it's easy to lapse into driving on the left. It's helpful to display a reminder, e.g. 'Think Right!', on your car's dashboard.

- Alcohol is a major factor in many road accidents and drink-driving laws are strict in Greece, where the permitted blood-alcohol concentration is 50mg of alcohol per 100ml of blood, as in most other EU countries. Fines for exceeding the alcohol limit are €150 for up to 80mg of alcohol and driving with a higher level is a criminal offence. A large percentage of fatalities on Greek roads are caused by drunk drivers.

- All motorists must carry a red breakdown triangle and a full set of spare bulbs and fuses. It's mandatory in Greece (and recommended everywhere) to carry a fire extinguisher and a first-aid kit. You cannot carry a petrol can. The Greek national motoring organisation (ELPA, 🖳 www.elpa.gr) is on hand in main towns and on major roads to help motorists who break down and are members of a foreign motoring organisation such as the British AA, RAC or AAA. ELPA has centres in main towns and on the main islands. Dial 174 for information and 104 in an emergency. If you aren't a member and call out the ELPA, you must pay full membership costs.

- Main roads in Greece are designated priority roads, shown by signs. On secondary roads *without* priority signs and in built-up areas, you must give way to vehicles coming from your RIGHT. **Failure to observe this rule is the cause of many accidents.** The priority rule was fine when there was little traffic, but nowadays most countries (Greece included) realise the necessity of having 'stop' or 'give way' signs at junctions, although 'give way' signs are uncommon. Most Greek motorists no longer treat priority as a God-given right, although many still pull out without looking. The priority to the right rule usually also applies in car parks, but never when exiting *from* car parks or dirt tracks. If you're ever in doubt about who has the right of way, it's wise to give way (particularly to large trucks!).

- The wearing of seat belts is *compulsory* in Greece and includes passengers in rear seats when seat belts are fitted. Children under the age of 12 aren't permitted to ride in the front of a vehicle. A baby under nine months of age must be strapped into a cot on a rear seat and an infant aged from nine months to three years must have an approved child safety seat. You can be fined for not wearing a seat belt. Note that if you have an accident and weren't wearing a seat belt, your insurance company can refuse to pay a personal injury claim.

- Jumping a red light in Greece can result in a fine of around €150 and even not dipping your headlights in town can result in a fine of €30. **Be warned!**

- Horns should only be used in emergencies, particularly in towns at night, when lights should usually be flashed to warn other motorists or pedestrians. Fines are imposed for unnecessary use of the horn.

- Always come to a complete stop when required at intersections and ensure that you stop behind the white line. Intersections are a favourite spot for police patrols waiting for motorists to put a wheel a few centimetres over the line.

- White or yellow lines mark the separation of traffic lanes. A solid single line, or two solid lines, means no overtaking in either direction. A solid line on your side of the road, means that overtaking is prohibited in your direction. You may overtake only when there's a single broken line in the middle of the road, or double lines with a broken line on your side of the road. No overtaking may also be shown by the international sign of two cars side by side (one red and one black).

- Always check your rear view and wing mirrors carefully before overtaking, as motorists often seem to appear from nowhere and zoom past at a 'zillion' miles an hour, especially on country roads. If you drive a right-hand drive (RHD) car in Greece you should take extra care when overtaking – the most dangerous of all driving manoeuvres.

- Many motorists seem to have an aversion to driving in the inside lane on a three-lane motorway, in effect reducing it to two lanes. It's illegal to overtake on an inside lane unless traffic is being channelled in a different direction. Motorists must indicate before overtaking and when moving back into an inside lane after overtaking, e.g. on a motorway. In many parts of Greece slower moving vehicles are expected to use the hard shoulder if another vehicle wishes to overtake. It's said that all two-lane roads in Greece actually have three lanes – one in each direction and a third down the middle (or one for going, one for coming back and one for dying in)!

- Be particularly wary of moped riders and cyclists. It isn't always easy to see them, particularly when they're hidden by the blind spots of a car or are riding at night without lights. Many young moped riders seem to have a death wish and tragically hundreds of them lose their lives each year. They are constantly pulling out into traffic or turning without looking or signalling. **Follow the example set by other motorists, who, when overtaking mopeds and cyclists, usually give**

them a wide . . . WIDE berth. If you knock them off their bikes you may have a difficult time convincing the police that it wasn't your fault; far better to avoid them (and the police).

- Cars mustn't be overloaded, particularly roof-racks, and luggage weight shouldn't exceed that recommended in manufacturers' handbooks. Greek police make spot checks and fine offenders around €30 on-the-spot for overloaded cars.

- Be careful where you park, particularly in cities where your car can be clamped or towed away in a flash. *Never* park across entrances, at bus stops or taxi ranks, in front of fire and ambulance stations and schools (which may be indicated by coloured kerbstones), or near pedestrian crossings. Always check parking signs carefully and look for kerb markings (ask someone if you aren't sure whether parking is permitted). Police are empowered to confiscate the number plates of vehicles parked illegally, although this usually only affects Greek-registered vehicles (but you should still ensure that your vehicle is parked legally).

- The use of a mobile phone while driving isn't permitted unless you have a hands-free device.

- All motorists in Greece must be familiar with the local highway code, available from book shops.

Car Rental

Multinational car rental companies such as Alamo, Avis, Europcar, Hertz, National and Thrifty have offices in most large towns and major airports in Greece, but on smaller islands there's often only a local company. If you're visiting in high season, you should reserve a rental car before arriving.

Car rental in Greece is expensive, particularly for short periods, and includes VAT at 18 per cent (13 per cent in the Dodecanese, North-Eastern Aegean and the Sporades). There are also optional extras such as collision damage waiver (CDW) of around €12 daily, without which you're liable for at least the first €500 of damage. High season weekly rates with unlimited mileage start at around €180 for a small model such as an Opel Corsa without air-conditioning. Rates for a larger car (e.g. a Nissan Almera or Renault Megane) with air-conditioning start at €275. Rates are reduced considerably for longer rental periods, e.g. a month or longer and during 'quiet' times when you may be able to negotiate a better deal. Local rental companies are usually cheaper than the nationals, although cars must be returned to the pick-up point. Older cars can also be hired from many garages at lower rates than those charged by the national car-hire companies, although they aren't always in good condition.

To hire a car in Greece you must be aged at least 21, although a few companies have a higher age of 23, and for certain categories of vehicles the age limit is 25. Drivers must have held a full licence for a minimum of one year and most companies have an upper age limit of 60 or 65. If a credit card isn't used, there's usually a cash deposit of a minimum of €100 per day. If you wish to take your hire car on a ferry or to another country, you must have written authorisation from the rental company.

Note that many car rental contracts state in the small print that you aren't permitted to use normal cars on dirt tracks, which are commonly found on many Greek islands and in the countryside. If any damage is done to the undercarriage, you will liable for this. Rental cars can be ordered with a luggage rack and child seats can be fitted free or for a small extra charge. You can also hire a 4-wheel-drive vehicle (useful in the more remote parts of Greece and on country roads), station wagon, minibus, prestige luxury car, armoured limousine or a convertible. Manual and automatic vehicles are also available. Minibuses accessible to wheelchairs can also be hired. Vans and pick-ups are available from the major rental companies by the hour, half-day or day, or from smaller local companies (which are often cheaper).

Moped & Motorbike Rental

In common with many Mediterranean countries, moped and motorbike travel is very popular in Greece and a practical alternative to a car on many islands. The accident rate is, however, extremely high and foreigners are often among the fatalities. Many companies offer mopeds and motorbikes for hire, particularly on the islands and daily hire costs from €10 for a moped and from €20 for a motorbike. Third party insurance is usually included, but medical expenses may not be. If you want to rent a moped or motorbike, bear the following in mind:

- Motorbikes over 50cc require a special driving licence (Category A in the UK). For mopeds under 50cc a standard driving licence will do. Note that some rental companies will rent you a motorbike up to 90cc on a standard licence, but this is illegal.

- Helmets must be worn at all times and if you have an accident when you aren't wearing one, you won't be covered by the insurance policy. Fines for not wearing a helmet are around €80.

- Take extra care when driving on tracks and gravel roads (common on many islands), particularly if you aren't familiar with motorbike riding.

- If there are two people, it's usually safer to hire two mopeds or a powerful motorbike.

- If you're visiting Greece, make sure your travel insurance policy includes cover for injuries resulting from a motorbike accident – many policies don't.

- Rental mopeds or motorcycles cannot be taken on ferries in Greece.

3.

YOUR DREAM HOME

Once you have considered possible locations for your dream home in Greece, you must decide on the type of property that will best suit your requirements and consider the purchase options and the fees associated with buying.

When buying property anywhere, it isn't wise to be in too much of a hurry – and Greece is no exception. It's a wise or lucky person who gets his choice absolutely right first time, which is why most experts recommend that you rent before buying unless you're absolutely sure of what you want, how much you wish to pay and where you want to live. Have a good look around in your chosen region(s) and obtain an accurate picture of the types of property available, their relative prices and what you can expect to get for your money.

However, before doing this, you should make a comprehensive list of what you want (and don't want) from a home, so that you can narrow the field and save time on wild goose chases. In most areas, properties for sale include derelict, unmodernised and modernised farmhouses and village homes, modern townhouses and apartments with all mod cons, and a wide choice of detached bungalows and villas. You can also buy a plot of land and have an individual, architect-designed house built to your own specifications.

 To reduce the chances of making an expensive error when buying in an unfamiliar region, it's often prudent to rent a house for a period (see Renting Before Buying on page 109).

Experts agree that you should rent for a minimum of a year in Greece, which allows you time to become familiar with the region and the climate, and gives you plenty of time to look around for a home at your leisure. There's no shortage of properties for sale in Greece and whatever kind of property you're looking for, you'll have an abundance to choose from. Wait until you find something you fall head over heels in love with and then think about it for another week or two before rushing headlong to the altar! One of the advantages of buying property in Greece is that there's often another 'dream' home around the next corner – and the second or third dream home is often even better than the first.

Don't delay too long as good properties at the right price don't remain on the market for long.

If you're looking for a holiday home, you may wish to investigate mobile homes or a scheme that restricts occupancy of a property to a number of weeks each year. These include shared ownership, leaseback, timesharing and a holiday property bond (see page 133). Don't rush into any of these schemes without fully researching the market and before you're absolutely clear about what you want and what you can realistically expect to get for your money.

RESEARCH

The secret of successfully buying a home in Greece is research, research and more research. A successful purchase is much more likely if you thoroughly investigate the towns and communities in your chosen area, compare the range and prices of properties and their relative values, and study the procedure for buying property.

The more research you do before buying a property the better, which should (if possible) include advice from those who already own a home there, from whom you can usually obtain invaluable information (often based on their own mistakes). Although mixing a holiday with a property purchase is common practice, it isn't advisable as most people are inclined to make poor decisions when their mind is fixed on play, rather than business.

 Some people make expensive (even catastrophic) errors when buying a home in Greece, often because they don't do sufficient research and are simply in too much of a hurry – often setting themselves impossible deadlines in which to buy a property or business, e.g. a few days or a week – and often end up bitterly regretting their rash decision.

Publications & Exhibitions

Property exhibitions are now commonplace in the UK and Ireland, and are increasingly popular with prospective buyers who can get a good idea of what's available and make contact with estate agents and developers. Note, however, that exhibitions tend to represent only the most popular parts of Greece, e.g. Corfu, Crete, Halkidiki, Kefallonia, the Peloponnese and Rhodes. **Appendix A** includes a list of the main exhibition organisers in the UK and Ireland. Some exhibitions charge an admission fee. Outbound Publishing (1 Commercial Road, Eastbourne, East Sussex BN21 3XQ, UK, ☎ 01323-726040, 💻 www.outbound publishing.com) publish *World of Property*, a quarterly magazine containing many properties for sale in Greece (and other countries) and they and others organise property exhibitions throughout the British Isles. Property is also advertised for sale in English-language newspapers and magazines in Greece and abroad (see **Appendix B**) and on the internet.

This chapter is designed to help you decide what sort of home to buy and help you avoid problems (see below). It also contains information about renting, estate agents, the cost of property, fees, buying a resale or a new home, community properties, timeshare and part-ownership schemes, retirement homes, inspections and surveys, renovation and restoration, building your own home and selling your home.

AVOIDING PROBLEMS

The problems associated with buying property abroad have been accentuated in the last decade or so, during which the property market in many countries has gone from boom to bust and back again. From a legal viewpoint, Greece is a relatively safe place in which to buy a home, with buyers having a high degree of protection under local law. However, the pitfalls must never be ignored! The possible dangers haven't been highlighted in order to discourage you, but simply to ensure that you go into a purchase with your eyes open and to help you avoid problems (forewarned is forearmed!).

Legal Advice

It cannot be emphasised too strongly that anyone planning to buy property in Greece must take expert, independent legal advice.

SURVIVAL TIP
Never sign anything or pay any
money, until you have sought legal advice in a
language in which you're fluent, from a lawyer who's
experienced in Greek property law.

If you aren't prepared to do this, you shouldn't even think about buying a property in Greece! Most people who experience problems take no precautions whatsoever when purchasing property abroad and of those who do take legal advice, many do so only after having already paid a deposit and signed a contract (or when they hit problems).

You will find that the relatively small price – when compared with the cost of a home – of obtaining legal advice is excellent value for money, if only for the peace of mind it affords. Trying to cut corners to save on legal costs is foolhardy in the extreme when tens of thousands of euros are at stake. However, be careful whom you engage, as some lawyers are sometimes part of the problem rather than the solution! Don't pick a lawyer at random, but engage one who has been highly recommended by someone you can trust.

Employing Professionals

There are professionals speaking English and other languages in some areas of Greece, and expatriate estate agents, architects, builders and surveyors also practise here. However, don't assume that because you're dealing with a fellow countryman, he'll offer you a better deal or do a better job than a Greek (the opposite is often true). It's wise to check the credentials of professionals you employ, whatever their nationality.

 It's never advisable to rely solely on advice proffered by those with a financial interest in selling you a property, such as a builder, developer or estate agent, although their advice may be excellent and totally unbiased. Avoid 'cowboy' agents and anyone who does property deals on the side – such as someone you meet in a bar – as dealing with them often leads to heartache and it could also be dangerous!

Problems

Among the possible problems associated with buying property abroad are: properties bought without a legal title; properties built illegally without planning permission; properties sold that are subject to embargoes; properties sold with forged deeds; properties with missing infrastructure; builders or developers going bust; developer's loans being undischarged after completion and undischarged mortgages from the previous owner; intermediaries disappearing with the seller's proceeds; overcharging by vendors (particularly when selling to foreigners); property being difficult to sell in some areas, particularly if there are problems with a development; properties sold to more than one buyer; and even properties sold that don't exist!

Note that old properties often have a number of owners, all of whom must agree to sell, and that trees, e.g. carob, citrus and olive, may belong to a number of people who don't own the land! Properties may not have been legally inherited by the heirs and there have been cases where the buyers have had to pay the inheritance taxes. Title deeds have been a big problem in the past, although this is rare nowadays. Buyers must also accept their share of the blame. It's a common adage that many buyers 'leave their brains behind at the airport' when buying property in Greece and it's certainly true that some people do incredibly irresponsible things, such as (on occasion) literally handing over bags full of cash to agents or owners without any security. **It's hardly surprising that people are occasionally defrauded!**

Mistakes

Common mistakes made by buyers in Greece include:

● Buying in the wrong area (**rent first!**);
● Buying a home that's difficult to resell;
● Buying a property for renovation and grossly underestimating the restoration costs;
● Not having a survey done on an old property;
● Not using the services of a good lawyer or not taking legal advice;
● Not including the necessary conditional clauses in the contract;
● Buying a property for business, e.g. to convert to self-catering accommodation, and being too optimistic about the income; and taking on too large a mortgage.

It's normal practice in Greece to declare a lower price in the title deed than actually paid, although you must take care that you don't declare too low a price. See **Assessed Tax Value** on page 122. Checks must be carried out both before signing a contract **and** before signing the deed of sale. Note that if you have a dispute over a property purchase in Greece it can take years to get it resolved in the courts, and even then there's no guarantee that you will receive a satisfactory outcome.

Buying Off Plan

Many problems can arise when buying off plan, i.e. unbuilt properties, or a property on an unfinished development. Because of the problems associated with buying off plan, such as the difficulty in ensuring that you actually get what's stated in the contract and that the developer doesn't go bust, some experts have even advised buyers against buying an unfinished property. However, this isn't practical, because in a seller's market it's essential to buy off plan if you wish to buy a home in a popular development. A 'finished' property is a property where the building is complete in every detail (as confirmed by your own lawyer or architect), communal services have been completed, and **the entire** infrastructure is in place such as roads, parking areas, external lighting, landscaping, water, sewerage, electricity and telephone services. A builder or developer is supposed to provide buyers who purchase off plan through stage payments with an insurance policy that protects them against the builder going bust before construction is completed.

Buying Land

Before buying building land, ensure that it has planning permission or that planning permission will be a formality. Don't take the vendor's word for this, but make it a condition of the purchase of a building plot. See also **Building Your Own Home** on page 146.

Take Your Time

Many people have had their fingers burnt by rushing into property deals without proper care and consideration. It's all too easy to fall in love with the attractions of a home in the sun and to sign a contract without giving it sufficient thought. If you aren't absolutely certain, don't allow yourself to be rushed into making a hasty decision, e.g. by fears of an imminent price rise or of losing the property to another buyer who has 'made an offer'. Although many people dream of buying a holiday or retirement home in Greece, it's vital to do your homework thoroughly and avoid the 'dream sellers' (often fellow countrymen), who will happily prey on your ignorance and tell you anything in order to sell you a home.

RENTING BEFORE BUYING

If you're uncertain about exactly what sort of home you want and where you wish to live, you should rent for a period in order to reduce the chances of making a costly error.

SURVIVAL TIP
Renting before buying is even more
important for those planning to live permanently
or set up a business in Greece, when it isn't wise
to buy a home until you're certain that the
business will be a success.

If possible, you should rent a similar property to that which you're planning to buy, during the time of year when you plan to occupy it. Renting allows you to become familiar with the weather, the amenities and the local people; to meet other foreigners who have made their homes abroad and share their experiences; and, not least, to discover the cost of living at first hand. Provided that you still find Greece alluring, renting 'buys' you time to find your dream home at your leisure. This also gives you the chance to establish yourself among the locals as a 'serious' buyer in the area, a status that may mean you're offered property at a lower price. You may even wish to consider renting a home long term (or even 'permanently') as an alternative to buying, as it saves tying up your capital and can be surprisingly inexpensive in many regions. Some people let their family home and rent one abroad – and often make a substantial profit!

If you're looking for a rental property for a few months, e.g. three to six months, it's best not to rent unseen, but to rent a holiday apartment for a week or two to allow yourself time to look around for a longer-term rental. Properties for rent are advertised in local newspapers and magazines, particularly expatriate publications, and can also be found through property publications in many countries (see **Appendix B** for a list). Many estate agents offer both short and long-term rentals and developers may also rent properties to potential buyers. Holiday companies also rent properties, although only short-term. A rental contract is necessary when renting property in Greece, whether long or short-term.

Long-term Rentals

Greece doesn't have a flourishing long-term (i.e. one year or longer) rental market in resort areas, where it's more common for people to buy, and it can be difficult to find good long-term rentals for a reasonable rent. Most rental properties in resort areas, whether long or short-term, are let furnished – and often poorly equipped for permanent living – and long-term unfurnished properties are difficult to find. However, in major cities the opposite is the case, with long-term rental properties usually let unfurnished and furnished properties in short supply. Note that rental accommodation usually has no heating.

Rental costs vary considerably depending on the size (number of bedrooms) and quality of a property, its age and the facilities provided. However, the most significant factor affecting rents is the region, the town and the particular neighbourhood. A small, one or two-bedroom, unfurnished apartment, e.g. 50 to 75m², which rents for between €500 to €1,000 a month in an average Athens suburb, costs around 50 per cent less in most rural and resort areas outside the main tourist season. You should be able to strike a good bargain when renting out of the main season, when there's a glut of properties for rent. Some islands, e.g. Kefallonia, have a good long-term (up to 12 months) rental market and you can expect to pay from €300 a month for a one-bedroom property and from €400 a month for two bedrooms.

As well as the monthly rent, you must pay one month's rent as a deposit. If you have a long-term contract you may have to pay up to six months rent in advance. Long-term tenants usually pay for their own water and electricity consumption unless utilities are paid for on a communal basis, a common practice in older apartment blocks.

Short-term Rentals

Short-term rentals are always furnished and are usually for holiday lets or periods of up to a year. A short-term or temporary contract is necessary, which provides tenants with fewer rights than a long-term contract. There's an abundance of self-catering properties for rent in Greece, including apartments, cottages, farmhouses, townhouses and villas. Rents for short-term rentals are usually higher than for long lets, particularly in popular holiday areas, where many properties are let as self-catering holiday accommodation. However, most owners let self-catering properties in resort areas at a considerable reduction during the 'low season', e.g. October to March. The rent for an average one or two-bedroom furnished apartment or townhouse during the low season is usually between €300 to €600 per month, for a minimum one or two-month let.

Rent is usually paid one month in advance with one month's rent as a deposit. Lets of less than a month are more expensive, e.g. €300 per week for a two-bedroom apartment in the low season, which is some 50 per cent (or less) of the rent in the high season. Many hotels and hostels also offer special low rates for long stays during the low season (see below). Note, however, that when the rental period includes the peak letting months of July and August, the rent can be prohibitively high.

Standards vary considerably, from dilapidated, ill-equipped apartments to luxury villas with every modern convenience. Always check whether a property is fully equipped (which should mean whatever you want it to mean) and whether it has central heating if you're planning to rent in winter. Rentals can be found by contacting owners advertising in the publications listed in **Appendix B** and through agents in most areas, many of who also handle rentals. See also **Chapter 9**.

Hotels & Motels

Hotel rates in Greece vary depending on the hotel rating – rates are set by the government for all hotels except those with the top 'L' rating – the time of year, the exact location and the individual establishment. You may be able to haggle over rates outside the high season and for long stays, for which many hotels offer special rates. Hotels located in large towns, cities and coastal resorts are the most expensive, and rates in cities such as Athens (while lower than in other European capitals) can be very high. However, inexpensive hotels can be found in most towns, where a single room can usually be found for around €25 and a double for under €50, although usually without a private bath or shower.

Minimum and maximum rates are set according to the facilities and the season, although there's no season in the major cities. Rates are considerably higher in tourist areas during the high season of July and August, when rooms at any price are hard to find. On the other hand, outside the main season, particularly in winter, many hotels offer low half or full board rates (even better rates are offered for stays of a week or longer).

Hotels aren't a cost-effective, long-term solution for home hunters, although there's usually little choice if you need accommodation for a short period only. Bed and breakfast accommodation is also available in Greece, although it isn't usually budget accommodation, in which case you need to choose a hostel.

Home Exchange

An alternative to renting is to exchange your home abroad with one in Greece for a period. This way you can experience home living for a relatively small cost and may save yourself the expense of a long-term rental. Although there's always an element of risk involved in exchanging your home with another family, most agencies thoroughly vet clients and have a track record of successful swaps. Homelink International claims 99 per cent of its clients enjoy successful swaps. There are home exchange agencies in most countries, many of which are members of the International Home Exchange Association (IHEA).

There are many home exchange companies in the US, including HomeLink International with over 12,500 members in around 50 countries (☎ USA 813 975 9825, 💻 www.swapnow.com). Two long-established home exchange companies in the UK are HomeLink International (☎ UK 01962-886882, 💻 www.homelink.org.uk), which publishes a directory of homes and holiday homes for exchange, and Home Base Holidays, 7 Park Avenue, London N13 5PG, UK (☎ 020-8886 8752, 💻 www.homebase-hols.com). The Home Exchange Guide by M. Simon and T. Baker (Poyeen Publishing) contains comprehensive information and advice.

House Hunting

There are many ways of finding homes for sale in Greece, including the following:

● Newspapers and magazines, including the English-language publications listed in **Appendix B**.

● Property exhibitions (see **Appendix A** for further details).

● The internet, where an increasing number of sites are dedicated to property in Greece. These can be found by typing in 'Greek property' or 'Crete property' in a search engine such as Google. Note that most property sites belong to or are linked to an estate agent.

● Visiting an area. Most Greek property owners sell privately and may have a 'For Sale' ('*Poleitai*') sign outside the property, although the best way to find property in villages and rural areas is to ask in the local bar or the local priest who knows everyone.

● Estate agents (see below).

ESTATE AGENTS

There are thousands of estate agents in Greece (over 2,500 in Athens alone) and many property sales in Greece, particularly those in resort areas and in towns, are handled by estate agents or developers' agents, especially those involving overseas buyers. It's common for foreigners in many countries, particularly the UK, to use an agent in their own country who works in co-operation with a foreign agent or developer. Most agents in popular areas of Greece now have staff who speak English and other foreign languages, so don't be discouraged if you don't speak Greek.

Most agents offer after-sales services and will help you arrange legal advice, insurance, utilities, and interior decorators and builders. Some offer help and advice on obtaining planning permission and permits for new buildings or restoration projects. Many agents, particularly on popular islands, provide construction and restoration services, including the supervision of building projects on your behalf. They may even offer a full management and rental service for non-resident owners. Note, however, that agents often receive commissions for referrals and therefore you may not receive independent advice.

Qualifications

Estate agents in Greece are regulated by law and must be professionally qualified and licensed. If possible, you should choose an agent who's a

member of a professional association such as the Hellenic Association of Realtors (☎ 2108-232 931, 🖳 www.sek.gr), whose members must follow a code of ethics, or the Federation of Greek Real Estate Agents (☎ 2104-933 001, 🖳 www.e-mesites.gr). You may be afforded extra protection if an agent is a member of an international organisation, such as the European Confederation of Estate Agents (CEI).

 If you pay a deposit to an agent, you must ensure that it's deposited in a separate bonded account.

Fees

There are no government controls on agents' fees in Greece, where an agent's commission (generally 2 to 5 per cent plus 18 per cent VAT) is paid by the vendor and buyer, and is usually included in the purchase price. Foreign agents located abroad often work with local agents and share the standard commission, so buyers usually pay no more by using them. However, check in advance whether this is the case and how much you're required to pay. When buying, also check whether you need to pay commission or any extras in addition to the sale price (apart from the normal fees and taxes associated with buying a property).

Viewing

If possible, you should decide where you want to live, what sort of property you want and your budget **before** visiting Greece. Obtain details of as many properties as possible in your chosen area and price range, and make a shortlist of those you wish to view. Usually the details provided by estate agents are sparse and few agents provide detailed descriptions of properties. Often there's no photograph, although many agents now post photographs on their websites. However, photographs don't usually do a property justice (on the other hand they may give a false impression!).

Note that there are no national property listings in Greece, where agents jealously guard their list of properties, although many work with overseas agents in areas popular with foreign buyers. Agents who advertise in foreign journals or who work closely with overseas agents usually provide coloured photographs and a full description, particularly for the more expensive properties. Agents vary enormously in their efficiency, enthusiasm and professionalism, and the best agents provide an abundance of information. If an agent shows little interest in finding out exactly what you want, you should go elsewhere.

Corfu Estate Agents
Acharavi, Corfu
Lefteris Tsoukalas - Licensed Real
Estate Agent

For your Dream Home on the Magical Island of Corfu

We have a selection of properties available to meet your needs

Permanent
Homes

Holiday
Villas

Old village
houses for
renovation

Land

Visit our regularly updated website and view all our current properties at:
www.corfuestateagents.com

E-mail: info@corfuestateagents.com

Office Telephone: (0030) 26630 64494
(0030) 26630 64624

Lefteris Tsoukalas: Mobile (0030) 6947269111
Anne Tsoukalas: Mobile (0030) 6947269114
Sarah Wood: Mobile (0030) 6947269115

If you're using a foreign agent, confirm (and reconfirm) that a particular property is still for sale and the price, before travelling abroad to view it.

Many estate agents have websites, so you can check what's on offer from the comfort of your home, although sites rarely show all properties for sale or the latest properties on their books.

An agent may ask you to sign a document before showing you any properties, which is to protect his commission should you obtain details from another source or try to deal directly with the owner. You're usually shown properties personally by agents and won't be given the keys (especially to furnished properties) or be expected to deal with tenants or vendors directly. You should make an appointment with an agent rather than simply turn up and ask him to show you a property. If you make an appointment and cannot keep it, you should call and cancel it.

If you happen to be on holiday, it's acceptable to drop in unannounced to have a look at what's on offer, but don't expect an agent to show you properties without an appointment. If you view properties during a holiday, it's best to do so at the beginning so that you can return later to inspect any you particularly like a second or third time. Agents don't usually work during lunch hours or on Saturdays and Sundays.

You should try to view as many properties as possible during the time available, but allow sufficient time to view each property thoroughly, to travel between properties and take breaks for sustenance. Although it's important to see a sufficient number of properties to form an accurate opinion of price and quality, don't try to see too many properties in one day, as it's easy to become confused over the merits of each property. If you're shown properties that don't meet your specifications, tell the agent immediately. You can also help the agent narrow the field by telling him exactly what's wrong with the properties you reject.

It's sensible to make notes of both the good and bad features and take lots of photographs of the properties you like, so that you're able to compare them later at your leisure (but keep a record of which photos are of which house!). It's also wise to mark each property on a map so that you can return later on your own if you wish without getting lost. The more a property appeals to you, the more you should look for faults and negative points – if you still like it after stressing the negative points, it must have special appeal.

Viewing Trips

Many agents and developers arrange viewing trips and may provide inexpensive accommodation for prospective buyers – some may even refund the cost of a viewing trip if you buy a property. By all means take advantage of inspection flight offers, but don't allow yourself to be pressured into buying on a viewing trip. Always allow yourself sufficient time to view and compare properties offered by a number of agents and developers. A long weekend isn't enough time to have a good look around, unless you already know exactly what you want to buy and where, or are coming to view just a few properties.

Legal Advice

Never allow yourself to be pressurised into a purchase and always take independent expert legal advice. Some agents pressurise clients into signing contracts and paying deposits quickly, alleging there are queues of other clients waiting to buy the property (which may be true!). Some property owners also try to pressurise clients into a purchase claiming legal advice isn't necessary. Your chances of solving any problems are greater if you take legal advice and all lawyers should have professional indemnity insurance. However, there are many reputable estate agents in Greece, particularly those on small islands or remote areas who have a local reputation to maintain.

PROPERTY PRICES

Greece has a fairly lively property market, although until the last decade or so it attracted few foreign buyers, mainly because of restrictions on foreign ownership. Until around 1990 there were few estate agents offering services to prospective foreign buyers, although more have appeared as Greece has become more popular. Greece is largely undeveloped with most areas as unspoilt as Portugal and Spain were 20 or 30 years ago. It has a largely untapped holiday-home market and many areas have good investment potential. There are strict controls over development and renovation to ensure that the local character is maintained, particularly in coastal and country areas. Old village houses are reasonably priced and in plentiful supply in most areas, although they usually require extensive modernisation and renovation and are seldom a good investment. Many foreign buyers buy a plot of land and build a new house. Note that you can expect to pay a premium for a coastal or island property.

Prices are stable in most areas and largely unaffected by world recessions. The main foreign buyers are the British, Germans and Scandinavians, who have been joined by Russian and other Eastern European buyers in recent years. The British tend to prefer the islands and the Peloponnese, and the Germans the mainland.

One of the things that attracts many buyers to Greece is the relatively low cost of property compared to many other European countries. Home ownership is one of the highest in Europe (over 80 per cent), although the locals don't generally buy property as an investment, and you shouldn't expect to make a quick profit when buying property in Greece. Property prices have risen considerably in the last decade, although not by as much as in some other countries. The biggest rises have been seen on some popular Greek islands, where prices have risen at a much faster rate since the country joined the European Union and restrictions on foreign ownership were largely abolished for EU citizens (see **Restrictions** on page 19).

Note that there's sometimes a tendency to over-charge foreigners in some areas of Greece, therefore it's important to compare local prices (i.e. what the locals are paying!) or find a good agent. Prices in winter tend to be lower than those advertised in the summer and if you spend several months in an area and establish yourself as a 'serious' buyer among the locals, your chances of buying for a lower price may increase. In contrast to the wild fluctuations seen in some countries, property prices generally rise slowly and steadily in Greece, and are usually fairly stable, particularly in rural areas where there's little local demand and few non-resident owners. The exception to this is Athens where prices have increased sharply over the last few years.

Apart from obvious factors such as size, quality and land area, the most important consideration influencing the price of a house is its location. Property is least expensive in rural areas (on the mainland in Greece), where a farmhouse or village house may cost the same as a studio apartment on a popular island or in a fashionable resort. The quality of property varies considerably in respect to materials, fixtures and fittings, and workmanship. Value for money also varies enormously and you should compare at least five to ten properties to get a good idea of their relative values. Most property is sold freehold.

When property is advertised, the total living area in square metres (written as m^2) and the number of bedrooms are usually stated. When comparing prices, compare the cost per square metre of the habitable or built area, excluding patios, terraces and balconies, which should be compared separately. If you're in any doubt about the size of rooms you should measure them yourself, rather than rely on the measurements provided by a vendor or agent. Note that a garage is rarely provided with apartments or townhouses, although there may be a private parking space or a communal off-road parking area. Some apartment blocks have underground garages, and lock-up garages may be sold separately for apartments and townhouses. Villas usually have their own car port or garage. Note that without a garage, parking can be a nightmare, particularly in cities or busy resort towns, developments in summer and even some villages.

Costs vary considerably depending on the location and whether you buy a new or an old property. Athens is expensive – not that many foreigners would choose to live here unless they work in the capital. New apartments on the islands cost from around €70,000 for one bedroom, €100,000 for two bedrooms and €120,000 for three bedrooms, although they can be much higher in a fashionable resort, Athens or on a popular island. A new two-bedroom townhouse or villa costs from around €105,000, although prices rise to €200,000 or more in a good location on a small island. A three-bedroom, two-bathroom villa costs from around €150,000 (from €200,000 with a pool) and a four-bedroom villa on a large plot from at least €300,000.

Inland properties are much cheaper than coastal properties. Old stone houses are common in many areas (particularly Crete) and can be purchased from as little as €50,000. However, renovation costs are likely to be at least twice the purchase price, depending on how much of the original structure you can retain. Note that most old village houses tend to be small, e.g. 50 to 75m², with only a few rooms and probably not a bathroom or toilet.

Property	Price Range (€)
1-bedroom apartment	70,000 – 150,000
2-bedroom apartment	90,000 – 350,000
2-bedroom townhouse	95,000 – 250,000
2-bedroom bungalow/maisonette	100,000 – 300,000+
Village house	50,000 – 200,000
Farmhouse (restored)	160,000 – 300,000
Stone house	150,000 – 500,000+
3-bedroom detached villa	150,000 – 500,000+
Luxury villa	350,000 – 1,000,000+

FEES

A variety of fees are payable when you buy a property in Greece, which usually adds between 10 and 15 per cent to the price, which is higher than in many other countries.

Assessed Tax Value

Most fees are based on the 'assessed tax value' (*antikimeniki acsia*) of the property, which is usually lower than the actual price paid. How much lower depends on the location of the property – property in resort areas or on islands tends to have a higher tax value than that in remote or less popular areas. The 'assessed tax value' is calculated by the local tax authorities based on government tables using criteria such as the location, size and characteristics of a property. It's this value that's usually declared on the final purchase contract (title deeds). In some rural areas the value can be negotiated, but in most areas it's fixed. You should ask your lawyer to ascertain the 'assessed tax value' of the property you plan to buy and to obtain confirmation in writing. Declaring below the 'assessed tax value' leads to heavy fines as well as potential problems when you sell the property. Greece, in common with other EU countries (e.g. Portugal), plans to increase the 'assessed tax values' to bring them more into line with actual market values by January 2006.

The fees payable when buying a property in Greece may include the following:

● Purchase or transfer tax;

● Value Added Tax (new constructions only);

● Land registry fees;

● Notary's fees;

● Lawyer's fees;

● Community or municipal tax;

● Surveyor's fee (optional);

● Selling agent's fees;

● Utility fees.

Purchase Tax

The main fee is purchase (or transfer) tax, which is based on the 'assessed tax value' (see **Assessed Tax Value** above). Purchase tax is payable by the buyer at 7 per cent on the first €15,000 and at 9 per cent on the remainder, unless the property is situated in an area covered by a public fire protection service (this includes most areas that are popular with foreign buyers). If this is the case, the rates are increased to 9 per cent on the first €15,000 and 11 per cent on the remainder. For example, if the property you're buying is in an area with a fire service and is valued at

€100,000, you would pay a total of €10,700 purchase tax (€1,350 on the first €15,000 plus €9,350 on the remaining €85,000).

Purchase tax must be paid before the final purchase contract is signed and the notary requires proof of payment (the receipt) in order to authorise the sale. The intricacies of purchase tax make it almost mandatory to obtain legal advice before proceeding with a property purchase.

Value Added Tax

New constructions with a building licence issued from January 2005 are subject to value added tax (VAT) at the rate of 18 per cent. New constructions with building licences issued before January 2005 aren't subject to VAT regardless of when building work is completed.

Land Registry Fees

Land registry fees are from 0.3 to 0.5 per cent of the 'assessed tax value' plus a small sum for stamp duties and certificates.

Notary's Fees

The fees for the notary, who draws up the final purchase contract and officiates the sale, are usually between 1 and 2 per cent of a property's 'assessed tax value'. Fees also include small set charges for each sheet and document included in the contract.

Legal Fees

Legal fees for the conveyancing (see page 174) involved in a sale are up to 1 per cent of the 'assessed tax value'. The actual fee depends on the value of the property. You and your lawyer should agree the fees in writing beforehand. Engaging a lawyer and paying legal fees is optional, but highly recommended.

Community or Municipal Tax

A community tax at 3 per cent of the property transfer tax is paid to the local municipality for general public services such as road maintenance. Note that this tax is paid at the same time as the purchase tax to the central tax office.

Surveyor's Fees

If you employ a surveyor to inspect a building or plot of land, the fee will depend on the type of survey, any special requirements and the value of the property or land. A survey costs from €250.

Selling Agent's Fees

Estate agent's fees (generally between 2 and 5 per cent of the purchase price) are usually paid by both parties, with the vendor and buyer paying half each. Sometimes an allowance is made for this when setting the sale price, so in effect the buyer pays.

Utility Fees

If you buy a new property you usually have to pay for electricity, gas and water connections, and the installation of meters. You should ask the builder or developer to provide the cost of connection to services in writing. In resale properties you will probably have to pay for the cost of new electricity and water contracts. See also **Utilities** on page 278.

Additional Fees

There may also be additional costs such as certificates proving the property has been built to legal standards and that it has not been affected by an earthquake.

Running Costs

In addition to the fees associated with buying a property, you should also take into account running costs. These include: local property taxes (see page 213); community fees for a community property (see page 131); garden and pool maintenance (for a private villa); household, i.e. building and contents, insurance (see **Chapter 8**); standing charges for utilities, e.g. electricity, gas, telephone and water; and a caretaker's or management fees if you leave a home empty or let it. Annual running costs usually average around 2 to 4 per cent of the cost of a property.

TYPES OF PROPERTY

Greece offers a wealth of different properties, from tiny holiday apartments to large stone mansions set in acres of land, with just about everything in between. Each region has a typical type of property, for example, stone mansions in the Peloponnese and Pelion peninsula, windmill properties in the Cyclades, or Venetian townhouses in the many harbour towns. The purchase and restoration of these typical homes is becoming popular among foreigners, especially those keen to establish small hotels or bed and breakfast businesses.

Below is a brief guide to the types of property available, including country properties.

Apartments

Apartments and flats abound in Greece and the vast majority of Greeks live in apartment blocks, particularly in towns and cities. There are also numerous purpose-built holiday apartment blocks in resort areas, although nothing like the scale found in Spain and Portugal.

The quality and size varies enormously, from tiny studio apartments crammed into blocks with '70s-style bathroom fittings, to spacious marble-floored apartments complete with all mod cons. Apartments in Greece tend to be in low-rise buildings, especially in resort areas where, unlike so many Spanish resorts, it's unusual to find more than three storeys. Prices range from €70,000 for a small one-bedroom apartment to over €1,000,000 or more for a luxury penthouse in Athens. New apartments tend to be more expensive, but the quality may be better. Bargain apartments can be found in most areas, although lower-priced properties usually require extensive modernisation and refurbishment. Older apartments often have communal heating and water services, which can be expensive if you aren't a full-time resident. Apartments aren't generally sold with a parking space.

Under Greek law all owners of apartments (regardless of their number or size) in Greece are members of the community of owners and must abide by the community's rules and regulations, and pay community fees or a service charge.

Advantages of apartments include low maintenance (once you have carried out any necessary work), security – especially if the block has 24-hour security or a concierge – and the use of communal gardens and swimming pool (and possibly other facilities such as tennis courts). Apartments situated in towns also have the added advantage of local facilities and amenities within walking distance. Disadvantages include noisy neighbours, poorly maintained communities and crowded complexes during holiday periods.

Townhouses

Two types of townhouse exist in Greece. Townhouses within a town itself usually have two or three storeys and are sometimes in need of renovation and restoration work. These properties often have balconies and/or a roof terrace with good views, with prices starting around €95,000. Advantages include low maintenance (once you have done any necessary renovation), the opportunity to interact with the local community and proximity to amenities. Disadvantages include noisy neighbours and possibly lack of parking space.

Townhouses built especially for holiday accommodation are available in resort areas and are usually part of purpose-built developments with swimming pools, gardens and possibly sports facilities, shops and restaurants. The quality of construction is usually high, which is reflected in prices starting at €115,000 for a one-bedroom townhouse. Advantages include low maintenance, the possibly of an income from letting and the use of communal facilities. Disadvantages may include noisy neighbours, over-crowding during the summer but too quiet in the winter (when many homes are empty) and possibly poorly maintained communities.

Detached Houses

Bungalows & Maisonettes

Small detached properties, often with only one floor and small front and back gardens or patios, are common in resort areas and known as bungalows or maisonettes. Most are new or of recent construction. Sizes range from small one-bedroom properties to larger three or four-bedroom homes. They are often in developments with up to 20 properties, although 8 to 12 are more usual, sharing a pool and possibly communal gardens. Prices start at €100,000 for one bedroom. Advantages are the privacy of a detached property, easy maintenance and shared communal facilities. Disadvantages may include limited living space and they may be too quiet for some out of season.

Villas

Villas in Greece tend to be large homes with at least three bedrooms, often of high quality with luxury specifications and set in extensive plots of land. Some have a swimming pool, but this is by no means standard. Prices start at €150,000 for properties in a poor location requiring renovation work and rise to over €5 million in a desirable beach location close to Athens. Advantages include privacy, plenty of space and good rental returns. On the other hand, villas require almost continual maintenance and running costs are high.

Village Houses

This is an increasingly popular option among foreigners in Greece and there are village properties for sale throughout the country. Possibilities range from tiny ruined buildings, often little more than an outhouse and needing complete restoration, to attractive modernised stone cottages. Most properties need some sort of restoration work, however, and many don't have a bathroom or toilet. Prices start at around €50,000, although a modernised property costs at least €80,000. Advantages of village houses include the chance to live among the locals and get a taste of the 'real' Greece, and the proximity to amenities. However, restoration costs can be high and some people find a village atmosphere claustrophobic.

Unusual Properties

Greece offers much more than conventional apartments and villas, and there are numerous possibilities to buy an unusual and unique property. If you're looking for something completely different you might wish to consider the following: a fortress, built to defend the coastline against pirates and complete with gun turrets; a monastery including stone-carved cloisters; an olive mill together with its original machinery and presses; or a windmill, which may be a working model. Unusual properties can be found in most areas, but the vast majority require extensive restoration and many are in isolated locations.

BUYING A NEW HOME

New properties are widely available and include coastal and city apartments and townhouses, golf and marina developments, and a wide range of individually designed bungalows and villas. Many new properties are part of purpose-built developments, which are planned as holiday homes and may not be attractive as permanent homes. If you're buying an apartment or house that's part of a community development, check whether your neighbours will be mainly locals or foreigners. Some people don't wish to live in a community consisting mainly of their fellow countrymen (or other foreigners) and this may also deter buyers when you wish to sell. On the other hand, some foreigners don't want to live in a Greek community, particularly if they don't speak the language.

Prices of new properties vary considerably depending on their location, size and quality. Most new homes have a steel (earthquake-resistant) frame with a reinforced concrete slab and hollow clay bricks. However, you can also have a new stone house built that is environmentally friendly and benefits from modern building methods, materials and amenities. Most apartments are relatively small, e.g. 75m², while townhouses and bungalows are usually between 100 and 150m². When sales are slow, some developers offer inducements to buyers, which may include 'free' inspection flights and accommodation. Bear in mind, however, that the cost of these 'gifts' is included in the price and you may be able to get an equivalent (or even larger) cash reduction by haggling.

It's often cheaper to buy a new home than an old property requiring modernisation or renovation, as the price is fixed, unlike the cost of renovation which can soar way beyond original estimates (as many people have discovered to their cost). If required (and permitted), a new property can usually be let immediately, and modern homes have good resale potential and are considered a good investment by local buyers. New properties are also covered by a warranty against structural defects. On the other hand, new homes may be smaller than older properties, have smaller gardens and rarely come with a large plot of land.

Most new properties are sold directly by property developers or builders, although they may also be marketed by estate agents. New developments may also have a sales office and/or a show house or apartment on site. When a building is purchased off plan, payment is made in stages as building work progresses. Typical payment schemes are 10 per cent deposit and the remainder on completion, or 10 per cent on deposit and three stage payments during construction. Homes can often be built in less than six months, although building work may not take place during the summer. **Note that it's important to ensure that each stage is completed satisfactorily before making payments.** If you're unable to do this yourself, you must engage an independent representative, e.g. an architect, to do it on your behalf. This service is also provided by some estate agents.

It isn't uncommon to have problems when buying a property off plan. According to investigations in various countries, many new properties have building defects or deficiencies and in many cases the contract conditions aren't adhered to, particularly regarding the completion date (properties are rarely completed on schedule) and the quality of materials used.

When buying a property off plan, you can usually choose the colour of your bathroom suites, wall and floor tiles, carpets, internal walls, external wall plaster, shutters, doors and timber finish. You may also be able to alter the interior room layout, although this may increase the price. Note that you should make any changes or additions to a property during the design stage, such as including a more luxurious kitchen, a chimney or an additional shower room, which will cost much more to install later.

The quality of new property in Greece is extremely variable and may be poorer than in northern European countries and North America, although the quality of construction is generally high. More expensive properties use a high proportion of imported fixtures and fittings, and many building materials may also be imported. The quality of a building and the materials used will be reflected in the price, so when comparing prices ensure that you're comparing similar quality. Cheaper properties aren't usually the best built, although there are exceptions. If you want a permanent rather than a holiday home, you're better off opting for high quality construction and materials.

New homes usually contain a high level of 'luxury' features, which may include: a full-size, fully-fitted kitchen (possibly with a microwave, hob/oven with extractor hood, dishwasher, fridge/freezer and washing machine); a utility room; large bathrooms (possibly en-suite to all bedrooms); a separate shower room and guest toilet; fitted carpets in bedrooms; double-glazing and shutters on all windows; stone, wood-burning fireplace; stone, ceramic or marble floors in kitchens and bathrooms, and terracotta-tiled floors in other rooms; tiled verandas, terraces and patios; oak wood doors; fitted wardrobes; communal satellite TV and telephone outlets. Options may include a Jacuzzi, barbecue, swimming pool, sauna/steam bath, wooden/parquet floors, pergolas, walkways/paved surfaces, landscaping, garage or car port, central heating and air-conditioning. Larger homes may also have maid's quarters or a separate guest apartment and a study.

Properties that are part of a development (see **Community Properties** on page 131) also have a wide range of communal facilities such as a swimming pool (or a number), tennis courts and landscaped gardens. If you wish to furnish a property for letting, many developers can do this for you and they may offer furniture packages that are generally good value for money.

Resale 'New' Homes

There are many advantages to buying a modern resale home rather than a brand new one in which you're the first occupant. These may include: a range of local services and facilities within an established development; the absence of 'teething troubles'; furniture and other extras included in the price; a mature garden and trees; and a larger plot of land. With a resale property, you can see exactly what you're getting for your money and the previous owners may have made improvements or added extras such as a swimming pool, which may not be fully reflected in the asking price. See also **Buying a Resale Home** below.

BUYING A RESALE HOME

Resale properties often represent good value, particularly in resort areas, where many apartments and townhouses are sold fully furnished, although the quality of furnishings varies considerably and may not be to your taste. Another advantage of buying a resale property is that you can see exactly what you will get for your money and you save the cost of installing water and electricity meters and telephone lines, or the cost of extending these services to a property. When buying a resale property in a development, you should ask the neighbours about any problems, community fees, planned developments and anything else that may affect your enjoyment of the property. Most residents are usually happy to tell you, unless of course they're trying to sell you their own property!

If you want a property with abundant charm and character, a building for renovation or conversion, outbuildings, or a large plot of land, you'll probably have to choose an old property. Although you can buy a new stone home, they invariably have less character than old renovated properties. Note, however, that many old homes are small, although they generally offer better value per m^2 than the same size new home. Traditional, stone-built houses are common throughout Greece, particularly in Crete, although the prices for 'ruins' are often farcical and have been driven up by demand in recent years. Note that you can buy a ruin from as little as €20,000, but you will need to carry out major renovation and modernisation which will greatly increase the price. A structurally sound property may cost as much as €50,000.

Many old homes lack basic services such as electricity, a reliable water supply and sanitation. Note that in order to obtain an electricity supply for older properties you may have to provide legal documentation showing the property's age (e.g. before 1956 on the island of Skopelos in the Sporades). Because the purchase price is usually low, many foreign buyers believe they're getting a wonderful bargain, without fully investigating the renovation costs. If you aren't into do-it-yourself in a big way, you may be better off buying a new or recently built property, as the cost of restoring an old property can be prohibitive. If you're planning to buy a property that needs restoration or renovation and you won't be doing the work yourself, obtain an **accurate** estimate of the costs **before** signing a contract. You should also consider having a survey carried out (see page 135) on a resale property, particularly a detached house, as major problems can be found even in properties less than five or ten years old. Be wary of buying a property designed for tourist accommodation, as these were often built with inferior materials and workmanship – cavity walls and good insulation are essential if a property is to be used as a permanent home.

Bear in mind that, if you buy and restore a property with the intention of selling it for a profit, you must take into account not only the initial price and the restoration costs, but also the fees and taxes included in the purchase. It's often difficult to sell an old renovated property at a higher than average market price, irrespective of its added value. The locals have little interest in old restored properties, which is an important point if you need to sell an old home quickly in an area that isn't popular with foreign buyers. **If you're buying for investment, you're usually better off buying a new home.**

Owners often advertise properties in the local and expatriate press (see **Appendix B**) or by simply putting a 'for sale' sign in a window. Note that, although you can save money by buying direct from an owner, particularly when he is forced to sell, you should **always** employ a lawyer to carry out the necessary checks (see **Conveyancing** on page 174). If you're unsure of the value of a property, you should obtain a professional valuation.

COMMUNITY PROPERTIES

Community properties are those with elements (whether a building, amenities or land) shared with other properties. They include apartments, townhouses, and single-family (detached) homes on a private estate with communal areas and facilities. In fact, the only properties that don't belong to a community are detached houses built on individual plots in public streets or on rural land. Community properties are owned through a system of part-ownership (similar to that of a condominium in the US) whereby each property owner also owns a share of the common elements of the building or development, including foyers, hallways, passages, lifts, patios, gardens, roads, and leisure and sports facilities (such as swimming pools and tennis courts). When you buy a community property, you automatically become a member of the community of owners.

Many community properties are located in or near coastal resorts and offer a range of communal facilities, which may include a golf course, swimming pools, tennis courts, a gymnasium or fitness club, and a bar and restaurant. Most developments have landscaped gardens and some also offer high security and a full-time caretaker. At the other extreme, cheaper, older developments may consist of tiny cramped studio

132 Your Dream Home

apartments with few, if any, amenities. Note that some community properties are planned as holiday homes and aren't attractive as permanent homes.

Advantages

The advantages of owning a community property include: increased security; lower property taxes than detached homes; a range of communal sports and leisure facilities; community living with lots of social contacts and the companionship of close neighbours; adequate off-road parking; no garden, lawn or pool maintenance; fewer of the responsibilities of home ownership; ease of maintenance; and the opportunity to live in an area where owning a single-family home would be prohibitively expensive, e.g. a beach front or town centre.

Disadvantages

The disadvantages of community properties may include: excessively high community fees (owners may have no control over increases); restrictive rules and regulations; a confining living and social environment and possible lack of privacy; noisy neighbours (particularly if neighbouring properties are let to holidaymakers); limited living and storage space; expensive covered or secure parking (or insufficient off-road parking); and acrimonious owners' meetings where management and factions may try to push through unpopular proposals (sometimes using proxy votes).

Cost

Community properties vary enormously in price and quality, e.g. from around €50,000 for a studio or one-bedroom apartment in an average location, to €200,000 or more for a luxury apartment, townhouse or villa in a prime location. Garages and parking spaces must usually be purchased separately, and a lock-up garage or a space in an underground car park can cost €8,000 to €15,000. If you're buying a resale property, check the price paid for similar properties in the same area or development in recent months, but bear in mind that the price you pay may have more to do with the seller's circumstances than the price fetched by other properties. Find out how many properties are for sale in a particular development; if there are many on offer you should investigate why, as there could be management or structural problems. If you're still keen to buy, you can use any negative points to drive a hard bargain.

Community Fees

Owners of community properties must pay fees for the upkeep of communal areas and for communal services. Charges are calculated according to each owner's share of a development or apartment building, and **not** whether they're temporary or permanent residents. Shares are usually calculated according to the relative size of properties, e.g. the owners of ten properties of equal size usually each pay 10 per cent of the community fees. The percentage to be paid is detailed in the property deed. Shares not only determine the share of fees to be paid, but also voting rights at general meetings.

Fees go towards: road cleaning; green zone maintenance (including communal and possibly private gardens); cleaning, decoration and maintenance of buildings; a caretaker or concierge; communal lighting in buildings and grounds; water supply, e.g. swimming pools and gardens; insurance; administration fees; community rates; maintenance of radio and TV aerials; and satellite TV charges. Always check the level of general and any special charges before buying a community property.

Fees are usually billed at fixed periods during the year and are adjusted at the end of the year when the actual expenditure is known and the annual accounts have been approved by the committee. If you're buying an apartment from a previous owner, ask to see a copy of the service charges for previous years and the minutes of the last annual general meeting, as owners may be 'economical with the truth' when stating service charges, particularly if they're high.

Community fees vary considerably according to the location and the communal facilities provided. Fees for a typical two-bedroom apartment in a well-maintained complex with good facilities are from €50 to €100 a month, although they can be much (much) higher for a luxury penthouse in a prestigious development. Note that high fees aren't necessarily a negative point (assuming you can afford them), provided that you receive value for money and the community is well managed and maintained. The value of a community property depends to a large extent on how well the development is maintained and managed. Note that if you own a holiday home, it's important to ensure that bills are paid in your absence so it's advisable to arrange for your community fees to be paid by direct debit.

TIMESHARE & PART-OWNERSHIP SCHEMES

If you're looking for a holiday home abroad, you may wish to investigate a scheme that provides sole occupancy of a property for a number of weeks each year. These include part-ownership, leaseback, timeshare and a holiday property bond.

 Don't rush into any of these schemes without fully researching the market and before you're absolutely clear what you want and what you can realistically expect to get for your money.

Part-ownership

Part-ownership includes schemes such as a group of people buying shares in a property-owning company and part-ownership between family, friends or even strangers. Part-ownership allows you to recoup your investment in savings on holiday costs while retaining equity in a property. A common deal is a four-owner scheme (which many consider to be the optimum number of part-owners), where you buy a quarter of a property and can occupy it for up to three months a year. However, there's no reason why there cannot be as many as 12 part-owners, with a month's occupancy each per year (usually divided between high, medium and low seasons).

Part-ownership offers access to a size and quality of property that would otherwise be unimaginable, and it's even possible to have a share in a substantial mansion, where a number of families could live together simultaneously and hardly ever see each other if they didn't want to. Part-ownership can be a good choice for a family seeking a holiday home for a few weeks or months a year and has the added advantage that (because of the lower cost) a mortgage may be unnecessary. Note that it's cheaper to buy a property privately with friends than to buy from an agent or developer who offers this sort of scheme, in which case you may pay well above the market value for a share of a property (check the market value of a property to establish whether it's good value). **Part-ownership is much better value than a timeshare and needn't cost much more.** Note, however, that a water-tight contract must be drawn up by an experienced lawyer to protect each co-owners' interests.

One of the best ways to get into part-ownership, if you can afford it, is to buy a property yourself and offer shares to others. This overcomes the problem of getting together a consortium of would-be owners and trying to agree on a purchase in advance, which is difficult unless it's just a few friends or family members. Many people form a local company to buy and manage a property, which can in turn be owned by a company in the part-owners' home country, thus allowing any disputes to be dealt with under local law. Each part-owner receives a number of shares according to how much he has paid, entitling him to so many weeks' occupancy a year. Owners don't need to have equal shares and can all be made direct title holders. If a part-owner wishes to sell his shares, he must usually give first refusal to the other part-owners, although if they don't wish to buy them and a new part-owner cannot be found, the property will need to be sold.

Timesharing

Also known as holiday ownership, vacation ownership, part-ownership or holidays for life, timeshare is a popular form of part-ownership and there's an increasing number of timeshare resorts in Greece. The best timeshare developments are on a par with luxury hotels and offer a wide range of facilities, including bars, restaurants, entertainment, shops, swimming pools, tennis courts, health clubs, and other leisure and sports facilities. If you don't wish to holiday in the same place each year, you should choose a timeshare development that's a member of an international organisation such as Resort Condominium International (☎ UK 0870-609 0141, 💻 www.rci.com) with 36 resorts around Greece, Interval International (☎ UK 0870-744 4222, 💻 www.interval world.com) with nine resorts or Marriott (☎ UK 0800-221 222, 💻 www. marriott.co.uk), with one hotel in Athens, which allow you (usually for an additional fee) to exchange your timeshare with one in another area or country.

Further information about timesharing can be obtained from the Timeshare Helpline (💻 www.timeshare.freeserve.co.uk), which provides help and advice for members. The Timeshare Consumers Association (UK, ☎ 01909-591 100, 💻 www.timeshare.org.uk) publishes several useful booklets as well as providing comprehensive information on their website.

INSPECTIONS & SURVEYS

When you have found a property that you like, you should make a close inspection of its condition. Obviously this will depend on whether it's an old house in need of complete restoration, a property that has been partly or totally modernised, or a modern home. One of the problems with a property that has been restored is that you don't know how well the job has been done, particularly if the owner did it himself. If work has been carried out by local builders, you should ask to see the bills.

Some simple checks you can do yourself include testing the electrical system, plumbing, mains water, hot water boiler and central heating.

Don't take someone's word that these are functional, but check them for yourself. If a property doesn't have electricity or mains water, check the nearest connection point and the cost of extending the service to the property, as it can be **very** expensive in remote rural areas. If a property has a well or septic tank, you should also have them tested. If there isn't a septic tank and no mains drainage in the area, check that the plot has sufficient room for a bulldozer access to dig the hole for the cesspit or septic tank.

An old property may show visible signs of damage and decay, such as bulging or cracked walls, rising damp, missing roof slates (you can check with binoculars) and rotten woodwork. Some areas are liable to flooding, storms and subsidence, and you should check an old property after a heavy rainfall, when any leaks should come to light. If you find or suspect problems, you should have a property checked by a builder or have a full structural survey carried out by a surveyor. You may also wish to have a property checked for termites and other infestations.

A local buyer wouldn't make an offer on an old property before at least having it checked by a builder, who will also be able to tell you whether the price is too high, given any work that needs to be done. However, it's unusual to have a survey on a property in Greece, particularly a property built in the last 10 or 20 years. Nevertheless, it isn't unusual to find serious faults with homes built in the '60s and '70s, many of which were built with inferior materials, and even relatively new buildings can have problems.

 It's important to check who the developer or builder was, as a major company with a good reputation is unlikely to cut corners.

If you're buying a detached villa, farmhouse or village house, especially one built on the side of a hill, it's **always** wise to have a survey carried out. Common problems in old buildings include rusting water pipes and leaky plumbing, inadequate sewage disposal, poor wiring, humidity and rising damp (no damp course), uneven flooring or no concrete base, collapsing façades, subsidence, and cracked internal and external walls. Some of these problems are even evident in developments less than five or ten years old. Generally, if you would have a survey done if you were buying a similar property in your home country, you should have one done in Greece.

You could ask the vendor to have a survey done at his expense, which, provided that it gives the property a clean bill of health, will help him sell it even if you decide not to buy. You can make a satisfactory survey a condition of a contract, although this isn't usual and a vendor may refuse or insist that you carry out a survey at your expense **before** signing the contract.

 If a vendor refuses to allow you to do a survey before signing a contract, you should look elsewhere.

Some foreign lenders require a survey before approving a loan, although this usually consists of a perfunctory valuation to ensure that a property is worth the purchase price. You can employ a foreign surveyor in some areas, although you must ensure that he is experienced in the idiosyncrasies of local properties and that he has professional indemnity insurance covering Greece (which means you can happily sue him if he does a bad job!). Professional surveyors who speak English work in most towns and large islands.

Always discuss with the surveyor exactly what will be included and, most importantly, what will be omitted from the survey (you may need to pay extra to include certain checks and tests). A full structural survey should include: the condition of all buildings, particularly the foundations, roofs, walls and woodwork; plumbing, electricity and heating systems; and anything else you want inspected such as a swimming pool and its equipment, e.g. the filter system or heating. A survey can be limited to a few items or even a single system only, such as the wiring or plumbing in an old house. You should receive a written report on the structural condition of a property, including anything that could become a problem in the future. Some surveyors will allow you to accompany them and provide a video film of their findings in addition to a written report.

Land

Before buying a home on its own plot of land, you should walk the boundaries and check fences, driveways, roads, and the overhanging eaves of buildings that might be encroaching upon the property. If you're uncertain about the boundaries, you should have the land surveyed, which is sensible in any case when buying a property with a large plot of land. When buying a rural property, you may be able to negotiate the amount of land you want included in the purchase. If a property is part of a larger plot of land owned by the vendor or the boundaries must be redrawn, you will need to engage a surveyor to measure the land and draw up a new plan.

You should also have a lawyer check the local municipal plans to find out what the land can be used for and whether there are any existing rights of way or animal grazing rights. If the land has trees, find out whom they belong to (there may be several owners). You can offer to buy the trees (although the owners may not sell) or continue to allow the owner(s) access to the land to prune and tend the trees. If you want to fell any trees permission is required and it may not be granted. Be wary of buying land in or near forested areas – forest fires in Greece strike every summer (fires in 2000 devastated large areas of the Peloponnese and a fifth of the island of Samos).

When considering buying land next to the sea, ensure that you will be allowed to build before you commit yourself to the purchase – permits are extremely difficult to obtain for plots next to the sea. If you're buying a property within 500m of the shoreline, you should be aware that different building regulations apply, which in many cases have strict specifications including roof shape, number of windows, etc. Finally you should double check that the plot is large enough to build on – many expatriates buy rural plots that are too small to build on.

Inspection Checklist

Below is a list of items you should check when inspecting a property. Note, however, that this is no substitute for an inspection or survey by a professional, or for legal checks by a lawyer.

Title

● Make sure that a property corresponds with the description in the title deeds.

● Check the number of rooms and the area of the property, terraces and the plot.

Note that if there are added rooms (e.g. an extension), terraces, a garage or a swimming pool that aren't mentioned in the property description, the owner should provide proof that planning permission was obtained. Additions or alterations to a property may require new title deeds for the entire property. If so, enquire whether the current owner will obtain the updated deeds before you buy or pay the costs if they're obtained on completion.

Plot

It's particularly important to make the following checks when buying a rural house or plot of land:

- Identify the boundaries of the plot. This may require the services of a land surveyor on unfenced rural properties.

- Check that there are no disputes over boundaries and ensure that any additions on your plot don't encroach on neighbouring plots.

- Check the rights of way over the plot. In rural areas, find out if your plot forms part of a grazing area or access route to other grazing areas for local animals.

- Check for streams and underground springs and whether any neighbours have rights to water on your land.

- If your plot isn't enclosed, check the local regulations regarding the height and type of boundary permitted.

Orientation

- Check the orientation of the property and how much sun it receives, particularly in winter, when north-facing properties are very cold and dark.

Exterior

- Check for cracks and damp patches on walls.

- Check for earthquake cracks and check that the property meets earthquake building regulations.

- On older properties, check that the walls are vertical and not bulging.

- Check that all the roof tiles are in place and that there's no sagging. Plants growing on a roof are an indication that it isn't well maintained. Note that gutters and drainpipes aren't common in Greek properties.

Interior

- Check for damp patches throughout a property, including inside cupboards and wardrobes.

- Check for cracks and damp patches on walls.

- Check that the floor is level and that the tiles are in good condition.

- Check the condition of doors and windows and whether they close properly.

- Check the woodwork for rot and signs of wood-boring insects, such as woodworm and termites (termites are difficult to detect unless damage is extensive).

Furniture & Fittings

- Check what is included in the sale.
- Check that any appliances included in the sale are in good working order.

Space

- Check that there's sufficient for your needs, particularly if you plan to live permanently in a property.
- If it's an apartment, you may wish to enquire whether there's the possibility of obtaining additional storage space within the building.

Parking

- Check that there are sufficient parking spaces for your family's needs – note that street parking is in very short supply in most areas.
- Check whether there's the possibility of buying or renting a garage or parking space within a building or complex nearby.

Utilities

- Check that water/electricity/gas supplies are functional, particularly the hot water supply.
- Enquire about heating/cooling units in the house and the annual costs.

Rural Properties

- Check the reliability of the electricity supply.
- If there's no electricity supply, find out whether you can connect to the mains supply or whether you can install alternative means (e.g. solar panels). See **Electricity** on page 279.
- Check the water supply. If a property's water is provided by wells, make sure that there's sufficient for your needs.
- Find out whether a property has a septic tank or cesspit and have it checked. Make sure that its size is sufficient for your needs.

Garden/Land

- Check whether the garden will need extensive maintenance, and if so, how much a gardener will cost (if you cannot do it yourself). If you aren't prepared to pay for a gardener, check what it will cost to create a low-maintenance garden.

● On rural land, find out whether the trees require maintenance, e.g. olive and fruit trees, and investigate what you can do with the crops after the harvest.

● On rural land including olive and fruit trees, find out whom the trees belong to. Trees often belong to several owners who have the right to access the land to tend the trees.

Swimming Pool

● Check that the pool and equipment (especially the pump) is in good working order.

● Look for cracks on the pool structure and the condition of the paving around the pool.

● Enquire how much the pool costs to maintain a year and how much it will cost to refill it, e.g. if it's emptied in winter.

● If a property doesn't have a swimming pool, check that there's room to build one and that the terrain is suitable.

SWIMMING POOLS

It's common for foreign buyers to install a swimming pool at a detached home in Greece. If you're letting, this will greatly increase your rental prospects and the rent you can charge. Many self-catering holiday companies won't take on properties without a pool. There are many local swimming pool installation companies or you can buy and install one yourself. Above ground pools are the cheapest, but they're unsightly and recommended only for those who cannot afford anything better. A better option is a liner pool, which can be installed by anyone with basic DIY skills. A liner pool measuring 8 x 4 metres costs around €12,000. A saline water option costs a bit more, but provides better quality water and lower maintenance costs. A concrete, fully tiled pool of 8 x 4 metres costs from €12,000 to €17,500 installed, including filtration and heating, and can be almost any shape.

Note that you need planning permission to install a pool and should apply at least a few months in advance. Pools require regular maintenance and cleaning. If you have a holiday home or let a property, you will need to employ someone to maintain your pool (you may be able to get a local family to look after it in return for using it).

RENOVATION & RESTORATION

Many old country or village homes purchased by foreigners in Greece are in need of total restoration, renovation or modernisation. Before buying a property requiring restoration, you should consider the alternatives. A relatively small extra sum spent on a purchase may represent better value than spending the money on building work. It's often cheaper to buy a restored or partly restored property than a ruin in need of total restoration, unless you're going to do most of the work yourself. The price of most restored properties doesn't reflect the cost and amount of work that went into them and many people who have restored a 'ruin' would never do it again and advise others against it.

SURVIVAL TIP
Before buying a property that needs
renovation or restoration, it's vital to obtain accurate
estimates of the work involved from one or more
reliable local builders. You should budget for costs
to be much higher than quoted, as it isn't unusual
for the cost to escalate wildly from
original estimates.

In general, the locals don't care for old homes and much prefer modern apartments and villas with all mod cons.

Checks

It's vital to check a property for any obvious faults, particularly an old property. Most importantly, a building must have sound walls, without which it's cheaper to erect a new building! Almost any other problem can be fixed or overcome (at a price). A sound roof that doesn't leak is desirable, as ensuring that a building is waterproof is the priority if funds are scarce. Don't take a vendor's or agent's word that a roof or anything else can be repaired or patched up, but obtain expert advice from a local builder. Sound roof timbers are also important, as they can be expensive to replace.

Old buildings often need a damp-proof course, timber treatment, new windows and doors, a new roof or extensive re-roofing, a modern kitchen and bathroom, re-wiring and central heating. Electricity and mains water should already be connected, as they can be expensive to extend to a property in a remote area (this also applies to a telephone line).

If a house doesn't have electricity or mains water, it's important to check the cost of extending these services to it.

Many rural properties have a spring or well as their water supply, which is usually fine, but you should check the reliability of the water supply – wells can and do run dry! If you're seeking a waterside property, you should check the frequency of floods and, if commonplace, ensure that a building has been designed with floods in mind, e.g. with electrical installations above flood level and solid tiled floors.

Planning Permission & Building Permits

If modernisation of an old building involves making external alterations, such as building an extension or installing larger windows or new doorways, you will need planning permission from the local town hall. If you plan to do major restoration or building work, you should ensure that a conditional clause is included in the contract stating that the purchase is dependent on obtaining planning permission (copies of the applications must be sent to the notary or lawyer handling the sale). **Never start any building work before you have official permission.**

Obtaining planning permission can take months and many people employ a local expert, often known as a *méson*, whose knowledge of local bureaucracy and probable friendship with local civil servants usually facilitates the process.

Depending on the area, different rules apply so find out what the local regulations are before committing yourself to any restoration projects. In some areas, it's only possible to obtain planning permission for restoration for rural properties on smaller plots (usually under 4,000m²) if they were built before a certain date, e.g. 1920. Many towns and villages in Greece are conservation areas and buildings within these areas are subject to strict regulations and can usually have few exterior changes made to them. The island of Hydra is a National Monument and any changes to buildings there are strictly controlled and require planning permission just to change the exterior paint colour!

DIY or Builders?

One of the first decisions you need to make regarding restoration or modernisation is whether to do all or most of the work yourself or have it done by professional builders or local artisans. A working knowledge of Greek is essential for DIY, especially the words associated with building materials and measurements (renovating a house in Greece will also greatly improve your ability to swear in Greek!). Note that when restoring a period property, it's important to have a sensitive approach to restoration. You should aim to retain as many of a building's original features as possible and stick to local building materials, reflecting the style of the property. When renovations or 'improvements' have been botched, there's often little that can be done except to start again from scratch.

It's important not to over-modernise an old property, to the extent that much of its natural rustic charm and attraction is lost. Note that even if you intend to do most of the work yourself, you will still need to hire craftsmen for certain jobs. Bear in mind that it can be difficult to find good craftsmen, who are in high demand and short supply in some areas.

 Note that even if you do all the work yourself, you must make a payment to the social security authority (IKA) who will charge you a percentage of the amount you would have paid to them had the work been done by builders!

Employing Others

The complexity and time-consuming nature of doing up a property yourself, means it's often much easier to employ someone to do it for you. If you employ workmen in Greece you must declare this to the social security authorities (IKA) and pay social security contributions for the workers.

There are numerous companies specialising in restoration work, particularly in areas popular with foreign buyers, e.g. Crete and Kefallonia. These companies carry out all the restoration work including obtaining necessary permits and licences. Typical payments are 40 per cent of the total cost at the start of the work, 30 per cent halfway through and the remaining 30 per cent at the end. Ask around for recommendations and to see examples of properties the company has restored previously.

Finding a Builder

When looking for a builder, you should obtain recommendations from local people you can trust, e.g. neighbours and friends. Note that estate agents, lawyers and other professionals aren't always the best people to ask, as they may receive commissions. Always obtain references from

previous customers. It may be better to use a local building consortium or contractor than a number of independent tradesmen, particularly if you won't be around to supervise them (although it will cost you a bit more). On the other hand, if you supervise the work yourself using local handpicked craftsmen, you can save money and learn a great deal into the bargain.

Supervision

If you aren't on the spot and able to supervise work, you should hire a 'clerk of works' such as an architect to oversee it, particularly if it's a large job, or it can drag on for months (or years) or even be left half-finished. This will add to the bill but is usually worthwhile. Be careful whom you employ if you have work done in your absence, and ensure that your instructions are accurate in every detail. Always make certain that you understand exactly what has been agreed and, if necessary, get it in writing (with drawings). It isn't unknown for foreign owners to receive bills for work done in their absence that shouldn't have been done at all!

 If you don't speak Greek, it's even more important to employ someone to oversee building work. Progressing on sign language and a few words of Greek is a recipe for disaster!

Quotations

Before buying a home abroad that needs restoration or modernisation, it's essential to obtain an accurate estimate of the work and costs involved. You should obtain written estimates from at least two builders before employing anyone. Note that for quotations to be accurate, you must detail exactly the work required (e.g. for electrical work this would include the number of lights, points and switches), and the quality of materials to be used. If you have only a vague idea of what you want, you will receive a vague and unreliable quotation. Make sure that a quotation includes everything you want done and that you fully understand it. You should fix a date for the start and completion of work and, if you can get a builder to agree to it, include a penalty for failing to finish on time. After signing a contract it's usual to pay a deposit, the amount of which depends on the size and cost of a job.

Cost

Building work such as electrical work, masonry and plumbing is costed by the square metre or metre. The cost of restoration depends on the type of work involved, the quality of materials used and the region. As a rough guide you should expect the cost of totally renovating an old 'habitable' building to be at least equal to its purchase price and possibly much more. How much you spend on restoring a property will depend on your purpose and the depth of your pockets. If you're restoring a property as an investment, it's easy to spend much more than you could ever hope to recoup when you sell it. On the other hand, if you're restoring a property as a holiday or permanent home, there's no limit to what you can do and how much money you can spend.

Always keep an eye on your budget (which will inevitably be too low – you should have a contingency fund of at least 25 per cent of your budget) and don't be in too much of a hurry. Some people take many years to restore a holiday home, particularly when they're doing most of the work themselves. It isn't unusual for buyers to embark on a grandiose renovation scheme, only to run out of money before it's completed and be forced to sell at a loss.

BUILDING YOUR OWN HOME

If you want to be far from the madding crowd, you can buy a plot of land and have an individual architect-designed house built to your own design and specifications or to a standard design provided by a builder. Note, however, that building a home abroad isn't recommended for the timid. Red tape and local business practices can make building your own home a nightmare and it's fraught with problems. Nevertheless, there are many excellent builders and construction companies in Greece, and building your own home allows you not only to design your home, but to ensure that the quality of materials and workmanship are first class. Remember, though, that properties must be built in the architectural styles of the region.

Checks

You must take the same care when buying land as you would when buying a home. The most important point is to ensure that it has been approved for building and that the plot is large enough and suitable for the house you plan to build. Minimum plot sizes vary and depend on whether the site is in a community (e.g. a village) or in the country.

Urban Plots

Plots within an urban area (including a village) vary in size, although the minimum is usually 250m² and you're generally allowed to build up to 40 per cent of the plot size. So if the plot measures 250m² the total ground floor area or footprint (not including terraces) cannot exceed 100m².

Rural Plots

Outside an urban area, restrictions are greater and the minimum plot size is usually 4,000m² (but may be 8,000m²) and you're generally allowed to build up to 5 per cent of the plot size. A plot with 4,000m² can therefore have a home with a footprint of up to 200m². Rural land may also be affected by forestry restrictions and in some areas you need a 'Certificate to Build' from the forestry authorities in order to obtain a building licence. Note that it's difficult to get permission to build on land near archaeological sites.

 The Greek government plans to increase the minimum plot size for rural plots to 6,000m² or 8,000m² in the near future.

It may be possible to build on agricultural land, but there are strict limits on plot and building sizes. If the plot is part of a development, the contract must state that the plan has been approved and give the date and authority. You should consult an architect before deciding to buy a plot, as it may be unsuitable for building, e.g. too steep or require prohibitively expensive foundations. Also check that there aren't any restrictions such as high-tension electricity lines, water pipes or rights of way that may prohibit or limit your building plans. You should also check that the boundaries are correct, as title deeds can be vague regarding measurements.

Always obtain confirmation in writing from the local town council that land can be built on. Don't assume that planning permission will be issued because neighbouring plots have houses on them – they could well be illegal. Confirm also: that road access has been approved (without which building isn't possible); whether building is restricted, and if so, in what way; whether the road is subject to a widening scheme; and whether electricity and water services can be provided and at what cost.

Before buying land for building, ensure that the purchase contract is dependent on obtaining the necessary planning permission. Obtain a receipt showing that the plot is correctly presented in the local property register and check for yourself that the correct planning permission has been obtained (don't simply leave it to the builder). If planning permission is flawed, you may need to pay extra to improve the local infrastructure, or the property may even have to be demolished! Note that it can take a long time to obtain planning permission in Greece.

Most builders and developers offer package deals that include the land and the cost of building a home. However, it isn't always wise to buy the plot from the builder who's going to build your home and you should shop around and compare separate land and building costs.

 If you decide to buy a package deal from a builder, you must insist on separate contracts for the land and the building, and obtain the title deed for the land before signing a building contract.

Cost

Land

Land is expensive in Greece and there are minimum plot sizes for each size of building. Land area is expressed in *stremmattas* (units of 1,000m² or around a quarter of an acre). In Greece, the average cost of a 4,000m² plot in a rural area is around €40,000, although building plots vary considerably in price and a small (e.g. 250m²) 'urban' plot near the coast can cost as much as €18,500.

Permits

Building permits, which can be obtained through registered architects and engineers, are also expensive. Fees are regulated by the government and are around €35 to €45 per m², i.e. €7,000 to €9,000 for a 200m² house. Half the permit fee is paid before work starts and the remainder later. Note also that providing services to a property in a remote rural area may be prohibitively expensive.

Construction Costs

The average cost of building a new home is from around €350 per m², although if you choose higher quality fittings and materials the cost can easily reach €1,000 per m². Costs are higher on the islands and range from €400 to €500 per m² because all materials have to be shipped in.

Finding an Architect & Builder

When looking for an architect and builder, you should obtain recommendations from local people you can trust, e.g. neighbours and friends. Note that estate agents and other professionals aren't always the best people to ask, as they may receive commissions (and therefore won't be independent). You can also obtain valuable information from expatriates in local bars and from the owners of properties in an area that you particularly like. Many Greek architects speak English, and there are also architects from other EU countries working in Greece. Note that architects' fees are fixed by the government and calculated as a percentage of the total cost of a project.

An architect should be able to recommend a number of reliable builders, but you should also do your own research, as the most important consideration when building a new home is the reputation (and financial standing) of the builder. You should also be wary of an architect with his 'own' builder (or a builder with his own architect), as it's the architect's job to ensure that the builder does his work according to the plans and specifications – so you don't want their relationship to be too cosy. Inspect other homes a builder has built and check with the owners as to what problems they've had and whether they're satisfied. If you want a house built exactly to your specifications, you will need to supervise it every step of the way or employ an architect to do so for you. Without close supervision it's possible (even likely) that your instructions **won't** be followed.

Contracts

You should obtain written quotations from a number of builders before signing a contract. Note that one of the most important features of a home must be good insulation (against both heat and cold) and protection against humidity. The contract must include: a detailed building description and a list of the materials to be used (with references to the architect's plans); the exact location and orientation of the building on the plot; the building and payment schedule, which must be made in stages according to building progress; a penalty clause for late completion; the retention of a percentage, e.g. 2 to 5 per cent, of the building costs as a 'guarantee' against defects; and how disputes will be settled. It may be difficult or impossible to get the builder to accept a penalty clause for late completion, as buildings are rarely completed on time. It should also be spelt out in the contract *exactly* what 'complete' means, as it's open to local interpretation.

Ensure that the contract includes: all costs, including the architect's fees (unless contracted separately); landscaping (if applicable); all permits and licences; and the connection of utilities (water, electricity, gas, etc.) to the house, not just to the building site. The only extra is usually the cost of electricity and water meters. Before accepting a quotation, you should have it checked by a building consultant to confirm that it's a fair deal. You should also check whether the quotation (which must include taxes) is an estimate or a fixed price, as sometimes the cost can escalate wildly due to contract clauses and changes made during building work.

 It's vital to have a contract checked by a lawyer, as building contracts are often heavily biased in the builder's favour and give clients very few rights.

Guarantees

Greek law requires a builder to guarantee his work against structural defects. An architect is also responsible for defects due to poor supervision, incorrect instructions given to the builder, or problems caused by poor foundations, e.g. subsidence. Note that it isn't uncommon to experience problems during construction, particularly regarding material defects. If you have problems, you must usually be extremely patient and persistent in order to obtain satisfaction. You should have a completed building checked by a structural surveyor and a report drawn up; if there are any defects, he should determine who was responsible for them.

SELLING YOUR HOME

Although this book is primarily concerned with buying homes in Greece, you may wish to sell your home at some time in the future. Before offering your home for sale, you should investigate the property market. For example, unless you're forced to, you shouldn't think about selling during a property slump when prices are depressed. It may be wiser to let your home long-term and wait until the market has recovered. It's also unwise to sell in the early years after purchase, when you will probably make a loss (unless the property was an absolute bargain). Having decided to sell, your first decision will be whether to sell it yourself (or try) or use the services of an estate agent. Although the majority of resale properties are sold by estate agents, a large number of people sell their homes privately in Greece. If you need to sell a property before buying a new one, this must be included as a conditional clause (see page 178) in the contract when buying a new home.

Price

It's important to bear in mind that property, like everything, has a market price, and the best way of ensuring a quick sale (or any sale) is to ask a realistic price. In the early to mid-'90s when prices plummeted and buyers dried up, many properties remained on the market for years largely because owners asked absurd prices. As in most countries, it's easier to sell a cheaper property, e.g. one priced below €150,000, than an expensive property. However, there's also a strong and constant demand for bungalows priced between €150,000 and €300,000, particularly if they're exceptionally attractive and in a popular area or a superb location.

If your home's fairly standard for the area, you can find out its value by comparing the prices of other homes on the market or those that have recently been sold. Most agents will provide a free appraisal of a home's value in the hope that you will sell it through them. However, don't believe everything they tell you, as they may over-price it simply to encourage you. You can also hire a professional valuer to determine the market value. You should be prepared to drop the price slightly, e.g. 5 or 10 per cent, and should set it accordingly, but shouldn't grossly over-price a home, which will deter buyers. Don't reject an offer out of hand unless it's ridiculously low, as you may be able to get a prospective buyer to raise his offer.

When selling a second home, you may wish to include the furnishings (plus major appliances) in the sale, which is a common practice in resort areas when selling a relatively inexpensive second home with modest furnishings. You should add an appropriate amount to the price to cover the value of the furnishings; alternatively, you can use them as an inducement to a prospective buyer at a later stage, although this isn't normal practice.

Presentation

The secret to selling a home quickly lies in its presentation (assuming that it's competitively priced). First impressions (both exterior and interior) are vital when marketing a property and it's important to present it in its best light and make it as attractive as possible to potential buyers. It may pay to invest in new interior decoration, new carpets, exterior paint and landscaping. A few plants and flowers can do wonders. Note that when decorating a home for resale, it's important to be conservative and not do anything radical, such as installing a red or black bathroom suite or painting the walls purple. White is a good neutral colour for walls, woodwork and porcelain.

It may also pay you to do some modernisation such as installing a new kitchen or bathroom, as these are of vital importance (particularly kitchens) when selling a home. Note, however, that although modernisation may be necessary to sell an old home, you shouldn't overdo it, as it's easy to spend more than you could ever hope to recoup on the sale price. If you're using an agent, you can ask him what you need to do to help sell your home. If a home is in poor repair, this must be reflected in the asking price and if major work is needed that you cannot afford, you should obtain a quotation (or two) and offer to knock this off the price.

Selling Your Home Yourself

While certainly not for everyone, selling your home privately is a viable option for many people and is particularly recommended when you're selling an attractive home in a sellers' market. It may allow you to offer it at a more appealing price, which could be an important factor if you're seeking a quick sale. How you market your home will depend on the type of property, the price, and the country or area from where you expect your buyer to come. For example, if your property isn't of a type and style or in an area that's desirable to local inhabitants, it's usually a waste of time advertising it in the local press.

Marketing

Marketing is the key to selling your home. The first step is to get a professional looking 'for sale' sign made (showing your telephone number) and erect it in the garden or place it in a window. Do some research into the best newspapers and magazines for advertising your property (see **Appendix B**), and place an advertisement in those that look most promising. You could also have a leaflet printed (with pictures) extolling the virtues of your property, which you could drop into local letterboxes or have distributed with a local newspaper (many people buy a new home in the vicinity of their present home). You may also need a printed fact sheet (if your home's vital statistics aren't included in the leaflet mentioned above) and could offer a 'reward' (e.g. €1,000) to anyone who finds you a buyer. Don't forget to market your home through local companies, schools and organisations, particularly if they have many foreign employees.

Finally, it may help to provide information about local financing sources for potential buyers. With a bit of effort and practice you may even make a better job of marketing your home than an estate agent! Unless you're in a hurry to sell, set yourself a realistic time limit for success, after which you can try an agent. When selling a home yourself, you will need to draft a contract or engage a lawyer to do it for you.

Using an Agent

Most owners prefer to use the services of an agent or agents, either in Greece or their home country, e.g. when selling a second home. If you purchased the property through an agent, it's often wise to use the same agent when selling, as he will already be familiar with it and may still have the details on file. You should take particular care when selecting an agent, as they vary considerably in their professionalism, expertise and experience (the best way to investigate agents is by posing as a buyer). Note that many agents cover a relatively small area, so you should choose one who regularly sells properties in your area and price range. If you own a property in an area popular with foreign buyers, it may be worthwhile using an overseas agent or advertising in foreign newspapers and magazines, such as the English-language publications listed in **Appendix B**.

Agents' Contracts

Before he can offer a property for sale, an agent must have a signed authorisation from the owner in the form of an exclusive or non-exclusive contract. An exclusive contract gives a single agent the right to sell a property, while a non-exclusive contract allows you to deal with any number of agents and to negotiate directly with potential buyers. Most people find that it's better to place a property with a number of agents under non-exclusive contracts. Exclusive contracts are rare and are for a limited period only, e.g. three to six months. Choose an agent who regularly sells properties in your price range and enquire how the property will be marketed and who will pay the costs. See also **Estate Agents** on page 114.

Agents' Fees

When selling a property, the agent's commission is usually paid by the buyer and vendor (half each) and may be included in the purchase price. Fees vary from 2 to 5 per cent, according to the price of a property, and are lower with an exclusive contract than with a non-exclusive contract.

Shop around for the best deal as there's fierce competition among agents to sell good properties (many agents 'tout' for properties to sell by advertising in the expatriate press).

 Note that if you sign a contract without reserving the right to find your own buyer, you must pay the agent's commission even if you sell your home privately!

Make sure that you don't sign two or more exclusive contracts to sell your home – check the contract and make sure you understand what you're signing. Contracts state the agent's commission, what it includes, and most importantly, who must pay it.

 Generally, you shouldn't pay any fees unless you require extra services and you should never pay the agent's commission before a sale is completed and you have been paid.

CAPITAL GAINS TAX

There is no capital gains tax for individuals in Greece.

> **IMPORTANT NOTE**
>
> As when buying a home, be very careful who you deal with when selling a home. Make sure that you're paid with a certified banker's draft before signing over your property to a buyer; once the deed of sale has been signed, the property belongs to the buyer, whether you have been paid or not. Take extra care if you plan to use an intermediary, as it isn't uncommon for a 'middle man' to disappear with the proceeds! Never agree to accept part of the sale price 'under the table'; if the buyer refuses to pay the extra money, there's nothing you can do about it (at least legally). Sellers have been known to end up with no property and no money! All sales should be conducted through a lawyer.

4.

MONEY MATTERS

One of the most important aspects of buying a home in Greece and living there (even for relatively brief periods) is finance, which includes everything from transferring and changing money to mortgages and taxes. If you're planning to invest in a property or a business in Greece financed with imported funds, it's important to consider both the present and possible future exchange rates. On the other hand, if you live and work in Greece and are paid in euros, this may affect your financial commitments abroad.

 If your income is received in a currency other than euros, it can be exposed to risks beyond your control when you live abroad, particularly regarding inflation and exchange rate fluctuations.

If you own a home in Greece it's advisable to employ an accountant or tax adviser to look after your financial affairs there and declare and pay your local taxes. You can also have your financial representative receive your bank statements, ensure that your bank is paying your standing orders, e.g. for utilities and property taxes, and that you have sufficient funds to pay them. If you let a home in Greece through a local company, the company may perform the above tasks as part of its services.

Although the Greeks prefer using cash to credit or charge cards, it's wise to have at least one credit card when visiting or living in Greece (Visa and Mastercard are the most widely accepted). Even if you don't like credit cards and shun any form of credit, they do have their uses, e.g. no-deposit car rentals, no pre-paying hotel bills (plus guaranteed bookings), obtaining cash 24 hours a day, simple telephone and mail-order payments, greater safety and security than cash, and above all, convenience. Note, however, that not all Greek businesses accept credit cards, particularly those in rural areas and on smaller islands.

SURVIVAL TIP
If you plan to live in Greece for long
periods, you must ensure that your income is
(and will remain) sufficient to live on, bearing in mind
devaluations (if your income isn't paid in local currency),
rises in the cost of living (see page 25), and unforeseen
expenses such as high medical bills or anything else
that may reduce your income.

Foreigners, particularly retirees, shouldn't under-estimate the cost of living and many are forced to return to their home countries after a few years. In the early '90s many pensioners with a fixed income paid in a foreign currency saw it fall dramatically as exchange rates worsened and the cost of living rose. The current high exchange rate for the euro (€1 = £1.45 in January 2005) means that pensioners from the UK get less for their pension than a year ago. The cost of living in Greece is still lower than in most other EU countries, although inflation is relatively high (3.7 per cent in 2004). If you're planning to live there permanently, it's wise to seek expert financial advice as it may provide the opportunity to reduce your taxes.

This chapter includes information about Greek currency, importing and exporting money, banking and mortgages.

GREEK CURRENCY

The Greek currency is the euro along with 11 other EU countries (Austria, Belgium, Finland, France, Germany, Ireland, Italy, Luxembourg, the Netherlands, Portugal and Spain). Euro notes and coins became legal tender on 1st January 2002, replacing the drachma. The euro is divided into 100 cents, and coins are minted to the value of 1, 2, 5, 10, 20 and 50 cents and €1 and €2. The 1, 2 and 5 cent coins are copper-coloured and the 10, 20 and 50 brass-coloured. The €1 coin is silver-coloured in the centre with a brass-coloured rim, and the €2 coin has a brass-coloured centre and silver-coloured rim. The reverse ('tail' showing the value) of euro coins is the same in all euro-zone countries, but the obverse ('head') is different in each country. Greek coins carry eight different designs: the 1, 2 and 5 cent coins depict ships from Greek history; the 10, 20 and 50 cent coins carry the images of leaders of the Greek independence struggle (Rigas-Fereos, Capodistrias and Venizelos respectively); the €1 coin depicts the owl of Athens; and the €2 coin shows the abduction of Europa by Zeus. All euro coins can, of course, be used in all euro-zone countries.

Euro banknotes are identical throughout the euro-zone and depict a map of Europe and stylised designs of buildings. Banknotes are printed in denominations of €5, €10, €20, €50, €100, €200 and €500 (worth over £300), the size increasing with their value. Euro notes have been produced using all the latest anti-counterfeiting devices; nevertheless you should be especially wary of €200 and €500 notes. The euro symbol may appear before the amount (as in this book), after it (commonly used by the Greeks, e.g. 25€) or even between the euros and cents, e.g. 25€10. When writing figures (for example, on cheques), a full stop/period (.) is used to separate units of millions, thousands and hundreds, and a comma to denote fractions, e.g. €2.500,50.

If possible, it's wise to obtain some euro coins and banknotes before arriving in Greece and to familiarise yourself with them. Bringing some euros with you (e.g. €50 to €100 in small notes) will save you having to change money on arrival at an airport (where exchange rates are usually poor). It's sensible not to carry a lot of cash and ideally you should avoid high value notes (above €50), which aren't widely accepted, particularly for small purchases or on public transport. Some establishments don't accept €200 and €500 notes at all. Beware of short-changing, which is common in some areas (always check your change, particularly when tendering a large note).

IMPORTING & EXPORTING MONEY

Exchange controls in Greece were abolished on 1st January 1990 and there are no restrictions on the import or export of funds. EU nationals are permitted to open a bank account in any country and to import (or export) unlimited funds in any currency. If you plan to export funds from Greece you need to prove to your bank that the transaction falls within permitted categories (i.e. the transaction is legal). For example, if you export funds as a result of selling your home, you will have to show a copy of the final purchase contract to your bank.

Cash

The import and export of sums over €10,000 (in any currency) must be declared at customs. Residents exporting over €10,000 in cash must present a Greek tax certificate stating that taxes have been paid in Greece. Non-residents must present proof, e.g. the 'pink slip' (see below) that the amount was declared on arrival.

Importing Funds for Property Purchase

When you import funds into Greece to buy a property, you should transfer the money to a Greek bank who will issue the corresponding 'exchange certificate', popularly known as the 'pink slip'. You should present this certificate with your first tax return otherwise you may be liable for income tax on the imported funds. See **Tax Return** on page 212 for more information.

International Bank Transfers

When transferring or sending money to or from Greece, shop around for the best exchange rates and the lowest costs. Banks are often willing to negotiate on fees and exchange rates when you're transferring a large amount of money.

 Don't be too optimistic about the exchange rate, which can change at short notice and can cost you thousands of euros more than you planned.

For example, if you're buying a home in Greece costing €150,000 and are paying in pounds sterling, this would be equal to £103,500 at an exchange rate of £1 = €1.45 (January 2005). However, if the £/€ exchange rate 'falls' to €1.35, it will cost you £111,000 – an increase of £7,500! (In May 2003 the exchange rate was £1 = €1.29!)

When transferring or sending money to (or from) Greece, you should be aware of the alternatives and shop around for the best deal. A bank-to-bank transfer can be made by a normal transfer or by a SWIFT electronic transfer. A normal transfer is supposed to take three to seven days, but it usually takes much longer (particularly when sent by mail), whereas a SWIFT electronic transfer **should** be completed in as little as two hours (although it usually takes at least a day). It's usually quicker and cheaper to transfer funds between branches of the same bank or affiliated banks than between non-affiliated banks.

If you plan to send a large amount of money abroad for a business transaction such as buying a property, you should ensure that you receive the commercial rate of exchange rather than the tourist rate. Shop around and compare your bank's rate with that of least one foreign exchange broker who specialises in sending money abroad (particularly large sums). The leading companies include Foreign Currency Direct (☎ UK 0800-328 5884, 💻 www.currencies.co.uk), Halewood (☎ UK 01753-859159, 💻 www.hifx.co.uk) and Moneycorp (☎ UK 020-7808 0500, 💻 www.moneycorp.com). When you have money transferred to a bank in Greece, make sure that you give the name, account number, branch number and the bank code; if money is 'lost' while being transferred, it can take weeks to locate it.

Always check charges and rates in advance and agree them with your bank (you may be able to negotiate a lower charge or a better exchange rate). It's usually better to convert money to euros before transferring it to Greece, in which case you shouldn't incur any charges in Greece, although some banks deduct commission, whatever the currency. Banks in EU countries are allowed only to pass on to customers costs incurred by the sending bank, and the money must be deposited in a customer's account within five working days. If you routinely transfer money between currencies, you should investigate

Fidelity Money Funds, which operate free of conversion charges and at wholesale rates of exchange.

Telegraphic Transfers

One of the quickest (it takes around 15 minutes) and safest methods of transferring cash is via a telegraphic transfer, e.g. Moneygram (☎ UK 0800-666 3947, 💻 www.moneygram.com) or Western Union (💻 www. westernunion.com), but it's also one of the most expensive, e.g. commission of 7 to 10 per cent of the amount sent! Money can be sent overseas via American Express offices by Amex card holders (using Amex's Moneygram service) to any other American Express office in just 15 minutes.

Bank Drafts & Personal Cheques

Another way to transfer money is via a bank draft, which should be sent by registered mail. However, if a bank draft is lost or stolen, it's impossible to stop payment and you must wait six months before a new draft can be issued. Bank drafts aren't treated like cash in Greece and must be cleared like personal cheques. It's also possible to send a cheque drawn on a personal account, although it can take a long time to clear (usually several weeks) and fees are high. It's possible to pay a cheque drawn on a foreign account into a local bank account, although it can take three or four weeks to clear. Note that personal cheques are rarely used in Greece.

Postcheques & Eurogiro

Giro postcheques issued by European post offices can be cashed (with a guarantee card) for up to €130 at main post offices in Greece. You can also send money to Greek post offices (Hellenic Post/ELTA) via the Girobank Eurogiro system from post offices in 15 European countries (including the UK); transfers sent by Eurogiro take between three and four days.

Obtaining Cash

An instant method of obtaining cash in Greece is to use a debit, credit or charge card from an automatic teller machine (ATM). Note that you'll need a PIN number. Many foreigners living in Greece (particularly retirees) keep the bulk of their money in a foreign account (perhaps an offshore bank) and draw on it with a cash card locally. This is an ideal solution for holidaymakers and holiday-homeowners, although homeowners will still need a local bank account to pay their bills. Visa, Mastercard, American Express and Diners Club cards are commonly accepted in major cities and tourist areas, although in remote rural areas cash is the most common and sometimes the only form of payment acceptable. Some shops may offer a discount for cash payment.

Most banks in major cities have foreign exchange windows and there are banks or *bureaux de change* with extended opening hours at major airports and railway stations in the main cities. Here you can buy or sell foreign currencies, buy and cash travellers' cheques, and obtain a cash advance on credit and charge cards. Note, however, that some Greek banks refuse to cash travellers' cheques. Bear in mind that airport banks and other outlets usually offer the worst exchange rates and charge the highest fees.

There are many private *bureaux de change* in Greece, with longer business hours than banks, particularly at weekends. Most offer competitive exchange rates and low or no commission (but always check). They're easier to deal with than banks, and if you're changing a lot of money you can also usually negotiate a better exchange rate. Never use unofficial moneychangers, who are likely to short change you or leave you with worthless foreign notes rather than euros. The official exchange rates for most European and major international currencies are listed in banks and daily newspapers.

Travellers' Cheques

If you're visiting Greece, it's safer to carry travellers' cheques than cash, although they aren't as easy to redeem as in some other countries, e.g. the US. For example, they aren't usually accepted by businesses, except some hotels, restaurants and shops, all of which usually offer a poor exchange rate. It's best to buy travellers' cheques in euros when visiting Greece. You can buy them from any Greek bank, usually for a service charge of 1 per cent. There should be no commission charge when cashing euro travellers' cheques at any bank in Greece (you must show your passport), although charges and rates vary considerably for travellers' cheques in other currencies. Banks usually offer a better exchange rate for travellers' cheques than for banknotes.

Always keep a separate record of cheque numbers and note where and when they were cashed. American Express provides a free, three-hour replacement service for lost or stolen travellers' cheques at all of their offices world-wide, provided that you know the serial numbers of the lost cheques. Without the serial numbers, replacement can take three days or longer. Most companies provide toll-free numbers for reporting lost or stolen travellers' cheques in Greece.

There isn't a lot of difference in the cost of buying Greek currency using cash, buying travellers' cheques or using a credit card to obtain cash from ATMs. However, many people carry only cash when visiting Greece, which is asking for trouble, particularly if you've no way of obtaining more cash locally, e.g. with a credit or debit card or travellers' cheques.

SURVIVAL TIP
One thing to bear in mind when travelling
anywhere is not to rely on only one source of funds!

BANKS

Greece generally has good banking facilities, which have improved considerably in recent years, although you may find Greek banks frustratingly slow and inefficient compared with their European counterparts. There are some 20 domestic banks operating in Greece which are divided into two groups: commercial banks and specialised credit institutions. The Bank of Greece (🖥 www.ethniki.gr) is the central (and largest) bank and monetary authority in Greece and is responsible for the supervision of credit institutions operating in the country. Other main banks include: Alpha Credit Bank (🖥 www.alpha.gr), the largest private bank; EFG Eurobank (🖥 www.eurobank.gr), the third-largest; Egnatia Bank (the Agricultural Bank, 🖥 www.egnatiabank.gr); and Piraeus Bank (🖥 www.piraeusbank.gr), currently under expansion. Several commercial banks are controlled to some extent by the state, although most are in the process of being merged with other banks or privatised. Most banks offer internet banking facilities which is a popular option in Greece.

There are also several foreign-owned banks represented in Greece, e.g. Barclays Bank, Citibank, HSBC, Natwest Bank and the Royal Bank of Scotland, mainly in Athens (branches are rare in the provinces with the possible exception of Thessaloniki).

Opening Hours

Greek banks are usually open from 8am to 2.30pm on Mondays to Thursdays and from 8am to 2pm on Fridays, although hours vary from town to town and even from branch to branch. Some branches in main cities and resorts have longer opening hours, which may include evenings and weekends. In small villages there may be a tiny bank office, open for a few hours a day or on certain days only. If you need to use teller services, you must take your passport as proof of identity (many Greek banks prefer this to a residence permit) and should be prepared for a **long** wait (Greek bank queues move very slowly). In many banks, transactions are performed in two parts (to keep the maximum number of people in 'employment'). A transaction involving a withdrawal must be approved or processed at one counter and then you need to queue to collect your money at the cash desk.

Opening an Account

You can open a bank account in Greece whether you're a resident or a non-resident. It's better to open a bank account in person than by correspondence from abroad. **Before choosing a bank, you should compare the fees charged for international money transfers and other services.** Ask your friends, neighbours or colleagues for their recommendations and go along to the bank of your choice and introduce yourself. You must be over 18 years old and provide proof of identity, e.g. a passport, your local address and papers to show the funds you have imported and the method used. You can open a bank account before arriving in the country via an overseas branch of any Greek bank (or a foreign bank operating in Greece), but your signature must be ratified before the account can be opened. Note that various types of bank account can be opened, including current accounts, foreign currency accounts and external accounts.

Most Greek banks provide a debit and cash withdrawal (ATM) card with current and savings accounts. Greek debit cards can also be used for purchases outside Greece. If you require a credit card, you should request one, but the bank may ask to see a recommendation from your bank in your home country before issuing one. Greek banks don't generally give loans (other than mortgages) to non-residents.

It isn't wise to close your bank accounts abroad when you're living permanently in Greece, unless you're absolutely certain that you won't need them in future. Even when you're resident in Greece, it's cheaper to keep some money in an account in a country that you visit regularly than to pay commission to convert foreign currency. Many foreigners living in Greece maintain at least two accounts, a foreign bank account for their international transactions and a local account for day-to-day business.

Offshore Banking

If you have a sum of money to invest or wish to protect your inheritance from the tax man, it may be worthwhile looking into the accounts and services (such as pensions and trusts) provided by offshore banking centres in tax havens such as the Channel Islands (Guernsey and Jersey), Gibraltar and the Isle of Man (some 50 locations world-wide are officially classified as tax havens). The big attraction of offshore banking is that money can be deposited in a wide range of currencies, customers are usually guaranteed complete anonymity, there are no double taxation agreements, no withholding tax is payable and interest is paid tax-free. Some offshore banks also offer telephone (usually seven days a week) and internet banking.

A large number of American, British and European banks, as well as various other international financial institutions, provide offshore banking facilities in one or more locations. Most institutions offer high-interest deposit accounts for long-term savings and investment portfolios, in which funds can be deposited in any major currency. Many people living abroad keep a local account for everyday business and maintain an offshore account for international transactions and investment purposes.

> **SURVIVAL TIP**
> Most financial experts advise investors
> not to rush into the expatriate life and invest their life
> savings in an offshore tax haven until they know what
> their long-term plans are.

Accounts have minimum deposits levels, which range from the equivalent of around €750 to €15,000 (e.g. £500 to £100,000) with some as high as €150,000 (£100,000). In addition to large minimum balances, accounts may also have stringent terms and conditions, such as restrictions on withdrawals or high early withdrawal penalties. You can deposit funds on call (instant access) or for a fixed period, e.g. from 90 days to one year (usually for large sums). Interest is usually paid monthly or annually; monthly interest payments are slightly lower than annual payments, although monthly payments have the advantage of providing a regular income. There are usually no charges if a specified minimum balance is maintained. Many accounts offer a cash card or a credit card (e.g. Mastercard or Visa) that can be used to obtain cash via ATMs world-wide.

When selecting a financial institution and offshore banking centre, your first priority should be the safety of your money. In some offshore banking centres, bank deposits are covered by a deposit protection scheme, whereby a maximum sum is guaranteed should a financial institution go to the wall (the Isle of Man, Guernsey and Jersey all have such schemes). Unless you're planning to bank with a major international bank (which isn't likely to fold until the day after the end of the world), you should check the credit rating of a financial institution before depositing any money, particularly if it doesn't provide deposit insurance. All banks have a credit rating (the highest is 'AAA') and a bank with a high rating will be happy to tell you (but get it in writing). You can also check the rating of an international bank or financial organisation with Moody's Investor Service (🖥 www.moodys.com). You should be wary of institutions offering higher than average interest rates; if it looks too good to be true, it probably is!

MORTGAGES

Mortgages or home loans are now widely available from most Greek banks who are now generally much more keen to lend money on property than they used to be, although some banks remain reluctant to lend to non-residents. The mortgage market is still relatively new and small compared to many other EU countries such as the UK and France – the outstanding mortgage debt in 2004 in Greece was a mere 14 per cent of the country's GDP compared to 64 per cent in the UK.

The amount you can borrow will depend on various factors such as your income, trade or profession, whether you're an employee or self-employed, and whether you're married, and if so, whether your partner works. Lenders may also have a maximum lending limit based on a percentage of your income, but this isn't required by law and many banks also have a minimum amount, e.g. €9,000. Most Greek banks will lend a maximum of 35 per cent of your monthly income so if you earn €3,000 a month the loan repayments cannot exceed €1,050 a month.

Mortgages are granted on a percentage of the 'assessed tax value', which is invariably below the market value (see page 122). Most banks offer mortgages of up to 100 per cent of this value, but the usual amount is a maximum of 75 per cent. The normal term is 20 years, although mortgages can be repaid over 5 to 30 years. 'Older' homebuyers must repay a mortgage before they are aged 74; for example, if you're 60 at the time of applying for a mortgage, the maximum term is 14 years.

To obtain a mortgage from a Greek bank, you need to complete the application form and present the original and a photocopy of your passport or residence card. Employees must present payslips from the previous three months, a certificate of salary from the previous year (P60 in the UK) and usually bank statements covering the last six months. The self-employed need to show copies of business accounts (usually for the last three years), bank statements from your business account for the past year and usually bank statements from your personal account covering the last six months. Note that all documents must usually be translated into Greek and stamped by the Greek embassy or consulate in your home country. Provided the paperwork is in order mortgages are usually approved within two to three weeks.

Greek mortgages are currently very competitive and in early 2005 variable interest rates were around 4 per cent and fixed rates ranged from 4.9 to 6 per cent. Greek Loan Tax of 0.12 per cent is added to the mortgage interest rate and paid to the state when you make your mortgage payments.

Note that you must add expenses and fees totalling from 10 to 15 per cent of the final purchase contract price, to the cost of a property. For example, if you're buying a property for €150,000 with an assessed tax value of €130,000 and obtain a mortgage for 75 per cent of the value (i.e. €97,500), you must pay the remaining 25 per cent of the value (€32,500), fees and expenses, plus the part of the price outside the assessed tax value (€20,000). There are numerous fees associated with mortgages including a pre-approval charge (e.g. €50), fixed charges ranging from €500 to €1,500 depending on the amount of the loan and pre-notation expenses of 0.825 per cent of the loan (paid to the mortgage registry). If you borrow between €60,000 to €300,000 you should expect to pay around €1,250 in costs. Mortgages usually have a cancellation fee. You can transfer a mortgage to another bank without charge if the mortgage has at least five years repayments outstanding, at least €15,000 remaining capital and you have a record of no repayment defaults.

SURVIVAL TIP
If you're a Greek taxpayer you can
claim a deduction for your Greek mortgage
against your tax liabilities.

Most banks are willing to finance the construction of a house, but you can only obtain a mortgage for a plot if you can show proof of an application for a building licence, which must be granted within 18 months of purchase of the plot. A bank usually advances the mortgage to the builder or developer in stages in line with the agreed stage payments. Banks also offer special mortgages for renovation or restoration work. Lenders usually require a life policy and building insurance for a property's full value. It's customary for a property in Greece to be held as security for a home loan, i.e. the lender takes a first charge on the property, which is recorded at the property registry. If a loan is obtained using a property as security, additional fees and registration costs are payable to the notary for registering the charge against the property.

Re-mortgaging

If you have equity in an existing property, either in Greece or abroad, then it may be more cost-effective to re-mortgage (or take out a second mortgage) on that property, rather than take out a new mortgage for a second home in Greece. It involves less paperwork, and therefore lower legal fees, and a plan can be tailored to meet your individual requirements. Depending on your equity in your existing property and the cost of your Greek property, this may enable you to pay cash for a second home. Note, however, that when a mortgage is taken out on a Greek property it's based on that property and not the individual, which could be important if you get into repayment difficulties.

Foreign Currency Loans

It's also possible to obtain a foreign currency mortgage, other than in euros (either in Greece or abroad), e.g. pounds sterling, Swiss francs or US dollars. In previous years, high Greek interest rates meant that a foreign currency mortgage was a good bet for many foreigners. However, you should be extremely wary about taking out a foreign currency mortgage, as interest rate gains can be wiped out overnight by currency swings and devaluations. It's generally recognised that you should take out a mortgage in the currency in which you're paid or in the currency of the country where a property is situated. In this case, if the foreign currency in which you have your mortgage is heavily devalued, you will have the consolation of knowing that the value of your Greek property will ('theoretically') have increased by the same percentage when converted back into euros.

When choosing between a euro and a foreign currency loan, take into account all costs, fees, interest rates and possible currency fluctuations. Irrespective of how you finance your purchase, you should always obtain professional advice. If you have a foreign currency mortgage, you must usually pay commission charges each time you transfer foreign currency into euros or remit money to Greece. If you let a second home, you may be able to offset the interest (pro rata) on your mortgage against letting income. For example, if you let a property for three months of the year, you can offset a quarter of your annual mortgage interest against your letting income.

SURVIVAL TIP
If you need to obtain a mortgage to
buy a home in Greece, shop around and compare
interest rates, terms and fees from a number of banks
and financial institutions – not just in Greece but
also your home country.

Bear in mind that mortgages in Greece are generally for a shorter period than in the UK and US, and therefore your repayments may be much higher than you expect.

5.

THE PURCHASE PROCEDURE

This chapter details the purchase procedure for buying a home in Greece. It's advisable to employ a lawyer before paying any money and, if necessary, have him check anything you're concerned about regarding a property that you're planning to buy. See also **Avoiding Problems** on page 106.

CONVEYANCING

Conveyancing (or conveyance) is the legal term for processing the paperwork involved in buying and selling a property and transferring the deeds of ownership. In Greece, some aspects of conveyancing, such as drawing up the final purchase contract/title deeds and witnessing the signatures, can be performed only by a public notary. A notary represents the government and one of his main tasks is to ensure that state taxes are paid on the completion of a sale.

 Note that a notary doesn't verify or guarantee the accuracy of statements made in a contract or protect you against fraud!

It's therefore vital to employ a lawyer (*dhikigóri*) to carry out the following checks:

- Verifying that a property belongs to the vendor or that he has legal authority to sell it. Note that when there's more than one owner, which is often the case in Greece, all owners must agree to the sale. **If a property has no deeds or isn't registered, you must be extremely wary.** The final transfer of ownership cannot take place until a separate title deed has been issued, which can take as long as two years; it's therefore important to check how long the title deed will take to obtain before signing a preliminary contract.

- Verifying that trees on rural properties belong to the owner or finding out who they belong to.

- Making sure that there are no tenants. If there are, you must ensure that you will obtain vacant possession.

- Checking that there are no pre-emption rights over a property and that there are no plans to construct anything that would adversely affect the value, enjoyment or use of the property such as roads, railway lines, airports, shops, factories or any other developments.

- Checking that the boundaries and measurements in the deeds are accurate. If possible, obtain a certificate from the property register containing an accurate physical description of the property and maps. When buying a property with a plot of land, the boundaries must be surveyed.

● Ensuring that building permits and planning permissions, e.g. building licence, water and electricity supply, and sewage connection, are in order and are genuine, and that a property was built in accordance with the plans.

● Checking that there are no encumbrances or liens, e.g. mortgages or loans, against a property or any outstanding debts, such as local taxes (rates), community charges, water, electricity or telephone. Note that if you buy a property on which there's an outstanding loan or taxes, the lender or local authority has first claim on the property and has the right to take possession and sell it to repay the debt. All unpaid debts on a property are inherited by the buyer.

● Finding out the correct 'assessed tax value' for the property and obtaining written confirmation of this (see **Assessed Tax Value** on page 122).

● Ensuring that proper title is obtained and arranging the necessary registration of ownership (see **Registration** on page 183).

Many estate agents will carry out the above checks for you and pass the information to your lawyer, but it's still wise to have your lawyer double-check. The cost of conveyancing depends on whether you employ a foreign or local lawyer or both (it's generally cheaper to use a local lawyer). Lawyers' fees in Greece are a maximum of 1 per cent of the 'assessed tax value'. Before hiring a lawyer, compare the fees charged by a number of practices and obtain quotations in writing. Always check what's included in the fee and whether it's 'full and binding' or just an estimate (a low basic rate may be supplemented by much more expensive 'extras'). You should also employ a lawyer to check the final purchase contract (see below) before signing it to ensure that it includes everything necessary, particularly any relevant conditional clauses.

Notary's Duties

In Greece, the final purchase contract is prepared by a public notary (*symvoleográfos*), who's responsible for ensuring that it's drawn up correctly and that the purchase price is paid to the vendor. He also certifies the identity of the parties, witnesses the signing of the final purchase contract, collects proof that the purchase tax has been paid, arranges for the property's registration (in the name of the new owner) in the local land registry or National Land Registry (see **Land Registries** on page 183) and collects any fees or taxes due.

Note, however, that a notary represents the state and **doesn't** protect the interests of the buyer or the seller and will rarely point out possible pitfalls in a contract, proffer advice or volunteer any information (as, for example, an estate agent usually will). Don't expect a notary to speak English or any language other than Greek (although some do) or to explain the intricacies of Greek property law.

Anyone buying (or selling) property abroad shouldn't even think about doing so without taking expert, independent legal advice. You should certainly never sign anything or pay any money before obtaining legal advice. Your lawyer should also check that the notary does his job correctly, thus providing an extra safeguard. It isn't wise to use the vendor's lawyer, even if this would save you money, as he is primarily concerned with protecting the interests of the vendor and not the buyer. See also **Avoiding Problems** on page 106.

PRELIMINARIES

Preliminary Contract

The first stage in buying a property in Greece is usually the signing of a preliminary contract drawn up by agreement between both parties, usually in consultation with their lawyers. Notaries can draw up a preliminary contract, although this is unusual. It's also possible to go to a notary in Greece and have him draw up the final purchase contract without having a preliminary contract, but, when you're paying a deposit (see below), it's necessary to have a preliminary contract drawn up. **Note that before signing a contract, it's important to have it checked by a lawyer.** One of the main reasons is to safeguard your interests by including any necessary conditional clauses (see below) in the contract.

Contracts are subject to a clear title being obtained and any necessary government permits. Builders, developers and estate agents often have ready-made contracts that are drafted to protect their own interests; these should be scrutinised by your lawyer. You should also instruct your lawyer to obtain the necessary permits and not leave it to an estate agent or developer. It's sometimes possible to sign an option or reservation agreement, where you pay a small deposit to secure a property for a period, e.g. 30 days, while waiting for funds to arrive from abroad. This deposit is usually lost if you back out of the purchase.

Deposit

When you sign the preliminary contract for a new or resale property or a plot of land you must usually pay a deposit (see below). If you're buying a resale or a new finished property (i.e. not off plan), you usually pay a deposit of 5 to 10 per cent when signing the contract (the percentage may be negotiable, but 10 per cent is normal), the balance being paid on completion when the final purchase contract is signed.

Deposits are refundable under strict conditions only, notably relating to any conditional clauses such as failure to obtain a mortgage. A deposit can also be forfeited if you don't complete the purchase transaction within the period specified in the contract. If you withdraw from a sale after all the conditions have been met, you won't only lose your deposit, but may also be required to pay the estate agent's commission.

The contract can be cancelled by either party, the buyer forfeiting his deposit or the vendor paying the buyer double the deposit. However, in some cases, if one of the parties wishes to withdraw from the sale, the other party can demand that he goes through with it or that he receives compensation for damages.

 Always make sure that you know exactly what the conditions are regarding the return or forfeit of a deposit.

Note that many estate agents don't have legal authority to hold money on behalf of their clients and that deposits should be kept only in a separate, bonded account. It isn't wise to make out cheques for deposits or other monies in the name of an estate agent.

Tax File Number

All foreigners purchasing property in Greece require a Greek Tax File Number (*Arithmo Forologiko Mitro*/ AFM – known as the 'A-Fi-Mi). This can be obtained from the local tax office usually within a few days of application. Your lawyer or representative can obtain this for you. The AFM must be presented to the notary at completion and is recorded on the final purchase contract. You also need an AFM if you wish to apply for a mortgage.

Importing Funds

The origin of funds used to buy property in Greece must be declared to the Bank of Greece using an official import document, popularly known as the 'pink slip'. You should open a local bank account (see page 165), through which all payments relating to the property purchase must take place (particularly if you're paying in stages). Your bank should provide you with an import form ('pink slip') for every transfer you have made from abroad. This will provide an accurate record of payments and show that they emanated from abroad.

Conditional Clauses

Contracts, whether for new or resale properties, usually contain a number of conditional clauses that must be met to ensure the validity of the contract. Conditions usually apply to events out of the control of either the vendor or buyer, although almost anything the buyer agrees with the vendor can be included in a contract. If any of the conditions aren't met, the contract can be suspended or declared null and void, and the deposit returned. However, if you fail to go through with a purchase and aren't covered by a clause in the contract, you will forfeit your deposit or could even be compelled to go through with a purchase.

Note that if you're buying anything from the vendor such as carpets, curtains or furniture that's included in the purchase price, you should have them listed in an inventory that is attached as an addendum to the contract. Any fixtures and fittings present in a property when you view it (and agree to buy it) should still be there when you take possession, unless otherwise stated in the contract (see also **Completion** on page 180). You should discuss with your lawyer whether conditional clauses are necessary.

There are many possible conditional clauses concerning a range of subjects, including the following:

- Being dependent on obtaining a mortgage;
- Obtaining planning permission and building permits;
- Obtaining special permits from the local authorities, e.g. non-EU nationals wishing to purchase property close to Greek borders require official permission (see **Restrictions** on page 19);
- Being unable to obtain a residence permit;
- Confirmation of the land area being purchased with a property;
- Plans to construct anything, e.g. roads, railways, etc, that would adversely affect your enjoyment or use of a property;
- Pre-emption rights or restrictive covenants over a property such as rights of way;

- Dependence on the sale of another property;
- Dependence on a satisfactory building survey or inspection.

Buying Off Plan

When buying an uncompleted property off plan, i.e. a property yet to be built or partly built, payment is made in stages. Stage payments vary considerably and may consist of the following: 10 per cent deposit and the remainder on completion, or 10 per cent on deposit and three stage payments during construction. Some of the final payment (e.g. 5 per cent) may be withheld for six months for maintenance and as 'insurance' against defects (see below). If a property is already partly built, the builder may ask for a higher initial payment, depending on its stage of completion.

The contract contains: the timetable for the property's completion; stage payment dates; the completion date and (possibly) penalties for non-completion; guarantees for building work; details of the builder's insurance policy (against non-completion); and a copy of the plans and drawings. The floor plan and technical specifications are signed by both parties to ensure that sizes and standard of construction are adhered to. The contract should also contain a clause allowing you to withhold at least 5 per cent of the purchase price for six months in case the builder fails to correct any faults in the property. The completion of each stage should be certified in writing by your own architect or lawyer before payments are made. It's important to ensure that payments are made on time, or you could forfeit all previous payments and the property could be sold to another buyer.

> **SURVIVAL TIP**
> It's important that the builder or
> developer has an insurance policy (or 'termination'
> guarantee) to protect your investment in the event that
> he goes bust before completing the property and
> its infrastructure. If he doesn't, you
> shouldn't buy from him!

See also **Avoiding Problems** on page 106 and **Conveyancing** on page 174.

Inheritance & Capital Gains Tax

Before registering the property, you should carefully consider the tax and inheritance consequences for those in whose name the property will be registered. Property can be registered in a single name; both names of a couple or joint buyers' names; the name or names of children, giving the parents sole use during their lifetime; or in the name of a local or foreign company (see below). However you decide to buy a property, it should be done at the time of purchase, as it will be more expensive (or even impossible) to change it later. Discuss the matter with your lawyer before signing a contract. See also **Inheritance & Gift Tax** on page 213. There's no capital gains tax in Greece.

Buying Through a Company

Properties in Greece can be purchased in the name of a Greek, foreign or offshore company, which may represent substantial savings on taxes, particularly inheritance taxes. However, there are numerous problems and costs associated with this kind of purchase and it's essential to obtain expert legal advice and weigh up the long-term advantages and disadvantages. This option is usually financially viable only for very expensive properties bought on a long-term basis. Note that offshore companies are now liable for a special annual tax in Greece, levied at 3 per cent of the company's value.

COMPLETION

Completion (or closing) is the name for the signing of the final purchase contract (deed), the date of which is usually one or two months after signing the preliminary contract, as stated in the contract (although it may be 'moveable'). Note that if there are several owners or inheritance procedures to go through before completion, this could take months and your lawyer will arrange an extension to the original preliminary contract.

Completion involves the signing of the final purchase contract, transferring legal ownership of a property and the payment of the balance of the purchase price, plus other payments such as the notary's or lawyer's fees, taxes and duties (although these may be paid earlier or later). When the necessary documents relating to a purchase have been returned to the notary or lawyer handling the sale, he will contact you and request the balance of the purchase price less the deposit and, if applicable, the amount of a mortgage. He will also send you a bill for his fees and taxes. At the same time, the notary should provide a draft final purchase contract (if he doesn't, you should request one), which should be complete and not contain any blank spaces to be completed later. If you don't understand the document, you should have it checked by your lawyer.

Final Checks

Property is sold subject to the condition that it's accepted in the state it's in at the time of completion, so you should be aware of anything that occurs between the signing of the preliminary contract and completion. Before signing the final purchase contract, it's important to check that the property hasn't fallen down or been damaged in any way, e.g. by a storm, vandals or the previous owner. If you have a lawyer or are buying through an agent, he should accompany you on this visit. You should also do a final inventory immediately prior to completion (the previous owner should already have vacated the property) to ensure that the vendor hasn't absconded with anything that was included in the price.

You should have an inventory of the fixtures and fittings and anything that was included in the contract or purchased separately, e.g. carpets, light fittings, curtains and kitchen appliances, and check that they're present and in working order. This is particularly important if furniture and furnishings (and major appliances) were included in the price. You should also ensure that expensive items, such as kitchen appliances, haven't been substituted by inferior (possibly second-hand) items. Any fixtures and fittings (and garden plants and shrubs) present in a property when you viewed it should still be there when you take possession, unless otherwise stated in the contract.

If you find that anything is missing or damaged or isn't in working order, you should make a note and insist on immediate restitution, such as an appropriate reduction in the amount to be paid. In such cases it's normal for the notary or lawyer to delay the signing of the deed until the matter is settled, although an appropriate amount could be withheld from the vendor's proceeds to pay for repairs or replacements.

SURVIVAL TIP
You should refuse to go through with the purchase if you aren't completely satisfied, as it will be difficult or impossible to obtain redress later.

If it isn't possible to complete the sale, you should consult your lawyer about your rights and the return of your deposit and any other funds already paid.

Signing

The final act of the sale is the signing of the final purchase contract, which takes place in the notary's office. Before the final purchase contract is signed, the notary or lawyer checks that the conditions contained in the preliminary contract have been met. The notary also checks the accompanying documents including the buyer's tax file number and the receipt of the payment of purchase tax (see **Purchase Tax** on page 122) by the buyer.

It's usual for all parties to be present when the deed of sale is read, signed and witnessed by the notary, although either party can give someone a power of attorney to represent them (see Power of Attorney below). This is quite common among foreign buyers and sellers and can be arranged by your lawyer. If a couple buys a property in both their names, the wife can give the husband power of attorney (or vice versa).

The notary reads through the final purchase contract, and both the vendor and buyer (or their representatives) must sign every sheet included in the contract, indicating that they've understood and accept the terms of the document. If you don't understand Greek, you should take along an interpreter – your lawyer may translate for you.

Power of Attorney

If for any reason you're unable to sign the final purchase contract in person, you may wish to give power of attorney to your lawyer beforehand. The power of attorney document can be as extensive or as limited you wish, but it should include authorisation to act on your behalf at completion and at tax offices (e.g. to obtain your tax file number and pay taxes).

The document can be drawn up in one of two ways: your lawyer sends you a power of attorney in Greek, which you take to the Greek embassy or consulate in your home country where it is legalised by the authorities; or your lawyer in your home country draws up a power of attorney, which is legalised by a public notary and authenticated with an official stamp (*apostille*). The document must then be officially translated into Greek.

If you choose to sign a power of attorney in Greek, make sure you know exactly what you're signing.

Payment

As stated under **Importing Funds** on page 177, the origin of funds used to buy property in Greece must be declared to the Bank of Greece using an official import document (the 'pink slip'). Proof that the funds have been imported must be produced at completion. The balance of the price (after the deposit and any mortgages are subtracted) must be paid by banker's draft or bank transfer. For many people the most convenient way is by banker's draft, which also means that you will have the payment in your possession (a bank cannot lose it!) and the notary can confirm it immediately. It also allows you to withhold payment if there's a last minute problem that cannot be resolved.

When the vendor and buyer are of the same foreign nationality, they can agree that the balance is paid in any currency and payment can also be made abroad. However, the final purchase contract must state the sale price in local currency, as taxes are paid on this price. At the time of signing, both the vendor and buyer declare that payment has been made in the agreed foreign currency. In this case the payment should be held by an independent lawyer or solicitor in the vendor's or buyer's home country. After paying the money and receiving a receipt, the notary or lawyer will usually give you a copy of the final purchase contract showing that you're the new owner of the property. You will also receive the keys!

Registration

After the final purchase contract is signed, the original is lodged at the land registry (*ipothikofilakio*) and the new owner's name is entered on the registry deed. It's important to send the signed deed to the land registry as soon as possible (the notary should do this), although the actual registration may take some time. Only when the deed has been registered do you become the legal owner of the property.

Land Registries

Until recently there was no centralised or co-ordinated system of registering property in Greece and property transactions were recorded by hand in small local land registries. Transactions were mainly recorded in the name of the people involved rather than the actual property. This system, still the only one in some parts of the country, means that a title search can take hours (or even days) as each cross reference is checked against others, a process that is open to error and omission.

To rectify this and to conform to EU directives, in 1995 Greece established a National Land Registry where all property will eventually be recorded and registered with an individual reference number and the names of current and past owners. This will facilitate checks on ownership and encumbrances and generally ensure a more secure purchase. The National Land Registry is far from complete and it's estimated that work will be finished by 2010. Meanwhile, many areas in Greece still rely on local land registries for registration of ownership.

6.

MOVING HOUSE

This chapter contains information about moving house, immigration and customs. It also contains checklists of tasks to be completed before or soon after arrival in Greece and when moving house, plus suggestions for finding local help and information.

SHIPPING YOUR BELONGINGS

After buying a home in Greece, it usually takes only a few weeks to have your belongings shipped from within continental Europe. From anywhere else it varies considerably, e.g. around four weeks from the east coast of America, six weeks from the west coast of America and the Far East, and around eight weeks from Australasia. Customs clearance is no longer necessary when shipping your household effects to Greece from another European Union (EU) country. However, when shipping your effects from a non-EU country to Greece, you should enquire about customs formalities in advance. If you fail to follow the correct procedure, you can encounter problems and delays and may be erroneously charged duty or fined. The relevant forms to be completed may depend on whether your home will be your main residence or a second home. Removal companies usually take care of the paperwork and ensure that the correct documents are provided and properly completed (see **Customs** on page 192).

It's recommended that you use a major shipping company with a good reputation. For international moves it's best to use a company that's a member of the International Federation of Furniture Removers (FIDI, 🖳 www.fidi.com) or the Overseas Moving Network International (OMNI, 🖳 www.omnimoving.com), with experience in Greece. Members of FIDI and OMNI usually subscribe to an advance payment scheme, which provides a guarantee whereby, if a member company fails to fulfil its commitments to a client, the removal is completed at the agreed cost by another company or your money is refunded. Some removal companies have local subsidiaries or affiliates, which may be more convenient if you encounter problems or need to make an insurance claim.

You should try to obtain at least three written quotations before choosing a company, as rates vary considerably. Removal companies should send a representative to provide a detailed quotation. Most companies will pack your belongings and provide packing cases and special containers, although this is naturally more expensive than packing them yourself. Ask a company how they pack fragile and valuable items, and whether the cost of packing cases, materials and insurance (see below) are included in a quotation. If you're doing your own packing, most shipping companies will provide packing crates and boxes.

Shipments are charged by volume, e.g. the square metre in Europe and the square foot in the US. You should expect to pay from €3,000 to €6,000 to move the contents of a three to four-bedroom house within western Europe, e.g. from London to Athens. If you're flexible about the delivery date, shipping companies will usually quote a lower fee based on a 'part load', where the cost is shared with other deliveries. This can result in savings of up to 50 per cent or more compared with a 'special' delivery.

```
SURVIVAL TIP
Whether you have an individual or
shared delivery, obtain the maximum transit period
in writing, otherwise you may have to wait
months for delivery!
```

Be sure to fully insure your belongings during removal with a well established insurance company. **Don't insure with a shipping company that carries its own insurance, as it will usually fight every euro of a claim.** Insurance premiums are usually 1 to 2 per cent of the declared value of your goods, depending on the type of cover chosen. It's prudent to make a photographic or video record of valuables for insurance purposes. Most insurance policies cover for 'all risks' on a replacement value basis. Note, however, that china, glass and other breakables can usually only be included in an all risks policy when they're packed by the removal company. Insurance usually covers total loss or loss of a particular crate only, rather than individual items (unless they were packed by the shipping company).

If there are any breakages or damaged items, they should be noted and listed before you sign the delivery bill (although it's obviously impractical to check everything on delivery). If you need to make a claim, be sure to read the small print, as some companies require clients to make a claim within a few days, although seven is usual. **Always send a claim by registered post.** Some insurance companies apply an excess of around 1 per cent of the total shipment value when assessing claims. This means that if your shipment is valued at €25,000 and you make a claim for less than €250, you won't receive anything.

If you're unable to ship your belongings directly to Greece, most shipping companies will put them into storage and some offer a limited free-storage period prior to shipment, e.g. 14 days.

```
┌─────────────────────────────────────────────────────┐
│                     SURVIVAL TIP                      │
│                  If you need to put your              │
│       household effects into storage, it's important to│
│         have them fully insured, as warehouses have   │
│                been known to burn down!               │
└─────────────────────────────────────────────────────┘
```

Make a complete list of everything to be moved and give a copy to the removal company. Don't include anything illegal with your belongings, e.g. guns, bombs, drugs or pornography, as customs checks can be rigorous and penalties severe. Provide the shipping company with **detailed** instructions for how to find your home abroad from the nearest motorway or main road, and a telephone number where you can be contacted.

After considering the shipping costs, you may decide to ship only selected items of furniture and personal effects and buy new furniture locally. If you're importing household goods from another European country, it's possible to rent a self-drive van or truck, although if you rent a vehicle outside Greece you usually need to return it to the country where it was hired. If you plan to transport your belongings to Greece personally, check the customs requirements in the countries you must pass through. Most people find it isn't advisable to do their own move unless it's a simple job, e.g. a few items of furniture and personal effects only. It's no fun heaving beds and wardrobes up stairs and squeezing them into impossible spaces! If you're taking pets with you, you may need to get your vet to tranquillise them, as many pets are frightened (even more than people) by the chaos and stress of moving house.

If you're moving permanently to Greece, take the opportunity to sell, give away or throw out at least half of your possessions. It will cut down your removal bill, clear your mind, and make life simpler, plus you will have the fun of buying new furniture that complements your new house.

Bear in mind when moving home that everything that can go wrong often does, so allow plenty of time and try not to arrange your move to your new home on the same day as the previous owner is moving out. That's just asking for fate to intervene!

Last but not least, if your home abroad has poor or impossible access for a large truck you must inform the shipping company (the ground must also be firm enough to support a heavy vehicle). Note that if your belongings need to be transferred to a smaller vehicle at the end of the road, carried a long distance, or if large items of furniture need to be taken in through an upstairs window or via a balcony, you may need to pay extra.

PRE-DEPARTURE HEALTH CHECK

If you're planning to take up residence in Greece, even for only part of the year, it's wise to have a health check before your departure, particularly if you have got a record of poor health or are elderly. If you're already taking regular medication, you should note that the brand names of drugs and medicines vary from country to country, and you should ask your doctor for the generic name. If you wish to match medication prescribed abroad, you will need a current prescription with the medication's trade name, the manufacturer's name, the chemical name and the dosage. Most drugs have an equivalent in other countries, although particular brands may be difficult or impossible to obtain abroad.

It's possible to have medication sent from another country and usually no import duty or value added tax is payable. If you're visiting a holiday home in Greece for a limited period, you should take sufficient medication with you to cover your stay, although in an emergency, a local doctor will write a prescription that can be taken to a local pharmacy. You should also take some of your favourite non-prescription drugs, e.g. cold and flu remedies (not readily available in Greece), creams, etc., with you, as they may be difficult or impossible to obtain locally or may be much more expensive. If applicable, also take a spare pair of spectacles, contact lenses, dentures or hearing aid.

IMMIGRATION

On arrival in Greece, your first task will be to negotiate immigration and customs. This presents few problems for most people, particularly European Union (EU) nationals. Greece is a signatory to the Schengen agreement (named after a Luxembourg village on the Moselle River), which came into effect in 1994 and introduced an open-border policy between member countries. Other Schengen members include Austria, Belgium, Finland, France, Germany, Iceland, Italy, Luxembourg, the Netherlands, Norway, Portugal, Spain and Sweden. Under the agreement, immigration checks and passport controls take place when you first arrive in a member country, after which you can travel freely between member countries without further checks.

When you arrive in Greece from a country that's a signatory to the Schengen agreement (see above), there are usually no immigration checks or passport controls, which take place when you first arrive in a Schengen member country. Officially, Greek immigration officials should check the passports of EU arrivals from non-Schengen countries (such as the UK and Ireland), although this doesn't always happen. If you're a non-EU national and arrive in Greece by air or sea from outside the EU, you must go through immigration for non-EU citizens. If you have a single-entry visa, it will be stamped by the immigration official.

 If you require a visa to enter Greece and attempt to enter without one, you will be refused entry.

In any case, unless you're simply on holiday, it may be wise to ask for a stamp in your passport as confirmation of your date of entry into the country.

If you're a non-EU national coming to Greece to live, work or study, you may be asked to show documentary evidence. Immigration officials may also ask non-EU visitors to produce a return ticket and proof of accommodation, health insurance and financial resources, e.g. cash, travellers' cheques and credit cards. The onus is on visitors to show that they don't intend to breach the immigration laws – immigration officials aren't required to prove that you will breach the immigration laws and can refuse anyone entry simply on the grounds of suspicion.

 Note that Greece will refuse entry to any foreigners, whatever their nationality, whose passport indicates that they've visited Northern Cyprus since November 1993.

CUSTOMS

The Single European Act, which came into effect on 1st January 1993, created a single trading market and changed the rules regarding customs for EU nationals. The shipment of personal (household) effects to Greece from another EU country is no longer subject to customs formalities. EU nationals planning to take up permanent or temporary residence in Greece are permitted to import their furniture and personal effects free of duty or taxes, provided that they were purchased tax-paid within the EU or have been owned for at least six months. When moving to Greece, you should make a detailed inventory of your belongings (although it's unlikely that anyone will check them) and provide the shipping company with a photocopy of your passport.

For further information about customs regulations, contact the Director of Customs, Ministry of Finance, 10 Karageorgi Servias Street,

10184 Athens (☎ 2103-375 000). Information about duty-free allowances can be found on page 268 and pets on page 268.

Visitors

Visitors' belongings aren't subject to duty or VAT when they're visiting Greece for up to six months (182 days). This applies to the import of private cars, camping vehicles (including trailers or caravans), motorcycles, aircraft, boats and personal effects. Goods may be imported without formality, provided that their nature and quantity doesn't imply any commercial aim. All means of transport and personal effects imported duty-free mustn't be sold or given away and must be exported when a visitor leaves the country. If you cross into Greece by road you may drive slowly through the border post without stopping (unless requested to do so). However, any goods and pets that you're carrying mustn't be subject to any prohibitions or restrictions (see page 36). Customs officials may stop anyone for a spot check, e.g. to search for drugs or illegal immigrants.

If you arrive at a seaport by private boat, there are no particular customs formalities, although you must show the boat's registration papers on request. A vessel registered outside the EU may remain in Greece for a maximum of six months in any calendar year, after which it must be exported or imported (when duty and tax must be paid). Foreign-registered vehicles and boats mustn't be lent or rented to anyone while in Greece.

Non-EU Nationals

Non-EU nationals planning to take up permanent or temporary residence in Greece are permitted to import their furniture and personal effects free of duty or taxes, provided they have owned them for at least six months. An application form must be completed (available from Greek consulates), plus a detailed inventory of the items to be imported showing their estimated value in euros, including the make, model and serial number of all electrical appliances. If you're importing carpets and/or rugs the inventory must also include details of the quality, quantity (in square metres) and colour. All items to be imported should be included on the list, even if some are to be imported at a later date. These documents must be signed and presented to a Greek consulate with your passport. If you won't be present when your effects are cleared by customs in Greece, a photocopy of the principal pages of your passport is required.

If you use a shipping company to transport your belongings to Greece, the company will usually provide the necessary forms and take care of the paperwork. Always keep a copy of forms and communications with customs officials, both in Greece and in your previous country of residence. Note that if the paperwork isn't in order, your belongings may end up incarcerated in a customs storage depot for a number of months. If you personally import your belongings, you may need to employ a customs agent at the point of entry to clear them. You should have an official record of the export of valuables from any country, in case you wish to re-import them later.

Prohibited & Restricted Goods

Certain goods are subject to special regulations, and in some cases their import and export is restricted or prohibited. This particularly applies to the following goods:

● Animal products and plants;

● Antiquities and archaelogical remains (see below);

● Certain goods and technologies with a dual civil/military purpose;

● Computers and cameras (see below);

● Firearms and ammunition;

● Medicines and medical products (except for prescribed drugs and medicines);

● Wild fauna and flora and products derived from them;

● Works of art and collectibles.

If you're unsure whether any goods you're importing fall into the above categories, you should check with the local customs authority. You can currently import two cameras, a video camera and a laptop computer. These items may be recorded in your passport when you enter Greece and you must have them in your possession when you leave.

Greek antiquities and archaeological remains are strictly protected by law and can only be exported with permission from the Archaeological Service in Athens (Hellenic Ministry of Culture, 20-22 Bouboulinas St, 1082 Athens, ☎ 2108-201 100, 🖳 www.culture.gr). Religious icons and other articles dating from before 1830 require an export certificate, which should be provided by the dealer or shop you bought them from.

Note that the import of illegal drugs (even small amounts) into Greece is a serious offence and offenders are liable to fines of up €300,000 and a prison sentence of between ten years and life!

EMBASSY REGISTRATION

Nationals of some countries are advised to register with their local embassy or consulate after taking up residence in Greece. Registration isn't usually compulsory, although most embassies like to keep a record of their country's citizens resident in Greece. US nationals can register with the US embassy in Greece online before they leave the US (⌨ https://travelregistration.state.gov/ibrs).

FINDING HELP

One of the major problems facing new arrivals in Greece is how and where to obtain help with day-to-day problems, such as finding accommodation, schooling and insurance. This book will be a great help, but in addition to the information provided here you will need detailed **local** information. How successful you are at finding local help depends on the town or area where you live, e.g. residents of cities and resort areas are better served than those living in rural areas, your nationality, language proficiency, your employer (if you work) and your sex (women are usually better catered for than men through women's clubs).

There's an abundance of information available in Greece, but little in English and other foreign languages. An additional problem is that much of the available information isn't intended for foreigners and their particular needs. You may find that your friends and colleagues can help, as they can often offer advice based on their own experiences and mistakes. **But take care!** Although they mean well, you're likely to receive as much false and conflicting information as accurate and helpful advice. (It may not be wrong but often won't apply to your situation or circumstances.)

Your town hall may be a good source of information, but you usually need to speak Greek to benefit and may still be sent on a wild goose chase from department to department. A wealth of useful information is available in major cities and resort towns, where foreigners are generally well-served by English-speaking clubs and expatriate organisations. Contacts can also be found through many expatriate publications (see

Appendix B), and many consulates provide their nationals with local information, including details of lawyers, translators, doctors, dentists, schools, and social and expatriate organisations.

CHECKLISTS

When moving permanently to Greece there are many things to be considered and a 'million' people to inform. Even if you plan to spend just a few months a year there, it may still be necessary to inform a number of people and companies in your home country. The checklists below are designed to make the task easier and help prevent an ulcer or a nervous breakdown (provided that you don't leave everything to the last minute). **Note that not all points are applicable to non-residents or those who spend only a few weeks or months each year in Greece.**

Before Arrival

The following are tasks that should be completed (if possible) before your arrival in Greece:

- Check that your family's passports are valid.

- Obtain a visa, if necessary, for all your family members (see page 26). Obviously this **must** be done before arrival in Greece.

- It's advisable to arrange health, dental and optical check-ups for your family before leaving your home country. Obtain a copy of health records and a statement from your private health insurance company stating your present level of cover.

- Arrange health and travel insurance for your family (see pages 221 and 230). This is essential if you aren't already covered by an international health insurance policy and won't be covered by Greek social security (IKA).

- Arrange inoculations and shipment for any pets that you're taking with you (see page 36).

- Visit Greece before your move to compare schools and to arrange schooling for your children (if applicable).

- Open a bank account in Greece (see page 165) and transfer funds. Give the details to any companies that you plan to pay by direct debit or standing order (e.g. utility and property management companies).

- If you don't already have one, it's advisable to obtain an international credit card or two, which will prove particularly useful in Greece.

- If you live in rented accommodation you will need to give your landlord notice (check your contract).

- Arrange shipment of your furniture and belongings by booking a shipping company well in advance (see page 188).

- Arrange to sell or dispose of anything you aren't taking with you (e.g. house, car and furniture). If you're selling a home or business, you should obtain expert legal advice as you may be able to save tax by establishing a trust or other legal vehicle. Note that if you own more than one property, you may need to pay capital gains tax on any profits from the sale of second and subsequent homes.

- If you're planning to export a car to Greece, you need to complete the relevant paperwork in your home country before you do this.

- Check whether you need an international driving licence or a translation of your foreign driving licence(s). Note that some foreigners are required to take a driving test before they can buy and register a car in Greece.

- Check whether you're entitled to a rebate on your road tax, car and other insurance. Obtain a letter from your motor insurance company stating your no-claims' discount.

- You may qualify for a rebate on your tax and social security contributions. If you're leaving a country permanently and have been a member of a company or state pension scheme, you may be entitled to a refund or may be able to continue payments to qualify for a full (or larger) pension when you retire. Contact your company personnel office, local tax office or pension company for information.

- Terminate any outstanding loan, lease or hire purchase contracts and pay all bills (allow plenty of time as some companies are slow to respond).

- Return any library books or anything borrowed.

- Obtain as many credit references as possible, for example from banks, mortgage companies, credit card companies, credit agencies, companies with which you have had accounts, and references from professionals such as lawyers and accountants. These will help you establish a credit rating in Greece.

- Take any documents that are necessary to obtain a residence permit plus certified copies, official translations and numerous passport-size photographs (students should take at least a dozen).

- Take all your family's official documents with you. These may include:
  - birth certificates;
  - driving licences;
  - marriage certificate, divorce papers or death certificate (if a widow or widower);
  - educational diplomas and professional certificates;
  - employment references and curriculum vitaes;
  - school records and student ID cards;
  - medical and dental records;
  - bank account and credit card details;
  - insurance policies (plus records of no claims' allowances);
  - receipts for any valuables.
- Inform the following:
  - Your employers (e.g. to give notice or arrange leave of absence) or clients if you're self-employed.
  - Your local town hall or municipality. You may be entitled to a refund of your local property or income taxes.
  - If it was necessary to register with the police in your home country (or present country of residence), you should inform them that you're moving abroad.
  - Your electricity, gas, water and telephone companies. Contact companies well in advance, particularly if you need to get a deposit refunded.
  - Your insurance companies (for example health, car, home contents and private pension), banks, post office (if you have a post office account), stockbroker and other financial institutions, credit card, charge card and hire purchase companies, lawyer and accountant, and local businesses where you have accounts.
  - Your family doctor, dentist and other health practitioners. Health records should be transferred to your new doctor and dentist in Greece, if applicable.
  - Your children's schools. Try to give a term's notice and obtain a copy of any relevant school reports or records from your children's current schools.
  - All regular correspondents, subscriptions, social and sports clubs, professional and trade journals, and friends and relatives. Give

them your new address and telephone number and arrange to have your post redirected by the post office or a friend. Give close friends, relatives and business associates a telephone number where you can be contacted in Greece.

- If you have a driving licence or car you will need to give the local vehicle registration office your new address in Greece and, in some countries, return your car's registration plates.

● If you will be living in Greece for an extended period (but not permanently), you may wish to give someone 'power of attorney' over your financial affairs in your home country so that they can act for you in your absence. This can be for a fixed period or open-ended and can be for a specific purpose only.

```
                         SURVIVAL TIP
              You should take expert legal advice
      before giving someone 'power of attorney' over any
                  of your financial affairs!
```

● Obtain some euros, as this will save you time on arrival and you may receive a better exchange rate.

● Finally, allow plenty of time to get to the airport, register your luggage, and clear security and immigration.

After Arrival

The following tasks should be completed after arrival in Greece (if not done before):

● Have your visa cancelled and your passport stamped, as applicable.

● If you took your car to Greece, you will need to have it re-registered in Greece.

● If you haven't brought a vehicle with you, rent one or buy one locally. Note that it's practically impossible to get around in rural areas without a car.

● Arrange whatever insurance is necessary such as health, car, household and third party liability.

● Contact offices and organisations to obtain local information.

● Make courtesy calls on your neighbours and the local mayor within a few weeks of your arrival. This is particularly important in small villages and rural areas if you want to be accepted and become part of the local community.

- Apply for a residence permit at the Aliens' Bureau or your local police station as soon as possible after arrival (see page 26).

- Apply for a social security card from your local social security office (IKA).

- Apply for a Greek driving licence (if necessary).

- Find a local doctor and dentist.

- Arrange schooling for your children (if applicable).

7.

TAXATION

An important consideration when buying a home in Greece, even if you're a non-resident, is taxation, which includes property tax, wealth tax, income tax (if you earn an income from a home) and inheritance tax. Note that there's no capital gains tax in Greece. If you live permanently in Greece, you will also have to pay Greek income tax on all your earnings.

Like most people, the Greeks hate paying taxes and tax evasion is a national sport. Most Greeks don't consider cheating the tax man a crime, and it's estimated that many self-employed people don't declare a substantial part of their income. However, the Greek authorities have tackled the problem of tax evasion by introducing compulsory tax returns (see **Liability** on page 208) on obvious signs of income or wealth, e.g. property, cars, motorbikes, boats and even swimming pools. As a result, **all** property owners in Greece must make an annual tax return.

If your tax affairs are investigated and you're found to have made a false declaration, even as a result of an 'innocent' mistake, the authorities often take a hard line. The tax authorities maintain computer records of tax declarations, employers and bank accounts to help them expose fraud, and if your perceived standard of living is higher than would be expected on your declared income, you may be suspected of fraud.

On the other hand, tax avoidance (i.e. legally paying as little tax as possible, if necessary by finding and exploiting loopholes in the tax laws) is highly recommended! Residents have a number of opportunities to legally reduce their taxes, while non-residents have very few or none at all, and moving to Greece (or another country) often provides opportunities for legal 'favourable tax planning'.

To make the most of your situation, it's advisable to obtain income tax advice before moving to Greece, as there are usually a number of things you can do in advance to reduce your tax liability, both in Greece and abroad. Be sure to consult a tax adviser who's familiar with both the Greek tax system and that of your present country of residence. For example, you may be able to avoid paying tax on a business abroad if you establish both residence and domicile in Greece before you sell it. On the other hand, if you sell a foreign home after establishing your principal residence in Greece, it becomes a second home and you may then be liable for capital gains tax abroad (this is a complicated subject and you should obtain expert advice). You should notify the tax authorities in your former country of residence that you're going to live permanently in Greece.

```
┌─────────────────────────────────────────────────┐
│                  SURVIVAL TIP                     │
│                 Before you decide to              │
│          live in Greece permanently, you should   │
│       obtain expert advice regarding Greek taxes. This will │
│       (hopefully) ensure that you take maximum advantage │
│            of your current tax status and that you │
│              don't make any mistakes that you      │
│                   will regret later.              │
└─────────────────────────────────────────────────┘
```

The Greek tax system is extremely complicated (most Greeks don't understand it), although most non-resident homeowners will find they have little contact with the system, particularly if they employ the services of a fiscal representative (see below). There's little information available in English (although an English-language section of the tax authorities' website – ▣ www.gsis.gr – is under construction), added to which, taxes change every year.

Disclaimer: Note that the tax rates referred to in this chapter are those available at the time of writing (January 2005) and are included for reference only. Rates in Greece are subject to frequent change (the new government has promised tax reform) and you're advised to check the current rates with an expert before making any decisions based on Greek tax rates.

TAX FILE NUMBER

All residents and non-resident foreigners with financial affairs in Greece must have a Tax File Number (*Arithmo Forologiko Mitro/AFM* – known as the '*A-Fi-Mi*'). An *AFM* is unique for each person and works as a form of identification for the Greek authorities. Without an *AFM* you won't be able to purchase property, buy a car or boat, import a foreign-registered car or obtain any kind of tax certificate from the authorities. Your *AFM* must be used in all dealings with the Greek tax authorities (e.g. when filing an annual tax return), when paying property taxes and in various other transactions.

You can apply for an AFM at the local tax office in the area where you're buying a property or living at the time. You need to present your passport and the number is usually issued within a few days of application. Your lawyer or representative can obtain an AFM on your behalf; to do this he needs a legalised copy of your passport plus written authorisation from you.

FISCAL REPRESENTATIVE

The term fiscal representative refers to any person or agent who provides tax and other financial services; this may be a professional, such as an accountant or tax adviser, or it may be a non-professional who merely deals with your financial affairs on your behalf.

It's highly recommended for non-resident property owners to have a fiscal representative in Greece who presents annual tax returns and receives communications from the tax authorities. A fiscal representative can also look after your financial affairs, e.g. receive your bank statements, make sure standing orders are being paid and that you have sufficient funds in your bank account to pay them. Your fiscal representative can also apply for a tax file number (AFM) on your behalf (see above). Most foreign residents employ a fiscal representative (usually an accountant) to manage their financial and/or taxation affairs.

Before employing a representative, you should obtain recommendations from friends, colleagues and acquaintances. Once you have appointed a fiscal representative, you should give him power of attorney to manage your financial affairs and he should inform the tax authorities that he's acting on your behalf. Note that many accountants, particularly those based on the islands, are very busy and it may be difficult to find one willing to take on new clients.

Professional fiscal representation including the handling of your financial affairs plus tax returns usually costs around €180 per year. The completion and filing of a single tax return costs between €15 and €30. There may be additional charges for handling tax administration – the cost depends on the complexity of your tax affairs. For the relatively small cost involved, most people (both residents and non-residents) are usually better off employing a professional to handle their tax and other financial affairs than doing it themselves, particularly as the regulations change frequently. You can also often save more than the representative's fee in avoided tax.

VALUE ADDED TAX

Value added tax (*foros prostithemenis axias*), was introduced in Greece on 1st January 1986, after the country joined the European Union. Most prices in stores are quoted inclusive of value added tax (VAT), although sometimes exclusive prices are quoted, e.g. for commercial goods. Certain goods and services are exempt from VAT, including medical services, legal and notarial services, post office services, building leases, agriculture and imports from other EU states. Exports are also exempt from VAT. On all other goods Greece levies three rates of VAT, as follows:

Rate	Applicability
4% (low)	Books and other printed materials; theatre tickets.
8% (reduced)	Food products; pharmaceutical products; medical equipment and ancillary goods; public transport; food and drink in coffee shops, cafeterias and restaurants; products and services relating to agricultural production.
18% (standard)	All other goods and services including new homes built with licences issued after January 2005.

On some of the Greek island groups such the Dodecanese, North-Eastern Aegean and the Sporades, the 18 and 8 per cent rates are reduced by 30 per cent (to 12.6 per cent and 5.6 per cent respectively) on all goods with the exception of tobacco products and vehicles.

All businesses in Greece must register for VAT and returns are normally filed monthly and due within two months of the end of the month to which they relate. Smaller enterprises with annual sales below a certain amount can file quarterly returns, when any tax due is paid when the return is filed. If you're self-employed, VAT returns must be filed via the internet.

VAT fraud is rife in Greece and payments are often paid in cash to avoid VAT. Note that it's necessary to have legitimate bills showing registered names and VAT numbers in order to reclaim VAT. Furnished property lettings are exempt from VAT, although you may need to charge clients VAT if you provide certain services.

VAT is payable on goods imported from outside the EU, but not on goods purchased from another EU country where VAT has already been paid, although you may be asked to produce a VAT receipt. Companies located in other EU countries may obtain a refund of VAT paid on goods and services purchased in Greece, and VAT may also be refunded to companies in a non-EU country when Greece has a reciprocal agreement with that country.

INCOME TAX

Greek income tax (*foros issodimatos*) is near the EU average, particularly for large families. However, when income tax is added to the high social security contributions and other indirect taxes, Greek taxes are among the highest in Europe. Major tax reforms have been introduced over the last few years and more are expected. Paying income tax in Greece rather than in another country can be advantageous, as there are more allowances than there are in some other countries. Nevertheless, if you're able to choose the country where you're taxed, you should obtain advice from an international tax expert.

Employees' income tax is deducted at source (i.e. pay-as-you-earn) by employers in Greece and employees aren't responsible for paying their own income tax, although most must still file a tax return. Non-residents who receive income from a Greek source or own assets in Greece (e.g. property or a car) must file an annual return with the main non-residents' tax office in Athens, which deals with Greeks and non-Greeks residing abroad with assets in Greece.

Liability

Your liability for Greek income tax (and certain other taxes) depends on where you're domiciled. Your domicile is normally the country you regard as your permanent home and where you live most of the year. For example, a foreigner working in Greece for a Greek company who has taken up residence in Greece and has no income tax liability abroad, is considered to have his tax domicile in Greece. A person can be resident in more than one country at any given time, but can be domiciled only in one country. The domicile of a married woman isn't necessarily the same as her husband's, but is determined using the same criteria as an independent person. Your country of domicile is particularly important when it comes to inheritance tax (see page 213). ou're considered to be a Greek resident and liable to Greek tax if **any** of the following apply:

- Your permanent home, i.e. family or principal residence, is in Greece.
- You spend over 183 days in Greece during any calendar year.
- You're employed or carry out paid professional activities in Greece, except when secondary to business activities conducted in another country.
- Your centre of vital economic interest, e.g. investments or business, is in Greece.

You must complete an income tax return in Greece if your annual income is over €3,000. Even if you have no taxable income at all, you must file a tax return if you meet **any** of the following conditions:

- You own a private car, a motorcycle with an engine capacity of more than 500cc, a pleasure boat or an aircraft.

- You own a property (see below).

- You're a partner in a Greek partnership, limited liability company or joint venture.

- You earn income from the letting of property or land.

- You're buying or constructing a building.

- You own a swimming pool of over 25m² (you must declare an income of at least €11,600 for an outdoor pool and at least €17,400 for an indoor pool).

These conditions were introduced by the tax authorities in an attempt to prevent tax fraud. When you declare your assets (including details such as the size of your home), the tax authorities apply a coefficient to each asset and from the resulting figure assume you have enough income to buy and maintain the asset. For example, if you declare a new car over 2,000cc, the authorities assume your annual income to be at least €21,000. Therefore you should declare at least this amount on your annual income tax return.

 This is a complicated matter and in order to avoid any nasty surprises you should consult a tax advisor.

Non-resident Property Owners

To avoid paying income tax on funds from abroad used to buy property, non-residents must produce the official import certificate (the 'pink slip') from the bank. This proves that the funds for the purchase were imported into Greece and are therefore exempt from income tax.

Double Taxation

Greek residents are taxed on their world-wide income, subject to certain treaty exceptions, although citizens of most countries (the US is a rare exception) are exempt from paying taxes in their home country when they spend a minimum period abroad, e.g. one year. The Greek government has double taxation treaties with many countries (see below), which are designed to ensure that income that has already been taxed in one treaty country isn't taxed again in another.

Treaties establish a tax credit or exemption on certain kinds of income, either in the country of residence or the country where the income is earned, and where applicable a double taxation treaty prevails over domestic law. Many people living abroad switch their investments to offshore holdings to circumvent often complicated double taxation agreements. If you're in doubt about your tax liability in your home country or another country where you have assets or from where you receive income, contact the tax authorities there for a ruling. Note that if you aren't living in Greece but have assets there, you're obliged by law to file a tax return listing your assets and any income you receive from them (see **Liability** above).

Greece has double taxation treaties with many countries, including Argentina, Austria, Belgium, Canada, Cyprus, the Czech Republic, Denmark, Egypt, Finland, France, Germany, Hungary, Iceland, Ireland, Italy, the Republic of Korea, Luxembourg, the Netherlands, Norway, Poland, Romania, the Slovak Republic, Sweden, Switzerland, the United Kingdom and the US.

Leaving Greece

Before leaving Greece, foreigners should pay any tax due for the previous year and the year of departure by applying for a tax clearance. A tax return should be filed prior to departure and includes your income and deductions from 1st January of the departure year up to the date of departure. Your local tax office will calculate the tax due and provide a written statement or certificate. When departure is made before 31st December, the previous year's taxes are applied. If this results in overpayment, a claim must be made for a refund.

Taxable Income

Income tax is payable on both earned and unearned income. Taxable income includes salaries, pensions, property, 'visible signs of wealth' (e.g. a car), property and investment income (dividends and interest), and income from professional, artistic, business or agricultural activities.

Allowances & Deductions

Before you're liable for income tax, you can deduct social security payments and certain costs from your gross income (allowances) and from the sum due after establishing your tax base (deductions). Most allowances and deductions apply only to residents and include the following:

- medical expenses for you and dependent family members;
- interest on mortgage loans taken out to buy your primary residence;
- rental payments;
- tuition fees for dependent children;
- donations to the Greek state under certain conditions and up to a certain amount;
- family expenditure for purchases of certain goods or services, including a computer;
- family allowances.

Calculation

The tax year in Greece is the same as the calendar year, i.e. 1st January to 31st December. Income tax rates for residents are shown below.

Employees & Pensioners		
Taxable Income (€)	**Tax Rate (%)**	**Cumulative Tax (€)**
Up - 10,000	0	0
10,000 - 13,400	15	510
13,400 - 23,400	30	3,510
Over 23,400	40	
Self-employed		
Taxable Income (€)	**Tax Rate (%)**	**Cumulative Tax (€)**
Up - 8,400	0	0
8,400 - 13,400	15	750
13,400 - 23,400	30	3,750
Over 23,400	40	

Non-residents

Income tax for non-residents is levied at the same rates as above except for the first band which is 5 per cent (not 0 per cent), unless 90 per cent of their income is from a Greek-source.

Tax Return

Tax returns must be filed by 1st March for the previous tax year, e.g. the return filed in March 2005 is for the year 2004. The deadline is extended to 16th April if your declared income includes income from individual commercial enterprises, and to 2nd May for income including employment or pensions and foreign income. Non-residents also have until 2nd May to file a return. No extensions are usually permitted and late filing incurs a penalty.

Married couples file joint returns, although tax is calculated separately on the income of each spouse and a net loss by one cannot be offset against the income of the other. The husband is responsible for filing a family's return and declaring his wife's income.

Greek tax returns are complicated, despite attempts to simplify them in recent years. Internet filing (TAXISnet) is now available, although tax returns are in Greek only. In 2003, the tax authorities offered a €118 reduction in tax to individuals who filed online – the incentive was so popular the system crashed!

The language used in tax returns is difficult for foreigners (and many Greeks) to understand, but local tax offices will usually help you to complete your tax return. You can make an appointment for a free consultation with your local tax inspector at your town hall. (Unless your Greek is fluent, you should take a translator with you). Alternatively, you can employ a tax accountant to complete your return (see **Fiscal Representative** on page 206).

WEALTH TAX

A wealth tax on property was re-introduced in Greece in 1997 and applies to all individuals and legal entities owning property there valued at over €243,600 for a single person and over €487,200 for a couple. The value of a property is based on the 'assessed tax value' (see page 122). After the deduction of the above allowances, tax is payable on a progressive scale ranging from 0.3 per cent to 0.8 per cent, as shown in the table below:

Taxable Amount (€)	Tax Rate (%)
Up to 146,750	0.3
146,751 – 293,500	0.4
293,501 – 440,250	0.5

440,251 – 733,750	0.6
733,751 – 1,027,250	0.7
Over 1,027,250	0.8

This means that a couple (with a total allowance of €487,200) owning a house worth €500,000 would pay tax on only €12,800 at 0.3 per cent, making a tax bill of €38.40. In practice, only owners of large and expensive properties are liable for this tax. There are plans to abolish the wealth tax at some point in the future.

PROPERTY TAX

All Greek property owners are liable for property taxes with the exception of Greek citizens and foreign residents buying their first home in Greece, who are exempt for a period. Otherwise, tax is levied at a rate of between 0.25 and 0.35 per cent of a property's market value by local municipalities, who also levy other fees and taxes to pay for local services, either directly or indirectly.

CAPITAL GAINS TAX

Greece levies no capital gains tax on property.

INHERITANCE & GIFT TAX

As in most countries, dying in Greece doesn't free you (or more correctly, your beneficiaries) from the clutches of the tax man. Greece imposes inheritance and gift taxes, called estate tax or death duty in some countries. **It's important for both residents and non-residents with property in Greece to decide in advance how they wish to dispose of their property, which if possible should be decided before buying a property.** Inheritance laws are complicated and professional advice should be sought from an experienced lawyer who understands both Greek inheritance law and the law of any other countries involved. Your will (see below) is also a vital component in reducing Greek inheritance and gift taxes to the minimum or delaying their payment.

Greece imposes inheritance tax on the world-wide assets of a deceased person who was domiciled in Greece. Similarly, property located in Greece and movable property situated abroad given by a Greek national or by a foreigner to a person domiciled in Greece is subject to gift tax. The tax rates for inheritance and gift tax are the same, although the amount of tax payable varies depending on the relationship of the beneficiary to the deceased or donor.

Relationships are categorised into the following four classes and three categories:

- **First Class/Category A** – Spouse and children, each of whom (children under 18 only) has a tax-free allowance of €300,000. Children over 18 have a tax-free allowance of €20,000.

- **Second Class/Category B** – Parents, aunts and uncles and their children each of whom has a tax-free allowance of €15,000.

- **Third Class/Category C** – Grandparents and their descendants, each of whom has a tax-free allowance of €5,000.

- **Fourth Class/Category C** – Distant relatives and non-relatives, each of whom has a tax-free allowance of €5,000.

Each category is taxed according to a different scale of rates, the highest rate in each case applying to assets valued at over €220,000, and each category is entitled to a different allowance, as shown in the tables below:

Category A		
Value of Estate (€)	**Tax Rate (%)**	**Cumulative Tax (€)**
Up to 20,000	0	0
20,001 – 60,000	5	2,000
60,001 – 220,000	10	18,000
Over 220,000	20	

Category B		
Value of Estate (€)	**Tax Rate (%)**	**Cumulative Tax (€)**
Up to 15,000	0	0
15,001 – 60,000	10	4,500
60,001 – 220,000	20	36,500
Over 220,000	30	

Category C		
Value of Estate (€)	Tax Rate (%)	Cumulative Tax (€)
Up to 5,000	0	0
5,001 – 60,000	20	11,000
60,001 – 220,000	30	59,000
Over 220,000	40	

WILLS

It's an unfortunate fact of life that you're unable to take your hard-earned money with you when you make your final exit. All adults should make a will, irrespective of how large or small their assets (each spouse should make a separate will). If a foreigner dies without a will (intestate) in Greece, his estate may be automatically disposed of under Greek law and the law regarding compulsory heirs (see below) applied.

A foreigner resident in Greece is usually permitted to dispose of his Greek assets according to the law of his home country, provided his will is valid under the law of that country. If you've lived in Greece for a long time, it may be necessary for you to create a legal domicile in your home country for the purpose of making a will.

A will made by a foreigner regarding Greek assets isn't invalidated because it doesn't bequeath property in accordance with Greek law. In practice, Greek law isn't usually applied to foreigners and the disposal of property (buildings or land) in Greece is governed by the national law of the deceased's home country unless there's a dispute among the beneficiaries, in which case Greek law is applied.

Law of Obligatory Heirs

Under Greek law, assets must be disposed of under the law of 'obligatory heirs' and the share depends on the relationship of the surviving relatives with the deceased. Relatives are divided into four classes (see **Inheritance & Gift Tax** above).

When a person dies leaving a surviving spouse and no other relatives, the entire estate goes to the spouse. If there's a surviving spouse and children, the estate is divided into four: a quarter for the spouse, with the remainder being divided equally between the children. If there are no children then the surviving spouse receives half the estate and the rest is divided between other relatives.

Types of Will

There are generally two kinds of Greek will, both of which are described below. Note that, where applicable, the rules regarding witnesses are strict and, if not followed precisely, can render a will null and void.

Although it isn't compulsory to have a Greek will for Greek property, it's advisable to have a separate will for any country in which you own property. When a person dies, assets can be dealt with immediately under local law without having to wait for the granting of probate in another country (and the administration of the estate is also cheaper). Having a Greek will for your Greek assets speeds up the will's execution and saves the long and complicated process of having a foreign will executed in Greece. Note that, if you have two or more wills, you must ensure that they don't contradict or invalidate one another. You should periodically review your will to ensure that it reflects your current financial and personal circumstances.

Open Will

An open will is normal in Greece and the most suitable kind of will for most people. It's usually drawn up by a lawyer who gives legal guidance on how you can leave your assets. The notary must know the will's contents in addition to three witnesses – who can be of any nationality – each of whom must sign the will. The notary is responsible for ensuring that the will is legal and correctly drawn up. He will give you a copy and retain the original. If you don't understand Greek, you will need an official translation into a language that you speak fluently.

Holographic Will

A holographic will is a will made in your own handwriting. It must be signed and dated and must be clearly drafted in order to ensure that your wishes are absolutely clear. No witnesses or other formalities are required. It can be voluntarily registered with a notary. On the death of the testator it must be authenticated before a judge, which will delay the will's execution.

Cost & Procedure

The cost of preparing a simple open will is from €200 to €300. Greek wills can be drawn up by Greek lawyers and notaries abroad, although it's cheaper to do it in Greece. Note also that marriage in Greece doesn't automatically revoke a will, as in some other countries.

Executors aren't normal in Greece and if you appoint one it may increase the inheritance tax payable. However, if you do appoint an executor, you should inform your heirs so that they will know who to notify in the event of your death. It isn't advisable to name a Greek bank or a lawyer who doesn't speak Greek as the executor, as they must instruct a Greek lawyer, whose fees will be impossible to control.

Your beneficiaries in Greece must produce an original death certificate or an authorised copy. If you die abroad, a foreign death certificate must be legally translated and notarised for it to be valid in Greece. The inheritance tax declaration and the payment of inheritance tax duties must be made within six months of your death if you die in Greece and within a year if you die abroad (otherwise a surcharge may result). Inheritance tax must be paid in advance of the release of any assets to be inherited in Greece, and beneficiaries may therefore need to borrow funds to pay the tax before they receive their inheritance. Note that the winding-up of an estate can take a long time in Greece.

Keep a copy of your will(s) in a safe place and another copy with your lawyer or the executor of your estate. Don't leave them in a bank safe deposit box, which in the event of your death is sealed for a period under Greek law. You should keep information regarding bank accounts and insurance policies with your will(s), but don't forget to tell someone where they are!

 Greek inheritance law is a complicated subject and it's important to obtain professional legal advice when writing or altering your will(s).

8.

INSURANCE

An important aspect of owning a home in Greece is insurance, not only for your home and its contents, but also for your family or friends when visiting the country. If you live in Greece permanently you will require additional insurance. It's unnecessary to spend half your income insuring yourself against every eventuality, but it's important to insure against an event that could precipitate a major financial disaster, such as a serious accident or your house being demolished by a storm or earthquake. The cost of being uninsured or under-insured can be astronomical.

 It's vital to ensure that you have sufficient insurance when visiting your home abroad, which includes travel insurance, building and contents insurance, and health insurance (covered in this chapter), as well as continental car insurance (including breakdown insurance) and third party liability insurance.

As with anything connected with finance, it's important to shop around when buying insurance, as simply collecting a few brochures from insurance agents or making a few telephone calls could save you a lot of money.

SURVIVAL TIP
Not all insurance companies
are equally reliable or have the same financial
stability, and it may be better to insure with a large
international company with a good reputation
than with a small local company, even if this means
paying a higher premium.

Read insurance contracts carefully and make sure that you understand the terms and the cover provided before signing them. Some insurance companies will do almost anything to avoid paying claims and will use any available legal loophole, therefore it pays to deal only with reputable companies (not that this provides a foolproof guarantee). Policies often contain traps and legal loopholes in the small print and it's sometimes wise to obtain legal advice before signing a contract.

In all matters regarding insurance, you're responsible for ensuring that you and your family are legally insured in Greece. Regrettably you cannot insure yourself against being uninsured or sue your insurance agent for giving you bad advice! Bear in mind, that if you wish to make a claim on an insurance policy, you may be required to report an incident to the police within 24 hours (this may also be a legal requirement). The law in Greece may differ considerably from your home country or your previous country of residence, and you should **never** assume that it's the same. If you're uncertain about your rights you should obtain legal advice for anything other than a minor claim. Under EU rules, an insurance company registered in an EU member country can sell its policies in any other EU country.

This chapter contains information on health insurance (state and private), household insurance, and holiday and travel insurance.

HEALTH INSURANCE

If you're visiting, living or working in Greece, it's extremely risky not to have health insurance for your family, because if you're uninsured or under-insured you could be faced with some very high medical bills. When deciding on the type and extent of health insurance, make sure that it covers **all** your family's present and future health requirements **before** you receive a large bill. A health insurance policy should cover you for **all** essential health care whatever the reason, including accidents, e.g. sports accidents, and injuries, whether they occur in your home, at your place of work or when travelling. Don't take anything for granted, but check in advance.

If you're planning to take up residence in Greece and will be contributing to Greek social security, you and your family will be entitled to subsidised or (in certain cases) free medical and dental treatment. The Greek national health system is operated by the *Idrima Kinonikon Asfalisseon* (IKA). When you start work or retire to Greece you must obtain a medical booklet (*iatrico vivliario*) from your local IKA office, which must be presented each time you visit a doctor or hospital. Doctor and hospital treatment within the Greek system is free, but you will be charged 25 per cent of the cost of prescriptions (pensioners pay 10 per cent).

Most foreign residents also subscribe to a complementary health insurance fund that pays the portion of medical bills that isn't paid by social security. Residents who don't contribute to social security should have private health insurance, which is mandatory for non-EU residents when applying for a visa or residence permit. Note that some foreign insurance companies don't provide sufficient cover to satisfy Greek regulations, therefore you should check the minimum cover necessary with a Greek consulate in your country of residence.

If you live in a remote area of Greece that isn't covered by a local IKA office, you'll have to pay the cost of any medical treatment in advance and re-claim it from the nearest IKA office. However, the refund will be only a proportion of the cost (up to around 85 per cent) and you will be responsible for the balance. If you receive treatment under these circumstances, it's necessary to obtain receipts and documentation in order to make a claim.

Visitors

Visitors spending short periods in Greece, e.g. up to a month, should have a travel health insurance policy (see page 230), particularly if they aren't covered by an international health policy. If you plan to spend up to six months in Greece you should either take out a travel policy, a special long-stay policy or an international health policy, which should cover you in your home country and when travelling in other countries. Note that premiums vary considerably and it's important to shop around. Most international health policies include repatriation or evacuation (these may be optional), which may also include shipment (by air) of the body of a person who has died abroad to his home country for burial. Note that an international policy also allows you to choose to have non-urgent medical treatment in the country of your choice.

Most international insurance companies offer health policies for different areas, e.g. Europe, world-wide excluding North America, and world-wide including North America. Most companies offer different levels of cover, for example, basic, standard, comprehensive and prestige levels of cover. There's always an annual limit on the total annual medical costs, which should be at least €300,000 (although many provide cover of up to €1.2 million), and some companies also limit the fees for specific treatment or care, such as specialists' fees, operations and hospital accommodation. A medical examination isn't usually required for international health policies, although pre-existing health problems are excluded for a period, e.g. one or two years.

Claims are usually settled in major currencies and large claims are usually settled directly by insurance companies (although your choice of hospitals may be limited). Always check whether an insurance company will settle large medical bills directly, because if you're required to pay bills and claim reimbursement from an insurance company, it can take several months before you receive your money (some companies are slow to pay). It isn't usually necessary to translate bills into English or another language, although you should check a company's policy. Most international health insurance companies provide emergency telephone assistance.

The cost of international health insurance varies considerably depending on your age and the extent of cover. Note that with most international insurance policies, you must enrol before you reach a certain age, e.g. between 60 and 80, to be guaranteed continuous cover in your old age. Premiums can sometimes be paid monthly, quarterly or annually, although some companies insist on payment annually in advance. When comparing policies, carefully check the extent of cover and exactly what is included and excluded from a policy (often this is indicated only in the **very** small print), in addition to premiums and excess charges.

In some countries, premium increases are limited by law, although this may apply only to residents of the country where a company is registered, and not to overseas policyholders. Although there may be significant differences in premiums, generally you get what you pay for and can tailor premiums to your requirements. The most important questions to ask yourself are: does the policy provide the cover required and is it good value for money? If you're in good health and are able to pay for your own out-patient treatment, such as visits to your family doctor and prescriptions, then the best value may be a policy covering only specialist and hospital treatment.

Residents

If you contribute to Greek social security, you and your family are entitled to free or subsidised medical and dental treatment. Benefits include general and specialist care, hospitalisation, laboratory services, discounted drugs and medicines, basic dental care, maternity care, appliances and transportation (four-fifths of the cost is paid by IKA). The vast majority of the Greek population is covered by the *Idrima Kinonikon Asfalisseon* (IKA), Greece's public health scheme, including retired EEA residents (with a residence permit) receiving a state pension. If you aren't entitled to public health benefits through payment of Greek social security or being in receipt of a state pension from another EU country, you must usually have private health insurance and must present proof of your insurance when applying for your residence permit. If you're an EU national of retirement age, who **isn't** in receipt of a pension, you may be entitled to public health benefits if you can show that you cannot afford private health insurance.

Anyone who has paid regular social security contributions in another EU country for two full years prior to coming to Greece is entitled to public health cover for a limited period from the date of their last contribution. Social security form E-106 or the European

Health Card (EHC) must be obtained from the social security authorities in your home country and be presented to the local provincial office of IKA in Greece. Similarly, pensioners and those in receipt of invalidity benefits must obtain form E-121 or the EHC from their home country's social security administration. Retirees living in Greece and receiving a state pension from another EU country are entitled to free state health benefits.

You will be registered as a member of IKA and given a social security card, a list of local medical practitioners and hospitals, and general information about services and charges. If you're receiving an invalidity pension or other social security benefits on the grounds of ill health, you should establish exactly how living in Greece will affect those benefits. In some countries there are reciprocal agreements regarding invalidity rights, but you must confirm that they apply to you. Citizens of EU countries can make payments in their home country entitling them to use public health services in Greece and other EU countries.

Further information about Greek social security can be obtained from IKA (☎ 520-055 564, 🖳 www.ika.gr.en/english).

Private Health Insurance

If you aren't covered by Greek social security, you should take out private health insurance. It's advantageous to be insured with a company that will pay large medical bills directly. Most private health insurance policies don't pay family doctors' fees or pay for medication that isn't provided in a hospital, or there's an 'excess' payment that often exceeds the cost of treatment. Most will, however, pay for 100 per cent of specialists' fees and hospital treatment in the best hospitals.

Generally, the higher the premium, the more choice you have regarding doctors, specialists and hospitals. You should avoid a company that reserves the right to cancel a policy when you reach a certain age, e.g. 65 or 70, or which increases premiums sharply as you get older, as trying to take out a new policy at the age of 65 or older at a reasonable premium is difficult. If you already have private health insurance in another country, you may be able to extend it to cover you in Greece.

Private health insurance is popular among the Greeks and there are numerous national companies offering policies, including Alico AIGlife (🖳 www.alico.gr), Ethniki Asfalistiki (🖳 www.ethniki-asfalistiki.gr), Generali (🖳 www.generali.gr) and La Vie Assurance (🖳 www. iatriko.gr). Foreign private health insurance companies with policies covering Greece include AXA PPP Healthcare (🖳 www.axappp healthcare.com), BUPA International (🖳 www.bupa-intl.com), Exeter

Friendly Society (🖥 www.exeterfriendly.co.uk) and International Health Insurance (🖥 www.ihi.com). Note that almost all hospitals and clinics included under foreign private health insurance schemes are situated in Athens or Thessaloniki.

Changing Employers or Insurance Companies

When changing employers or leaving Greece, you should ensure that you have continuous health insurance. If you and your family are covered by a company health plan, your insurance will probably cease after your last day of employment. If you're planning to change your health insurance company, you should ensure that important benefits aren't lost, e.g. existing medical conditions won't usually be covered by a new insurer. When changing medical insurance companies, you should inform your old company if you have any outstanding bills for which they're liable.

Reciprocal Health Agreements

If you're entitled to social security health benefits in another EU country or in a country with a reciprocal health agreement with Greece, you will receive free or reduced cost medical treatment there. If you live in the EU, you should apply for the European Health Card (EHC) – provided you're entitled to treatment from your local social security office – at least three weeks before you plan to travel to Greece. An EHC is open-ended and valid for life. However, you must continue to make social security contributions in the country where it was issued. It covers emergency hospital treatment but doesn't include prescribed medicines, special examinations, X-rays, laboratory tests, physiotherapy or dental treatment. If you use the EHC in Greece, you must sometimes pay in advance and apply for a reimbursement from Greek social security (instructions are provided with the card), which can take months.

Note, however, that you can still receive a large bill from a Greek hospital, as your local health authority assumes only a percentage of the cost!

Greece has reciprocal social security agreements with EU member states and Switzerland, Argentina, Brazil, Egypt, Libya, New Zealand, Uruguay, the US and Venezuela. Note, however, that the US doesn't have a reciprocal health agreement with Greece and therefore American students and other Americans who aren't covered by Greek social security **must** have private health insurance in Greece. British visitors or Britons planning to live in Greece can obtain information about reciprocal health treatment from the Department of Social Security, Pensions and Overseas Benefits, Newcastle-upon-Tyne, NE98 1BA, UK (☎ 0191-218 7777, 🖳 www.dwp.gov.uk).

HOUSEHOLD INSURANCE

Many foreign property owners don't insure their homes in Greece with occasional disastrous consequences. Comprehensive household insurance in Greece is essential and should include the building, its contents and third party liability. These are usually contained in a multi-risk household insurance policy. Policies are offered by both local and international insurance companies, whose policies are similar, although foreign companies tend to charge higher premiums.

Building

Although it isn't compulsory, it's wise to take out property insurance that covers damage to a building due to fire, smoke, water, explosion, storm, freezing, snow, theft, vandalism, malicious damage, acts of terrorism, impact, broken windows and other natural catastrophes (such as falling trees). Insurance should include glass, external buildings, aerials and satellite dishes, gardens and garden ornaments. Bear in mind that most of Greece lies in an earthquake zone (most buildings on the island of Kefallonia were destroyed in an earthquake in 1953 and many in Athens were ruined in a 1999 earthquake), therefore you should ensure that damage caused by earthquakes is included.

Cover for earthquakes, lightning damage and subsidence is usually included in a standard policy nowadays, but you should check exactly what's **excluded** and what it will cost to include extra risks. Policies for building insurance in areas with a high risk of earthquakes are likely to be considerably more expensive – building insurance premiums in Athens tripled after the 1999 earthquake.

Note that if a claim is the result of a defect in design or construction, e.g. the roof is too heavy and collapses, the insurance company won't pay up (another reason why you should have a survey before buying!).

Property insurance is based on the cost of rebuilding your home and should be increased each year in line with inflation. **Make sure that you insure your property for the true cost of rebuilding.** It's important to have insurance for storm damage, which can be severe in some areas. If floods are one of your concerns (flash floods aren't uncommon), make sure that you're covered for water coming in from ground level, not just for water seeping in through the roof. **Always read the small print of contracts.** If you own a home in an area that has been hit by a succession of natural disasters (such as floods and/or earthquakes), your insurance premiums may be increased dramatically or your policy may even be cancelled.

Contents

Contents are usually insured for the same risks as a building (see above) and are usually insured for their replacement value (new for old), with a reduction for wear and tear for clothes and linen. Valuable objects are covered for their actual declared and authenticated value. Most policies include automatic indexation of the insured sum in line with inflation. Contents insurance may include accidental damage to sanitary installations, theft, money, replacement of locks following damage or loss of keys, frozen food, alternative accommodation cover, and property belonging to third parties stored in your home. Some items, however, are usually optional, including credit cards, frozen foods, emergency assistance (plumber, glazier, electrician, etc.), redecoration, garaged cars, replacement pipes, loss of rent, and the cost of travel to Greece for holiday homeowners. Many policies include personal third party or legal liability, e.g. up to €300,000, although this may be an option.

Items of high value must usually be itemised and photographs and documentation (e.g. a valuation) should be provided. Some companies recommend or insist on a video film of belongings. When claiming for contents, if possible you should produce the original bills (always keep bills for expensive items) and should bear in mind that replacing imported items may be much more expensive if you need to buy them locally. Note that contents policies usually contain security clauses and if you don't adhere to them a claim won't be considered. If you're planning to let a property, you may be required to inform your insurer.

A building must be secure with good locks and many companies offer a discount if properties have steel reinforced doors, high security locks and alarms (particularly alarms connected to a monitoring station). An insurance company may send someone to inspect your property and advise on security measures. Policies pay out for theft only when there are signs of forcible entry and you aren't usually covered for thefts by a guest or tenant (but you may be covered for thefts by domestic personnel). All-risks policies offering a world-wide extension to a household policy covering jewellery, cameras and other items aren't usually available from Greek companies, but are available from a number of foreign companies.

Community Properties

If you own a property that's part of a community development (see page 131), building insurance is included in your service charges, although you should check exactly what's covered. You must, however, still be insured for third party risks in the event that you cause damage to neighbouring apartments or buildings, e.g. through a flood or fire.

Holiday Homes

Premiums are generally higher for holiday homes because of their high vulnerability (particularly to burglaries) and are often based on the number of days a year a property is inhabited and the interval between periods of occupancy. Cover for theft, storm, flood and malicious damage may be suspended when a property is left empty for an extended period. **Note that you're required to turn off the water supply at the mains when vacating a building for more than 72 hours.** It's possible to negotiate cover for periods of absence for a hefty surcharge, although valuable items are usually excluded. If you're absent from your property for long periods, e.g. more than 60 days a year, you may also be required to pay an excess on a claim arising from an occurrence that takes place during your absence (and theft may be excluded). You should read all small print in policies.

Where applicable, it's important to ensure that a policy specifies a holiday home and **not** a principal home. In areas with a high risk of theft, e.g. major cities and most resort areas, an insurance company may insist that you fit extra locks, e.g. two locks on external doors, including a mortise deadlock, internal locking shutters and security bars or metal grilles on windows. A policy may specify that all forms of protection on doors must be used whenever a property is unoccupied, and that all other forms, e.g. shutters, must also be used when a property is left empty for more than a few days. Some companies may not insure holiday homes in high risk areas.

It's unwise to leave valuable or irreplaceable items in a holiday home or a home that will be vacant for long periods. Note that some insurance companies will do their utmost to find a loophole which makes you negligent and relieves them of their liability. Always check that the details listed on a policy are correct, otherwise your policy could be void.

Insuring Abroad

It's possible and legal to take out building and contents insurance in another country for a property in Greece (some foreign insurance companies offer special policies for holiday homeowners), although you must ensure that a policy is valid under European Union (EU) law. The advantage is that you will have a policy you can understand and will be able to handle claims in your own language. This may seem like a good option for a holiday home in Greece, although it's usually more expensive than insuring with a local company and can lead to conflicts when the building is insured with a local company and the contents with a foreign company, e.g. in some countries, door locks are part of the contents and in others they constitute part of the building. Most experts advise that you insure a Greek property (building and contents) with a local insurance company through a local agent.

Rented Property

Your landlord will usually insist that you have third party liability insurance. A lease requires you to insure against `tenant's risks', including damage you may make to the rental property and to other properties if you live in an apartment, e.g. due to flood, fire or explosion. You can choose your own insurance company and aren't required to use one recommended by your landlord.

Premiums

Premiums are usually calculated on the size of the property, either the habitable area in square metres or the number of rooms, rather than its value. As a rough guide, building insurance costs around €20 per €10,000 of value insured, e.g. a property valued at €100,000 will cost around €200 a year to insure. Contents insurance costs from around €35 per €5,000 of value insured (e.g. a premium of €140 for contents valued at €20,000) and may be higher for a detached villa than an apartment. Detached, older and more remote properties often cost more to insure than apartments and new properties. If you have an index-linked policy, cover is increased each year in line with inflation.

Claims

If you wish to make a claim, you must usually inform your insurance company in writing (by registered letter) within two to five days of an incident or 24 hours in the case of theft. Thefts should also be reported to the police within 24 hours, as the police statement (of which you need a copy for your insurance company) usually constitutes irrefutable evidence of your claim. Check whether you're covered for damage or thefts that occur while you're away from a property and are therefore unable to inform your insurance company immediately.

Take care you don't under-insure your house contents and that you periodically reassess their value and adjust your insurance premium accordingly. You can arrange to have your cover automatically increased annually by a fixed percentage or amount by your insurance company. If you make a claim and the assessor discovers that you're under-insured, the amount of the claim will be reduced by the percentage you're under-insured. For example, if you're 50 per cent under-insured, your claim for €15,000 will be reduced by half to €7,500. You must usually pay an excess for each claim.

HOLIDAY & TRAVEL INSURANCE

Holiday and travel insurance is recommended for all who don't wish to risk having their holiday or travel ruined by financial problems. As you're probably aware, anything can and often does go wrong with a holiday, sometimes before you even get started (particularly if you **don't** have insurance). The following information applies equally to both residents and non-residents, whether they're travelling to or from Greece or within either country. No-one should visit Greece without travel and health insurance!

Travel insurance is available from many sources, including travel agents, insurance companies and brokers, banks, automobile clubs and transport companies (airline, rail and bus). Package holiday companies and tour operators also offer insurance policies, some of which are compulsory, too expensive and don't provide adequate cover. You can also buy 24-hour accident and flight insurance at major airports, although it's expensive and doesn't offer the best cover. Before taking out travel insurance, carefully consider the range and level of cover you require and compare policies. Short-term holiday and travel insurance policies may include: cover for holiday cancellation or interruption; missed flights; departure delay at both the start and end of a holiday (a common occurrence); delayed, lost or damaged baggage; personal effects and money; medical expenses and accidents (including evacuation home); flight insurance; personal liability and legal expenses and default or bankruptcy insurance, e.g. a tour operator or airline going bust.

Health Cover

Medical expenses are an important aspect of travel insurance and you shouldn't rely on insurance provided by reciprocal health arrangements (see page 225), charge and credit card companies, household policies or private medical insurance (unless it's an international policy), none of which may provide adequate cover. The minimum medical insurance recommended by experts is €300,000 in Greece and the rest of Europe, and €1.2 million for the rest of the world. If applicable, check whether pregnancy related claims are covered and whether there are any restrictions for those over a certain age, e.g. 65, as travel insurance is becoming increasingly more expensive for those aged over 65. You may prefer a policy that pays a hospital directly, rather than having to pay yourself and make a claim later. If you do need to make a claim, then you must keep your medical receipts.

Always check any exclusion clauses in contracts by obtaining a copy of the full policy document, as not all relevant information will be included in an insurance leaflet. High risk sports such as off-road trekking, para-sailing, scuba-diving, motorcycling and other 'risky' pursuits should be specifically covered and **listed** in a policy if applicable (there's usually an additional premium), as these pursuits are usually excluded from general cover. Special winter sports policies are available and are more expensive than normal holiday insurance ('dangerous' sports are excluded from most standard policies). Third party liability cover should be €2.4 million in North America and €1.2 million in the rest of the world. Note that this doesn't cover you when you're using a car or other mechanically propelled vehicle.

Cost

The cost of travel insurance varies considerably, depending on where you buy it, how long you intend to stay abroad and your age. Generally, the longer the period covered, the cheaper the daily cost, although the maximum period covered is usually limited, e.g. six months. With some policies an excess (deductible) must be paid for each claim. As a rough guide, travel insurance for Greece (and most other European countries) costs from around €40 for one week, €60 for two weeks and €100 for a month for a family of four (two adults and two children under 16).

Annual Policies

For people who travel abroad frequently, whether on business or pleasure, an annual travel policy usually provides the best value, but check carefully to find out exactly what it includes. Many insurance companies offer annual travel policies for a premium of around €150 for an individual (the equivalent of around three months insurance with a standard travel insurance policy), which are excellent value for frequent travellers. Some insurance companies also offer an 'emergency travel policy' for holiday homeowners who need to travel abroad at short notice to inspect a property, e.g. after a severe storm or robbery.

The cost of an annual policy may depend on the area covered, e.g. Europe, world-wide (excluding North America) and world-wide (including North America), although it doesn't usually cover travel within your country of residence. There's also a limit on the number of trips a year and the duration of each trip, e.g. 90 or 120 days (the longer the better). An annual policy is usually a good choice for owners of a holiday home in Greece who travel there frequently for relatively short periods. However, check exactly what's covered (or omitted), as an annual policy may not provide adequate cover.

9.

LETTING

Many people planning to buy a holiday home in Greece are interested in owning a property that will provide them with an income, e.g. from letting, to cover the running costs and help with mortgage payments. Letting a home for a few weeks or months in the summer can more than recoup your running costs (see page 124) and pay for holidays. Note that it's difficult to make a living providing holiday accommodation in most areas, as the season is too short and there's often too much competition.

 If you're planning to let a property, it's important not to overestimate the income, particularly if you're relying on letting income to help pay the mortgage and running costs.

The letting season varies with the region, although on most islands it runs from May to October (around 24 weeks) when charter flights are available. The season is longer in Athens and nearby resort areas, e.g. around 30 weeks. However, you're unlikely to achieve this many weeks' occupancy and you should budget for around half of these figures, even when letting full time. Note that the rental market in Greece isn't as well as developed as in many other popular holiday destinations. In addition, there has been a slump in the tourist market in both 2003 and 2004, and tour operators aren't optimistic about figures for the immediate future. Apartments in Athens have year-round letting potential, whereas apartments in resort areas and villas tend to be in demand during the summer months only.

> **You may be unable to meet all your mortgage payments and running costs from rental income, even if a property is available to let year-round. Most experts recommend that you don't buy a home in Greece if you need to rely on rental income to pay for it.**

Buyers who over-stretch their financial resources often find themselves on the rental treadmill, constantly struggling to raise sufficient income to cover their running costs and mortgage payments.

See also **Buying for Investment** on page 19.

RULES & REGULATIONS

Letting Licence

If you let a property in Greece, you're required by law to obtain a licence from the Greek National Tourist Organisation (EOT), which has offices in the main towns and on most islands as well as in the UK (☎ 210-870 7000, 🖥 www.gnto.gr). Bear in mind that this involves a great deal of paperwork (see below), is expensive and takes time, therefore you should apply for the licence well in advance. In some areas where the rental market is saturated, the EOT has stopped issuing licences.

 If you plan to make an income from letting, find out if licences are available in the area where you plan to buy before committing yourself to a purchase.

Requirements for the licence vary depending on the area and the type of property you plan to rent (e.g. self-catering villa, apartment or bed and breakfast), but generally include the following:

For the applicant:

● Certificate of no criminal record (available from the police in your home country or from the Greek police if you're resident);

● Completed application form;

● Health certificate if a non-EEA national (see **Health Certificate** on page 29);

● Latest tax return;

● Signed declaration of intention to rent.

For the property:

● Certificate issued by a qualified architect stating that plumbing and sewerage (including cesspits) meet official requirements.

● Environmental Survey: This is provided by a local architect who must inspect the property to ensure that it's suitable for rental. The survey can cost up to €1,500.

● Fire Certificate: The property is inspected by the local chief fire inspector who checks the property for adequate fire exits and fire extinguishers, and for fire hazards in the immediate area. Fire extinguishers must also be inspected and stamped annually.

● Original and a copy of the planning permission and/or building licence.

● Proof that payment of local taxes is up-to-date.

● Proposed rental agreement or contract.

● Statement from an architect certifying that the property conforms to earthquake building regulations.

Some areas have specific regulations for swimming pools (see **Swimming Pools** on page 141).

Many foreigners use the services of a lawyer or architect to help them obtain the licence, a process that's easier if you understand Greek and know the right people. Most people find architects are generally co-operative and willing to help. Once you have the licence (and have recovered from the stress of obtaining it!) you should renew it every year, which costs around €100.

Some foreigners let property without obtaining a licence and apparently have no problems with the authorities. This is, however, illegal and could lead to serious problems. If a guest at your property has an accident and you don't have a licence, you could be prosecuted and face a prison sentence. You may also find that locals in your area who have gone to the trouble and expense to obtain a licence report you to the local tax authorities who will undoubtedly take legal action.

Contracts

Most people who do holiday letting in Greece have a simple agreement form that includes a property description, the names of the clients, and the dates of arrival and departure. However, if you do regular letting you may wish to check with a lawyer that your agreement is legal and contains all the necessary safeguards. If you plan to let to non-English speaking clients, you should have a letting agreement in Greek or other languages. If you use an agent, they will provide a standard contract.

Although the law is on your side, you should be aware that if a tenant with a short-term rental contract refuses to leave, it can take months to have him evicted. Note also that if you receive rent and accept a lessee without protest, you're usually deemed to have entered into a contractual relationship, even if there's no written contract.

Taxation

You should inform the local tax office if you plan to let your property and must comply with the following regulations:

● You must issue official tax receipts (including your tax number) for any rental payment received.

● You must declare your rental income annually and may have to pay tax on it. Rates in 2005 ranged from 0 to 40 per cent.

- In addition to income tax you're also liable for an annual property income tax levied at a flat rate depending on the size and category of the property you let. For example, an apartment in Category A (the highest) is liable for a payment of around €200 and a villa around €300. This tax changes annually.

- You must pay stamp duty (3.6 per cent of the rent) monthly.

Declaring rental income can be complicated, particularly as regulations change periodically so it's advisable to use the services of an accountant. See **Income Tax** on page 208 for further information regarding tax liability.

LOCATION

If income from a Greek home has a high priority, then the location (see also page 64) must be one of the main considerations when buying. When considering the location for a property you plan to let, you should bear in mind certain factors.

Climate

Properties in areas with a pleasant year-round climate such as Crete and Rhodes have greater rental potential, particularly outside high season. This is also important should you wish to use the property yourself outside the high season; for example you could let a property over the summer months when rental income is at its highest, and use it yourself in May or October and still enjoy fine weather. See **Climate** on page 20.

Proximity to an Airport

A property should be situated within easy reach of an airport, as most holidaymakers won't consider travelling more than 30 to 45 minutes to their destination after arriving at an airport. Choose an area with an airport with a good choice of flights from your home country. Note, however, that because most airports in Greece are served only by charter flights it's also advisable to choose an airport with frequent domestic flights from Athens. For further information on airports see page 75 and also the map on page 314.

Proximity to a Port

If your property is on an island without an airport or on part of an island that isn't easily accessible by road, make sure there are good ferry connections and that the property is within easy reach of a port. Further information about ports and ferry travel can be found in **Chapter 2**. The map on page 312 also provides information on the main ferry routes around the islands.

Public Transport & Access

It's an advantage if a property is served by public transport or is situated in a town where a car is unnecessary. If a property is located in a town within a maze of streets, you should provide a detailed map. However, if it's in the country where signposts are all but non-existent, you will need to provide not only a detailed map with plenty of landmarks, but you may also need to erect signs. Holidaymakers who spend hours driving around trying to find a place are unlikely to return or recommend it! Maps are also helpful for taxi drivers, who may not know the area.

Attractions

The property should be close to attractions and/or a good beach, depending on the sort of clientele you wish to attract. If you want to let to families, then a property should be within easy distance of leisure activities such as water parks, sports activities and night-life. For this reason it's best not to choose a very small island where leisure options can be quickly exhausted by holidaymakers. Note that some small islands have few attractions beyond good beaches. If you're planning to let a property in a rural area, it should be somewhere with good hiking possibilities, preferably near one of Greece's many national parks.

SWIMMING POOL

If you're planning to let your property, a swimming pool is obligatory in most areas, as properties with pools are much easier to let than those without, unless a property is situated on a beach, lake or river. It's usually necessary to have a private pool with a single-family home (e.g. a detached villa), although a shared pool is adequate for an apartment or bungalow. If you plan to let mainly to families, it's advisable to choose an apartment or bungalow with a 'child-friendly' communal pool, e.g. with a separate paddling pool or a pool with a shallow area. Country properties should have a private pool (some letting agencies won't handle properties without a pool). You can charge a higher rent for a property with a private pool and it may be possible to extend the letting season even further by installing a heated or indoor pool, although the cost of heating the pool may be higher than the rental return.

There are strict regulations regarding pool safety (including private pools) in Greece and some areas have special requirements, such as the depth(s) should be marked; life-belts provided; and if the pool has a depth over 2m, a lifeguard should be on duty. Check these requirements when you apply for the letting licence (see page 236).

SURVIVAL TIP
You should have third party
insurance covering accidents and injuries for guests
(and anyone) using your pool (and your
property in general).

LETTING RATES

Rental rates vary considerably depending on the season, the region, and the size and quality of a property. An average apartment or townhouse sleeping four to six in an average area can be let for between €300 and €600 per week, depending on the season, location and quality. At the other extreme, a luxury villa in a popular area with a pool and accommodation for 8 to 12 can be let for €1,000 to €3,000 per week in the high season. The high season includes the months of July and August and possibly the first two weeks of September.

The mid-season usually comprises June, late September and October (and sometimes also the Easter and Christmas periods), when rents are around 25 per cent lower than in high season; the rest of the year is usually the low season, which may extend from October to May, when rates are usually up to 50 per cent lower than in the high season. In winter, rents may drop as low as €75 to €150 per week for a two-bedroom apartment, although there may be a minimum let of around two months.

Note that rates usually include linen, gas and electricity, although electricity and heating (e.g. gas bottles) are usually charged separately for long winter lets.

Increasing Rental Income

Rental income can be increased outside the high season by offering special interest or package holidays – which can be organised in conjunction with local businesses or tour operators – to broaden a property's appeal and cater for larger parties. These may include:

- Activity holidays, such as golf, tennis, cycling, hiking or yoga;
- Cooking, gastronomy and wine tours/tasting;
- Arts and crafts such as painting, sculpture, photography and writing courses.

You don't need to be an expert or conduct courses yourself, but can employ someone to do it for you.

COSTS & EXPENSES

When letting your property, make sure you allow for the numerous costs and expenses that inevitably reduce the amount of profit you can expect to make. These may include: a letting agent's commission; cleaning between and during lets; laundry of household linen; garden and pool maintenance; maintenance of appliances; replacement of damaged or soiled items; and insurance and utility bills (note that electricity bills can be high if your property has air-conditioning or electric heating). Some property owners find that the costs and expenses account for as much as half of their rental income.

FURNISHINGS

If you let a property, it isn't advisable to fill it with expensive furnishings or valuable personal belongings. While theft is rare, items will eventually be damaged or broken. When furnishing a property that you plan to let, you should choose hard-wearing, dark coloured carpets, which won't show stains (although most properties have tiled or marble floors rather than carpets), and buy durable furniture and furnishings. Simple, inexpensive furniture is best in a modest home, as it will need to stand up to hard wear. Small, two-bedroom properties should have a sofa bed in the living room. Properties should generally be well equipped with cooking utensils, crockery and cutlery (including a kitchen knife that cuts!), and it's usual to provide bed linen and towels. Buy the best quality household linen you can afford. You may also need a cot or high-chair for young children. Electricity is usually included in the rent, with the possible exception of long winter lets.

Appliances should include a washing machine and microwave, and possibly a dishwasher and tumble dryer. Depending on the rent and quality of a property, your guests may also expect central heating, air-conditioning, covered parking, a barbecue and garden furniture (including loungers – particularly if you have a pool). Some owners provide bicycles and badminton and table-tennis equipment. It isn't usual to have a telephone, although you could install a credit card phone or one that receives incoming calls only.

KEYS

You will need several sets of spare keys (plus spare remote controls for electric gates, etc.), which will probably get lost at some point. If you employ a management company, its address should be on the key fob and not the address of the house. If you let a home yourself, you can use a 'key-finder' service, whereby lost keys can be returned to the key-finder company by anyone finding them. If you lose keys or they can be easily copied, you should change the lock barrels regularly (at least annually). You don't need to provide clients with keys to all external doors, only the front door (the others can be left inside the property). If you arrange your own letting, you can send keys to clients in your home country or they can be collected from a local caretaker. It's also possible to install a key-pad entry system, the code of which can be changed after each let.

CLEANING

A property should always be spotlessly clean when holidaymakers arrive and you should provide basic cleaning equipment. You will need to arrange for cleaning in between lets and also at regular intervals, e.g. weekly or twice-weekly, for lets of more than one week. If you use a local agent, they will usually arrange cleaning at your expense, currently from €5 to €10 an hour. If applicable, you will also need to arrange pool cleaning and a gardener.

USING AN AGENT

If you're letting a second home, the most important decision is whether to let it yourself or use a letting agent (or agents). If you don't have much spare time, you're better off using an agent, who will take care of everything and save you the time and trouble of advertising and finding clients. An agent will charge commission of between 20 and 40 per cent of gross rental income, although some of this can be recouped through higher rents. If you want your property to appear in an agent's catalogue, you must usually contact them the summer before you wish to let it (the deadline is usually September). Note that, although self-catering holiday companies may fall over themselves to take on a luxury property in Greece, the top letting agents turn down most properties they're offered.

There are numerous self-catering holiday companies operating in Greece, and many local estate agents also act as letting agents for holiday and long-term lets.

 Take care when selecting an agent, as it isn't unknown for them to go bust.

If possible, make sure that your income is kept in an escrow account and paid regularly or, even better, choose an agent with a bonding scheme who pays you the rent **before** the arrival of guests (some do). It's absolutely essential to employ a reliable and honest (preferably long-established) company, as anyone can set up a holiday letting agency and there are many 'cowboy' operators. Always ask a management company to substantiate rental income claims and occupancy rates by showing you examples of actual income received from other properties. Ask for the names of satisfied customers and check with them.

Things to ask a letting agent include:

● When the letting income is paid;

● What additional charges are made and what they're for;

● Whether they provide detailed accounts of income and expenses (ask to see samples);

● Who they let to, e.g. what nationalities and whether families, children or singles;

● How they market properties;

● Whether you're expected to contribute towards advertising and marketing costs;

● Whether you're free to let the property yourself and use it when you wish. Many agents don't permit owners to use a property during the peak letting season (July and August) and may also restrict their use at other times.

The larger companies market homes via newspapers, magazines, overseas agents and direct mail, and have representatives in a number of countries. Management contracts usually run for a year and should include arranging routine and emergency repairs; reading meters (if electricity is charged extra); general maintenance of house and garden, including lawn cutting and pool cleaning; arranging cleaning and linen changes between lets; advising guests on the use of equipment, and providing them with information and assistance (24 hours a day in the case of emergencies).

Agents may also provide someone to meet and greet clients, hand over keys and check that everything is in order. The actual services provided will usually depend on whether a property is a basic apartment or a luxury villa costing €1,000 or more a week. A letting agent's representative should also make periodic checks when a property is empty to ensure that it's secure and everything is in order. You may wish to check whether a property is actually let when an agent tells you it's empty, as it isn't unknown for some agents to let a property and pocket the rent (you can get a friend or neighbour to call round). Note that when letting a property short-term, you must check that it's permitted under the community rules and you may also be required to notify your insurance company.

DOING YOUR OWN LETTING

Some owners prefer to let a property to family, friends, colleagues and acquaintances, which allows them more control and with any luck the property will also be better looked after. In fact, the best way to get a high volume of lets is usually to do it yourself, although many owners use a letting agency in addition to doing their own marketing in their home country. You will need to decide whether you want to let to smokers or accept pets and young children – some people won't let to families with children under five due to the risk of bed-wetting. Some owners also prefer not to let to young, single groups. Note, however, that this reduces your letting prospects.

Rental Rates & Deposits

To get an idea of the rent you should charge, simply ring a few letting agencies and ask them what it would cost to rent a property such as yours at the time of year you plan to let it. They're likely to quote the highest rent you can charge. You should also check the advertisements in newspapers and magazines. Set a realistic rent, as there's usually a lot of competition. Add a returnable deposit, e.g. €150 to €300 (depends on the rent), as security against loss of keys and breakages. A booking deposit is usually refundable up to six weeks before the booking, after which it's forfeited. Most people have a minimum two-week rental period in July and August.

Advertising

If you wish to let a property yourself, there's a wide range of local and foreign newspapers and magazines in which you can advertise, e.g.

Dalton's Weekly (☎ UK 020-8329 0222, 💻 www.daltonsholidays.com) and newspapers such as the *Sunday Times* and *Sunday Telegraph* in the UK. Many of the English-language newspapers and magazines listed in **Appendix B** also include advertisements from property owners. You will need to experiment to find the best publications and days of the week or months to advertise. Note, however, that most owners find it's prohibitively expensive to advertise a single property in a national newspaper or magazine.

A cheaper and better method is to advertise in property directories such as Private Villas (☎ UK 020-8329 0195, 💻 www.privatevillas.co.uk) or on websites such as Owners Direct (☎ UK 01372-722 708, 💻 www. ownersdirect.co.uk) and Holiday Rentals (☎ UK 020-8743 5577, 💻 www.holiday-rentals.co.uk), where you pay for the advertisement and handle bookings yourself. Regional tourist agencies can put you in touch with local letting agents.

You can also advertise among friends and colleagues, in company and club magazines (which may even be free), and on notice boards in companies, stores and public places. The more marketing you do, the more income you're likely to earn, although you must also ensure that you provide a quick and efficient response to any enquiries. It also pays to work with other local people in the same business and send surplus guests to competitors (they will usually reciprocate). In addition to advertising locally and in your home country, you can also extend your marketing abroad (or advertise via the internet – see below). Note that it's usually necessary to have an answer machine and preferably also a fax machine.

Internet

Advertising on the internet is an increasingly popular option for property owners, particularly as a personalised website is an excellent advertisement and can include photographs, booking forms and maps, as well as comprehensive information about your property. You can also provide information about flights, ferries, car rental, local attractions, sports facilities and links to other websites. A good website should be easy to navigate (avoid complicated page links or indexes) and must include contact details, ideally via email. You can also exchange links with other websites.

Brochures & Leaflets

If you don't have a website containing photographs and information, ideally you should produce a coloured brochure or leaflet. This should contain external and internal pictures, comprehensive details, the exact location, local attractions and details of how to get there (with a map included). You should enclose a stamped addressed envelope when sending out details and follow up within a week if you don't hear anything. It's necessary to make a home look as attractive as possible in a brochure without distorting the facts – advertise honestly and don't over-sell your property.

Handling Enquiries

If you plan to let a home yourself, you will need to decide how to handle enquiries about flights and car rentals. It's easier to let clients do it themselves, but you should be able to offer advice and put them in touch with airlines, ferry companies, travel agents and car rental companies.

INFORMATION PACKS

Pre-arrival

After accepting a booking, you should provide guests with a pre-arrival information pack containing the following:

● A map of the local area and instructions on how to find the property;

● Information about local attractions and the local area (available free from local tourist offices);

● Emergency contact numbers in your home country (e.g. the UK) and Greece if guests have any problems or plan to arrive late;

● The keys, or instructions regarding where to collect them on arrival.

> **SURVIVAL TIP**
> It's ideal if someone can
> welcome your guests when they arrive, explain how
> things work, and deal with any special requests
> or problems.

Post-arrival

You should also provide an information pack in your home for guests, including the following:

● How things work such as kitchen appliances, TV/video, heating and air-conditioning;

- Security measures (see below);
- What not to do and possible dangers, for example, if you allow young children and pets, you should make a point of emphasising dangers such as falling into the pool;
- Local emergency numbers and health services such as a doctor, dentist and hospital;
- Emergency assistance such as a general repairman, plumber, electrician and pool maintenance (you may prefer to leave the telephone number of a local caretaker who can handle any problems);
- Recommended shops, restaurants and attractions.

Many people provide a visitor's book for guests to write their comments and suggestions, and some send out questionnaires. If you want to impress your guests, you can arrange for fresh flowers, fruit, a good bottle of wine and a grocery pack to greet them on their arrival. It's personal touches like this that ensure repeat business and recommendations; you may even find after the first year or two that you rarely need to advertise. Many people return to the same property year after year. Simply do an annual mail-shot to previous clients. **Word-of-mouth advertising is the cheapest and always the best.**

MAINTENANCE

If you do your own letting, you will need to arrange for cleaning and maintenance, including pool cleaning and a gardener, if applicable. Ideally you should have someone on call seven days a week.

Caretaker

If you own a second home in Greece, you will find it beneficial or even essential to employ a local caretaker, irrespective of whether you let it. You can have your caretaker prepare the house for your family and guests as well as looking after it when it isn't in use. If it's a holiday home, it's wise to have your caretaker check it periodically (e.g. weekly) and allow him to authorise minor repairs. If you let a property yourself, your caretaker can arrange for (or do) cleaning, linen changes, maintenance, repairs, gardening and pay bills. If you employ a caretaker or housekeeper you should expect to pay at least the minimum local hourly wage (currently €3.50) or for full-time employees, €560 a month.

Closing a Property for the Winter

Before closing a property for the winter, you should turn off the water at the mains (required by insurance companies) and drain pipes, remove fuses (except those for a dehumidifier or air-conditioner if you leave them on), empty food cupboards and the fridge/freezer, disconnect gas cylinders and empty rubbish bins. You should leave open interior doors and a few small windows (with grilles or secure shutters), plus wardrobes in order to provide ventilation. Lock the main doors, windows and shutters, and secure anything of value or leave it with a neighbour or friend. Check whether any essential work needs to be done before you leave and, if necessary, arrange for it to be done in your absence.

Most importantly, leave a set of keys with a neighbour or friend and arrange for them (or a caretaker) to check your property periodically.

SECURITY

Most people aren't security conscious when on holiday and you should therefore provide detailed instructions for guests regarding security measures and emphasise the need to secure the property when they go out. It's also important for them to be security conscious when in the property, particularly when having a party or in the garden, as it isn't unusual for valuables to be stolen while guests are outside.

Ideally, you should install a safe for your guests (and yourself while you're there) and leave the key or code for it in the property. When you or your guests leave the property unattended, it's important to employ all security measures available, including the following:

- Storing valuables in a safe (if applicable) – hiding them isn't a good idea, as thieves know **ALL** the hiding places;

- Closing and locking all doors and windows;

- Locking grilles on patio and other doors;

- Closing shutters and securing any bolts or locks;

- Setting the alarm (if applicable) and notifying the alarm company when absent for an extended period;

- Making it appear as if a property is occupied through the use of timers and leaving lights and a TV/radio on.

Bear in mind that prevention is always better than cure, as stolen possessions are rarely recovered.

If you have a robbery, you should report it to your local police station, where you must make a statement. You will receive a copy, which is required by your insurance company if you make a claim. See also **Home Security** on page 257.

10.

MISCELLANEOUS MATTERS

This chapter contains miscellaneous – but nevertheless important – information for homeowners in Greece, including crime, heating & air-conditioning, newspapers & magazines, postal services, public holidays, security, shopping, telephone, television and radio, and utilities.

CRIME

Greece is one of Europe's safest countries with a low crime rate and a well-deserved reputation for honesty. If you leave some personal belongings at a bar or café, you're likely to find them in the safe-keeping of the owner awaiting your return. Greeks are generally used to leaving their possessions unattended or unlocked, although there has been an increase in crime in recent years (blamed mainly on Albanian refugees, but often carried out by tourists), therefore you should ensure that your belongings are safely locked up or supervised. The worst crime areas include Omonia in Athens, the flea markets and the old section of the Athens' metro, where pickpocketting is rife. Theft of passports is also common in Athens. Sexual harassment (or worse) is fairly common in Greece and women should take particular care late at night and never hitchhike alone.

 Note that the possession of illegal drugs (even small amounts) is a very serious offence in Greece, where offenders are liable to fines of up €300,000 and a prison sentence of between ten years and life!

Police

There are three types of police in Greece, although only national police (*ethniki astynomia*) operate throughout the country. National police are in charge of traffic and crime prevention. Tourist police (*touristikí astynomia*), found in most large cities and resorts, assist tourists (they can usually provide a wealth of local information) and carry out official inspections of hotels and restaurants. Tourist police are a division of the local police, identified by flags on their jackets indicating the languages they speak. Athens has its own police force (*póleon astynomia*) with dark blue uniforms and white patrol cars. All police are armed in Greece. Dial 100 in an emergency or 171 for the tourist police.

HEATING & AIR-CONDITIONING

If you're used to central heating and like a warm house in winter, you will probably want central heating in Greece during winter, even in the warmest areas where winter nights can be chilly. Central heating systems may be powered by oil, gas, electricity, solid fuel (usually wood) or even solar power – see below. Whatever form of heating you use, it's important to have good insulation, without which around half of the heat generated is lost through the walls and roof. Note that many homes, particularly older and cheaper properties (but also some new ones), don't have good insulation and builders don't always keep to the regulations.

In cities, apartment blocks may have a communal central heating system which provides heating for all apartments, the cost of which is divided among the tenants. If you're a non-resident or absent for long periods you should choose an apartment with a separate heating system, otherwise you will be contributing towards your neighbours' bills when you aren't there.

Heating

Electric

Electric heating isn't particularly common, as it's expensive and requires good insulation and a permanent system of ventilation. You should avoid electric heating in regions with a cold winter, as the bills can be astronomical. However, a system of night-storage heaters operating on a night tariff can be economical. Some stand-alone electric heaters are expensive to run and are best suited to holiday homes. If you rely on electricity for your heating, you should expect to pay between €50 and €150 a month during the coldest months i.e. November to February. An air-conditioning system (see below) with a heat pump provides cooling in summer and economical heating in winter. Note that if you have electric central heating or air-conditioning, you will probably need to upgrade your power supply. See **Electricity** on page 279 for more information.

Gas

Stand-alone gas heaters using standard gas bottles are an inexpensive way of providing heating in areas with mild winters (such as Crete and Rhodes). Note that gas heaters must be used only in rooms with adequate ventilation and it can be dangerous to have too large a difference between indoor and outdoor temperatures. Gas poisoning due to faulty ventilation ducts for gas heaters, e.g. in bathrooms, isn't uncommon. It's possible to install a central heating system operating from standard gas bottles (Primus of Sweden is one of the leading manufacturers). Mains gas central heating is available only in Athens and Thessaloniki and is the cheapest to run. See **Gas** on page 284 for more information.

Solar Energy

The use of solar energy to provide hot water and heating is relatively rare in Greece, although it's on the increase. The amount of energy provided by the sun each year is equivalent to eleven gas bottles per square metre – the sun provides around 8,000 times the world's present energy requirements annually! A solar power system can be used to supply all your energy needs, although it's usually combined with an electric or gas heating system, as it cannot be relied upon for year-round heating and hot water. Solar power can also be used to provide electricity in a remote rural home, where the cost of extending mains electricity is prohibitive, or to heat a swimming pool.

The main drawback of solar energy is the high cost of installation, which varies considerably according to the region and how much energy you require. A 400-litre hot-water system costs around €3,000 and must be installed by an expert. The advantages are no running costs, silent and maintenance-free operation, and no (or very small) electricity bills. A system should last 30 years (it's usually guaranteed for ten years) and can be uprated to provide additional power in the future. Advances in solar cell and battery technology are expected to dramatically increase the efficiency and reduce the cost of solar power, which is tipped to become the main source of energy world-wide in the future.

Air-conditioning

In summer, the temperature in Greece frequently exceeds 40°C (104°F) and although properties are built to withstand the heat, you may wish to install air-conditioning. Note, however, that air-conditioning can have negative effects if you suffer from asthma or respiratory problems. You can choose from a huge variety of air-conditioners: fixed or moveable; indoor or outdoor installation; high or low power. Expect to pay around €600 for a unit sufficient to cool an average size room. An air-conditioning system with a heat pump and outside compressor provides cooling in summer and economical heating in winter. Many people fit ceiling fans for extra cooling in summer (costing from around €40), which are standard fixtures in some new homes.

Humidifiers & De-humidifiers

Central heating and air-conditioning dry the air considerably and may cause your family to develop coughs and other ailments. Those who find dry air unpleasant can install humidifiers that add moisture to the air. These range from simple water containers hung from radiators to electric or battery-operated devices. Humidifiers that don't generate steam should be disinfected occasionally with a special liquid available from chemists to prevent the build-up of bacteria.

On the other hand, if you're going to be using a holiday home only occasionally, it's worthwhile installing de-humidifiers, especially in the bedrooms, to prevent clothes and linen going mouldy. In some parts of Greece (e.g. the Ionian islands) where winters are very wet, a de-humidifier is a good way of keeping your house as dry as possible.

HOME SECURITY

Security is of paramount importance when buying a home in Greece, particularly if it will be left empty for long periods. Obtain advice from local security companies and neighbours.

 Bear in mind, however, that no matter how good your security, a property is rarely impregnable, so you should never leave valuables in an unattended home unless they're stored in a safe.

When moving into a new home, it's often wise to replace the locks (or lock barrels) as soon as possible, as you will have no idea how many keys are in circulation for the existing locks. This is true even for new homes, as builders often give keys to sub-contractors. In any case, you should change the external lock barrels regularly, e.g. annually, particularly if you let a home. If they aren't already fitted, it's best to fit high security (double cylinder or dead bolt) locks. In areas with a high risk of theft, e.g. resort areas and major cities, your insurance company may insist on extra security measures such as two locks on external doors, internal locking shutters, and exterior shutters or security bars on windows and patio doors on the ground, first and second floors of buildings. A policy may specify that all forms of protection on doors must be employed when a property is unoccupied.

You may wish to have a security alarm fitted, which is usually the best way to deter thieves and may also reduce your household insurance (see page 226). Ideally it should include all external doors and windows or have internal infra-red security beams. It may include a coded entry keypad (which can be frequently changed and is useful for clients if you let) and 24-hour monitoring – with some systems it's possible to monitor properties remotely via a computer from another country. With a monitored system, when a sensor detects an emergency, e.g. smoke or forced entry, or a panic button is pushed, a signal is sent automatically to a 24-hour monitoring station. The person on duty will telephone to check whether it's a genuine alarm (a password must be given) and if he cannot contact you or someone gives the wrong code, a security guard will be sent to investigate.

You can deter thieves by ensuring that your house is well lit at night and not conspicuously unoccupied. External security 'motion detector' lights (that switch on automatically when someone approaches), random timed switches for internal lights, radios and TVs, dummy security cameras, and tapes that play barking dogs (etc.) triggered by a light or heat detector may all help deter burglars. In rural areas, owners often take extra security measures such as fitting two or three locks on external doors, alarm systems, bars on doors and windows, window locks, security shutters and a safe for valuables. The advantage of bars is that they allow you to leave windows open without inviting criminals in (unless they're **very** slim).

 Note, however, that security bars must be heavy duty as cheap bars can easily be prised apart.

Many people also wrap a chain around their patio or balcony bars and secure them with a padlock when a property is unoccupied (although it might not withstand bolt-cutters). You can fit UPVC (toughened clear plastic) security windows and doors, which can survive an attack with a sledge-hammer without damage, and external steel security blinds (which can be electrically operated), although these are expensive. A dog can be useful to deter intruders, although it should be kept inside where it cannot be given poisoned food. Irrespective of whether you actually have a dog, a warning sign showing an image of a fierce dog may act as a deterrent. You should have the front door of an apartment fitted with a spy-hole and chain so that you can check the identity of visitors before opening the door.

Bear in mind that prevention is always better than cure, as stolen property is rarely recovered.

Holiday homes are particularly vulnerable to thieves, especially in rural areas, and are occasionally ransacked. No matter how secure your door and window locks, a thief can usually gain entry if he is sufficiently determined, often by smashing a window or even breaking in through the roof or by knocking a hole in a wall in a rural area! In isolated areas, thieves can strip a house bare at their leisure and an un-monitored alarm won't be a deterrent if there's no-one around to hear it. If you have a holiday home, you shouldn't leave anything of real value (monetary or sentimental) there and should have full insurance for your belongings (see page 226). One almost guaranteed way to protect a home when you're away is to employ a house-sitter to look after it. This can be done for short periods or for six months, e.g. during the winter, or longer if you have a holiday home. It isn't usually necessary to pay someone to house-sit for a period of six months or more, when you can usually find someone to do it in return for free accommodation. However, you must take care whom you engage and obtain references.

An important aspect of home security is making sure that you have an early warning of a fire by installing smoke detectors, which should be tested periodically to ensure that the batteries aren't exhausted. You can also fit an electric-powered gas detector that activates an alarm when a gas leak is detected.

When closing up a property for an extended period, e.g. over the winter, you should ensure that everything is switched off and that it's secure. If you vacate your home for a long period, you may also be obliged to notify a caretaker, landlord or insurance company, and to leave a key with a caretaker or landlord in case of emergencies. If you have a robbery, you should report it immediately to your local police station where you must make a statement. You will receive a copy, which is required by your insurance company if you make a claim.

There are many specialist home security companies in Greece who will inspect your home and provide free advice on security, although you should obtain at least two quotations before having any work done.

See also **Crime** above.

NEWSPAPERS & MAGAZINES

Greeks are avid newspaper readers and there are some 15 daily newspapers in Greece, of which the most popular are the *Eleftherotypia*, *Kathimerini* (an English-language version is distributed with the *International Tribune*, 🖳 www.ekathimerini.com) and *Ta Nea*, although only *Eleftherotypia* is considered to be good quality. There are also two

English-language newspapers: *Athens News* (💻 www.athensnews.gr), published weekly on Fridays and featuring world and Greek news and a weekly entertainment guide for the capital, and the *Aegena Times* (💻 www.aegeantimes.net), containing mainly Greek news. Both are widely available in Athens and the main resort areas. An English-language magazine, *Odyssey* (💻 www.odyssey.gr), is published bi-monthly and features political, travel and cultural articles. In Athens, *Athinorama* and *Time Out Athens* have weekly listings of entertainment in the capital, but most information is in Greek.

Many foreign newspapers and magazines are available at news kiosks in most resorts and cities, although outside the main season (May to September) they're usually available only in Athens and major resorts. Most publications arrive in Athens on the afternoon of the day of publication, although they may not be available until the next day and weekend availability varies considerably. Note that foreign publications are expensive and are the equivalent of around three times or more of the cover price (from at least €1.50 to €10).

POSTAL SERVICES

There's a post office (*tachidromío*), depicted by a yellow sign, in most towns and villages in Greece, where in addition to the usual post office services a range of other services are provided. These include telephone calls, telegrams, fax and telex transmissions, domestic and international cash transfers, and currency exchange. There's a *poste restante* service and mail can be collected for up to a month from main post offices (you need to show your passport to collect your mail).

Business hours for main post offices in towns and cities in Greece are usually from 7.30am to 2pm. In larger towns they usually stay open until around 7pm, Mondays to Fridays and also open from 8 or 9am until noon on Saturdays. Main post offices in major towns don't close for lunch and may also provide limited services outside normal business hours. In small towns and villages, post offices may close for lunch and may be also closed on one day a week. You shouldn't expect post office staff to speak English or other languages, although in resort areas some English may be spoken.

The Greek mail delivery service (operated by ELTA – Customer Service ☎ 800-118 2000, 💻 www.elta-net.gr, also in English) has a reputation as one of the slowest in Europe, although services have improved in recent years and aren't as bad as they're sometimes portrayed. Delivery times vary depending on where letters are posted, e.g. around three to eight days to European countries and five to eleven days to North America. Bear in mind that mail to and from Greek islands without an airport takes considerably longer to arrive at its destination. For important documents you should use the registered (*sistiméno*) service, although this is slow unless you also send it via the express (*katepígonda*) service. Airmail letters up to 20g cost €0.65 to all overseas destinations. Stamps can be purchased from small kiosks (*períptero*) located on street corners (which levy a 10 per cent surcharge), as well as from post offices. Note that when sending a parcel it needs to be inspected at the post office, therefore you shouldn't seal it in advance.

Standard post boxes in Greece are small, square yellow containers usually mounted on a post, possibly with two slots: one for local mail (*esorerikó*) and the other for overseas mail (*exoterikó*). Dark red post boxes are for the rapid mail service. It's best to use post boxes outside post offices only, as collection from other boxes is often erratic. The international postal identification, written before the four-digit postal code, is 'G' for Greece. Comprehensive information about the Greek postal service is available in English on the ELTA website (🖥 www.elta-net.gr).

Courier Services

The only guaranteed way to send something urgently is by courier or to 'send' letters by fax or e-mail. Express mail and courier services are provided by the post office, airlines, and international courier companies such as DHL, Federal Express and UPS.

PUBLIC HOLIDAYS

When a holiday falls on a Saturday or Sunday in Greece, another day isn't usually granted as a holiday unless the number of public holidays in a particular year falls below a minimum number. Holidays are occasionally moved to form long weekends and when a holiday falls on a Friday or Monday many businesses close for the entire holiday weekend (assuming they would normally work on a Saturday or Sunday). Note that foreign embassies and consulates in Greece usually observe local public holidays in addition to their own country's national holidays.

There are 11 statutory national public holidays a year in Greece plus local holidays, on which government offices, banks, post offices, most shops and restaurants, and many museums and ancient sites are closed. The following days are official national public holidays in Greece:

Date	Holiday
1st January	New Year's Day
6th January	Epiphany
Feb/March	First Sunday in Lent
25th March	Independence Day
March/April	Good Friday
March/April	Easter Sunday
1st May	Labour Day
15th August	Feast of the Assumption
28th October	Ohi Day
25th December	Christmas Day
26th December	St Stephen's Day

In addition to national public holidays, each province or town has its own feast days, fairs and pilgrimages. Easter is the most important festival in Greece and during Easter week every town and village dedicates its energies to religious ceremonies, feasting and celebrating. The ceremonies are particularly noteworthy on the islands of Hydra, Corfu and Kios. Carnival, three weeks before Lent, is celebrated throughout Greece, with the parades and festivities in Athens and Kefallonia among the most famous and colourful. Regional holidays aren't always official public holidays, but most local businesses are closed, sometimes for a number of days. Public holidays are marked (usually in red) on most calendars.

SHOPPING

Greece doesn't rate among Europe's great shopping countries, either for quality or bargains, with the exception of handmade arts and crafts, which are widely available at reasonable prices. Prices of many consumer goods such as TVs and stereo systems, computers, cameras, electrical apparatus and household appliances have fallen considerably in recent years, although they're still generally higher than in many other European countries, where there's more competition. Clothes aren't particularly good value and good quality clothing can be expensive, particularly if it's imported.

Considering its relatively small population, Greece has a surprisingly large number of shops, practically as many as Britain, a country with four times the population. Most Greek retail enterprises are family-run and it's unusual for a large family not to own some sort of shop. Consequently, shopping is a pleasant experience and an essentially social occasion. Recent years have seen the introduction of shopping centres and hypermarkets, although these are still relatively few and far between, unlike in most other European countries where they dominate. Shopping is excellent in Athens where there are several department stores, including Lambropouli, as well as foreign stores such as Bodyshop, Zara and the British-owned BHS. Shopping in Athens is concentrated around Ermou street. Marks & Spencer (British owned) have a store in Corfu. The biggest drawback to shopping in cities and towns is parking, which can be impossible, particularly in Athens. With the exception of street markets and some souvenir shops, where haggling over the price is part of the enjoyment, retail prices are fixed.

Among the best buys in Greece are the diverse handicrafts, including hand-woven textiles such as rugs, bags and knitwear, religious icons, ceramics, e.g. in Athens and Rhodes, leather goods (Chania on Crete has some of the best buys), Greek music and musical instruments, olive wood figures and jewellery. Gold jewellery, although of exceptional quality, is expensive and silver filigree is often cheaper and better value. Goods made throughout Greece are available from most souvenir shops, although they're usually cheaper when purchased in the area where they're made. Local wines and olive oil are also good buys.

It's important to shop around and compare prices in Greece, as they can vary considerably, even between shops in the same town. Note, however, that price differences often reflect different quality, so make sure that you're comparing similar products.

Greeks generally pay cash when shopping, although credit cards are widely accepted in major stores and those frequented by tourists. However, in remote areas and on some Greek islands you may find that only cash is accepted. In major cities and tourist areas you should be wary of pickpockets and bag-snatchers, particularly in markets and other crowded places. Don't tempt fate with an exposed wallet or purse or by flashing your money around.

Opening Hours

During the hotter summer months, shops are **usually** open on Mondays, Wednesdays and Saturdays from 9am until 2.30pm, and on Tuesdays, Thursdays and Fridays from 8.30am to 2pm and from 6 to 9pm. During the cooler months, shops open around half an hour later and close an hour earlier. Opening hours are, however, somewhat erratic and also depend on national and local public holidays and individual shopkeeper's preferences, although in most tourist areas they're open all day, seven days a week during the high season. Note that butchers and delicatessens aren't allowed to sell fresh meat in the afternoon and fishmongers are only open in the mornings.

Furniture & Furnishings

The kind of furniture you buy for your Greek home will depend on a number of factors, including its style and size, whether it's a permanent or holiday home, your budget, the local climate and not least, your personal taste. Holiday homes are often sold furnished, particularly apartments, although furniture may be of poor quality and not to your taste. However, buying a furnished property can represent a bargain, as the cost of the furnishings often isn't reflected in the price. If you're buying a new property as an investment for letting some developers or agents will arrange to furnish it for you.

If you plan to furnish a holiday home with antiques or expensive modern furniture, bear in mind that you will need adequate security and insurance. If you own a holiday home in Greece, it may be worthwhile shipping surplus items of furniture you have in your home abroad. If you intend to live permanently in Greece in the future and already have a house full of good furniture abroad, there's little point in buying expensive furniture in Greece. However, many foreigners who decide to live permanently in Greece find that it's better to sell their furniture abroad rather than bring it to Greece, as foreign furniture often isn't suitable for Greece's climate and house styles (and shipping is expensive).

A wide range of modern and traditional furniture is available in Greece at reasonable prices. Modern furniture is popular and is often sold in large stores in towns, e.g. To Epiplo (💻 www.toepiplo.gr), which has stores in several locations including Athens, Kalamata (Peloponnese) and Crete (Chania and Rethimnon). IKEA (💻 www.ikea.gr) has stores in Athens and Thessaloniki, and the Habitat chain has a store in Athens. Pine and cane furniture is inexpensive and widely available.

If you're buying a large quantity of furniture, don't be reluctant to ask for a reduction, as most stores will give you a discount. The best time to buy furniture and furnishings is during sales (particularly in winter), when prices of many items are slashed. Furniture stores may also offer special deals on complete furniture packages, e.g. from around €3,000 to totally furnish a two-bedroom apartment. It's possible for residents to pay for furniture and large household appliances over 12 months interest-free or over five years (with interest).

If you're looking for antique furniture at affordable prices, you may find a few bargains at antique and flea markets in rural areas. However, you must drive a hard bargain, as the asking prices are often ridiculous, particularly in tourist areas during the summer.

Household Goods

Household goods in Greece are generally of high quality and although the choice isn't as wide as in some other European countries, it has improved considerably in recent years. Electrical items have traditionally been more expensive in Greece, although the gap has narrowed and prices are now comparable (particularly in hypermarkets). Wide ranges of imported brands are usually available. White goods are mainly German or Italian.

Bear in mind when importing household goods that aren't sold in Greece, that it may be difficult or impossible to get them repaired or serviced locally. If you import appliances, don't forget to bring a supply of spares and consumables such as bulbs for a refrigerator or sewing machine, and spare bags for a vacuum cleaner. Note that the standard size of kitchen appliances and cupboard units in Greece isn't the same as in other countries and it may be difficult to fit an imported dishwasher or washing machine into a Greek kitchen. Check the size and the latest Greek safety regulations before shipping these items to Greece or buying them abroad, as they may need expensive modifications.

> **Greek washing machines take in cold water ONLY and heat it in the machine, which makes machines that take in hot water (such as those sold in the UK) obsolete in Greece.**

If you already own small household appliances it's worthwhile bringing them to Greece, as usually all that's required is a change of plug. However, if you're coming from a country with a 110/115V electricity supply such as the US, you will need a lot of expensive transformers (see page 281) and it's usually better to buy new appliances in Greece. Don't bring a TV or video recorder without first checking its compatibility, as TVs made for other countries often don't work in Greece without modification. If your need is only temporary, many electrical and other household items (such as TVs, beds, cots/highchairs, electric fans, refrigerators, heaters and air-conditioners), can be rented by the day, week or month.

Tools and do-it-yourself (DIY) equipment can also be rented in most towns. DIY supplies can be bought from hardware shops in towns and large villages. The German-owned DIY giant, Praktiker (⌨ www. praktiker.com), has stores in Athens, Patra, Larissa and Thessaloniki.

If you need kitchen measuring equipment and cannot cope with decimal measures, you will need to bring your own measuring scales, jugs, cups and thermometers. Note that foreign pillow sizes (e.g. American and British) aren't the same as in Greece.

Markets

Markets are a common sight in towns and villages throughout Greece and are an essential part of life, largely unaffected by competition from supermarkets and hypermarkets. They're colourful, entertaining and fun, and an experience not to be missed, even if you don't plan to buy anything (you find the real flavour of Greece in markets). Some towns have markets on only one or two days a week, while others stage them on virtually every day of the year and many towns have permanent indoor markets selling foodstuffs. There are different kinds of markets, including indoor markets, permanent street markets and travelling street markets (laïkí agorá) that move from neighbourhood to neighbourhood on different days of the week or month, although they usually have a fixed day in each neighbourhood. Prices are generally lower than in shops, although much depends on your bargaining skills (haggling is expected for expensive items or when buying in bulk). There's often a large central market in cities and many towns and city neighbourhoods have indoor or covered markets. Markets usually operate from around 7am to 2pm.

A variety of goods are commonly sold in markets, including household items, dry goods (along with a vast range of herbs) and fruit and vegetables. Specialist markets in Athens and other large cities sell antiques, books, clothes, stamps, postcards, medals, coins, birds and pets.

> **You should be wary of bargain-priced branded goods in markets and souvenir shops, such as watches, perfume and clothes, as they're invariably fakes.**

Food markets are highly popular, despite the presence of supermarkets and hypermarkets, and there are also fish markets in coastal towns. Food is invariably beautifully presented and includes fruit and vegetables (including many exotic varieties), fish, meat, live poultry, dairy products, bread and cakes, herbs, olives and olive oil. Food is usually cheaper and fresher in markets than in supermarkets, particularly if you buy what's in season and grown locally. You should arrive early in the morning for the best choice, although bargains can often be found when stall holders are packing up for the day.

All produce is clearly marked with its price per piece or kilogramme and usually there's no haggling over the price, although near the end of the day an offer may be accepted. When shopping for food in markets, vendors may object to customers handling the fruit and vegetables, although you needn't be shy about asking to taste a piece of fruit. It's advisable to take your own bag when buying fruit and vegetables, as carrier bags aren't always provided. When buying fruit and vegetables in markets, make sure that the quality of produce you're given is the same as on display, which isn't always the case. Queues at a particular stall are usually a good sign. Another good place to buy fresh fruit and vegetables is from roadside stalls set up in rural areas. Here the produce couldn't be fresher and is often grown by the seller himself.

Antique and flea markets are common throughout Greece. Athens in particular has several famous flea markets, including those at Monastiraki, Piraeus and Thission, which take place on Sundays from 6am to 2pm. Being close to the Middle East, Greece also has several bazaars, that are well worth a visit (particularly in Athens). At antique and flea markets, you shouldn't expect to find many (or any) bargains in the major cities, where anything worth buying is snapped up by dealers, although in small towns you may find some real bargains.

You should never assume that because something is sold in a market it will be a bargain, particularly when buying antiques, which aren't always authentic.

Note that in Greece it's illegal to buy, sell, possess or export antiquities that are over 100 years old and penalties for infringements are second only to those imposed for drug smuggling.

In many cases the local antique shops are cheaper and in particular those selling to local residents rather than tourists. Always haggle over the price of expensive items. To find out where and when local markets are held, enquire at your local tourist office or town hall.

Shopping Abroad

Shopping 'abroad' includes trips to Bulgaria, Cyprus, Italy and Turkey as well as shopping excursions further afield. A short trip to a neighbouring country makes an interesting day (or days) out and could save you money. Don't forget your passports or identity cards, car papers, visas (if required) and foreign currency (if applicable). There are no cross-border shopping restrictions within the EU for goods purchased duty and tax paid, provided goods are for personal consumption or use and not for resale. Although there are no restrictions, there are 'indicative' levels for items such as spirits, wine, beer and tobacco products, above which goods may be classified as commercial quantities.

Duty-free Allowances

If you travel to or from Greece to or from another EU country, you're entitled to import goods of an unlimited value as long as they're for your personal use, plus cigarettes and alcohol as listed below.

Note that the list is issued as a guide only and if you import more than the amounts shown below, you must be able to prove that the goods are for your personal use. If you cannot, they may be confiscated by customs officials. Note also that guidelines are subject to change and you should check with an official source before you import large amounts:

- 800 cigarettes;
- 400 cigarillos;
- 20 cigars;
- 1kg smoking tobacco;
- 90 litres wine (of which no more than 60 should be sparkling);
- 10 litres spirits;
- 20 litres fortified wine;
- 110 litres beer.

For each journey to a non-EU country travellers aged 17 or over (unless otherwise stated) are entitled to import the following goods purchased duty-free:

- One litre of spirits (over 22 degrees proof) **or** two litres of fortified wine, sparkling wine or other liqueurs (under 22 degrees proof);

- Two litres of still table wine;
- 200 cigarettes **or** 100 cigarillos **or** 50 cigars **or** 250g of tobacco;
- 60cc/ml of perfume;
- 250cc/ml of toilet water;
- Other goods, including gifts and souvenirs to the value of €175 (€90 for under 14s).

Duty-free allowances apply on both outward and return journeys, even if both are made on the same day, and the combined total (i.e. double the above limits) can be imported into your 'home' country. It's rarely worthwhile buying duty-free alcohol when travelling to Greece, as it's cheaper in Greek shops and supermarkets.

Claiming VAT

If you reside outside the EU and have been in Greece for at least 48 hours, you can reclaim value added tax (VAT) on single purchases over €120. An export sales invoice is provided by retailers listing purchases, which must be validated by a customs officer when leaving Greece (so don't pack purchases in your checked baggage). Your refund will be posted to you later or paid to a credit card account. With certain purchases, particularly large items, it's better to have them sent directly abroad, when VAT won't be added. Allow plenty of time at airports or ports for VAT claims.

TELEPHONE SERVICES

In recent years there has been extensive investment in communications services in Greece, including telephones (fixed and mobile), internet, fax, mail and courier services, and the country now enjoys a comparatively high standard of communications. The telephone service has been 'liberalised', although only one company, *Organismós Telepikononion Elládos* (OTE), offers a complete service, including the installation of telephone lines; others provide call and internet services only, but the market is very much dominated by OTE, originally a state-owned monopoly. The other main providers of private telephone services are FORTHnet and Tellas (with 5 and 8 per cent of the market share respectively). Competition in the market means there's been some reduction in the cost of calls, although Greece still has some of the highest telephone charges in the EU.

Installation & Registration

When moving into a new home in Greece with a telephone line, you must have the account transferred to your name. If you're planning to move into a property without an existing telephone line, you may want to get one installed, which costs from €30. To have a telephone installed or reconnected, you can visit your local OTE office (in all main towns and on large islands). You need to present your passport or residence permit, proof of your address such as a recent electricity bill, and a copy of your final purchase contract (title deeds) or rental contract. Alternatively, you can phone OTE (☎ 134) or fill out a form online (🖥 www.ote.gr, available in English).

Note that if your property is located in an area with no telephone junction box you will be charged for the installation of one and possibly the installation of telegraph poles as well. This is notoriously slow, as telephone pole workers may only service certain areas once or twice a year! Note also that in some areas there are no new numbers available, in which case you must join a waiting list until one becomes available.

SURVIVAL TIP
If a property doesn't have a telephone line, ensure that you will be able to get one installed within a reasonable time if it's important to you. You may also wish to check whether it's possible to have an ADSL (broadband) connection installed (see page 273).

Dialling Codes

There are no town codes as such in Greece, where each region has its own area code. All numbers now have ten digits and include the area code, which must be dialled whether you're making a local or regional call, or calling Greece from abroad. All fixed telephone numbers start with 2. Codes are listed in telephone directories.

If you're using a service other than OTE, you need to dial the company's prefix, e.g. 1789 for FORTHnet and 1738 for Tellas. For example, to call Athens ☎ 2100-123 456 with FORTHnet you dial ☎ 1789-2100 123 456.

For information on international calls see below.

Line Rental

If you have a private line, the monthly line rental or service charge is around €12 (plus 18 per cent VAT). OTE has a 'Holiday Line Plan' designed for owners of second homes in Greece under which you pay six months line rental and can use the phone for six months a year: 15 days both sides of Easter Sunday, from 1st June to 30th September and from 15th December to 15th January. This scheme offers substantial savings on line rental charges, although you cannot choose the months when your phone is 'active'. Further information can be found on the OTE website (🖳 www.ote.gr).

Call charges

Call charges in Greece are among the highest in the EU, although they've been reduced in recent years and now vary depending on the company; it's best to shop around and use the cheapest one for the call you're making. OTE has several schemes offering substantial savings on calls. For information on services and tariffs, contact FORTHnet (☎ 801-100 1000, 🖳 www.forthnet.gr), OTE (☎ 134, 🖳 www.ote.gr) or Tellas (☎ 13800, 🖳 www.tellas.gr). All three companies have comprehensive websites in English. Note that the call charges are usually quoted in minutes, but in practice the price of calls is based on the number of seconds it lasts. Rates listed below were correct in January 2005.

Local Calls

Local calls cost the same with FORTHnet and Tellas (€0.024 a minute) and Tellas charges €0.023 a minute at weekends. OTE has a very complicated way of calculating call charges and local calls cost €0.026 for the first two minutes with the remainder of the call costing €0.0004 per second!

Long-distance Calls

Long-distance calls with FORTHnet cost €0.05 a minute Mondays to Saturdays and €0.024 a minute on Sundays. Tellas charges €0.052 a minute Mondays to Fridays and €0.044 a minute at weekends. OTE has a flat rate of €0.026 for the first 25 seconds and €0.001 per second after that.

International Calls

Calls to the EU, North America and Australia cost €0.19 per minute with FORTHnet; and €0.202 per minute from Mondays to Fridays and €0.19

a minute at weekends with Tellas. OTE charges €0.0035 per second for calls to the EU and €0.0041 per second for calls to North America and Australia.

It's possible to make direct International Direct Dialling (IDD) calls to most countries from both private and public telephones. Many foreigners buy discount international phone cards, available from kiosks and local shops.

A full list of country codes is shown in the information pages of telephone directories, plus area codes for main cities and tariffs. To make an international call you dial 00, the country code, the area code (without the first zero) and the subscriber's number.

Bills

Bills are sent out by OTE every two months and you're allowed 30 days to pay, while FORTHnet and Tellas bill monthly. VAT at 18 per cent is levied on all charges and itemised bills are provided. Bills can be paid in cash at most banks, at OTE offices, post offices or via a bank account. You can also have your telephone bill paid by direct debit from a bank account, which is advisable for holiday-home owners as it helps ensure that you aren't disconnected for non-payment. Note that banks make a small charge for this. All companies offer the facility to check your bill and telephone usage via the Internet.

Emergency Numbers

Emergency numbers are listed at the front of all telephone directories (white and yellow pages) and are as follows:

Ambulance	☎ 166
Emergency Traveller Assistance	☎ 112
Fire Brigade	☎ 199
Forest Fire	☎ 191
Police	☎ 100
Tourist Police	☎ 171 (Athens)
	☎ 210 171 (outside Athens)

Emergency calls are free. There are free SOS telephones on motorways and main highways. Dial 121 to report telephone or line problems.

Fax

If you're planning to take a fax machine to Greece, check that it will work there or that it can be modified. Most fax machines made for other European countries will operate in Greece, although getting them repaired locally may be impossible unless the same machine is sold there. Faxes can be purchased from OTE and purchased or rented from telephone and business equipment retailers.

Public fax services are provided by main post offices in most towns and by some travel agencies.

Public Telephones

All public telephones in public places in Greece take phone cards (*telekarta*) only, which can be purchased for €3, €5 and €9 from kiosks and newsagents. Calls using a phone card are expensive, although you can buy discount phone cards, which offer substantial savings. To use these cards you first dial an access code and then the subscriber's number. Public phones in bars and hotels may be coin-operated. You can also make calls from an OTE office.

Mobile Telephones

Mobile phones are extremely popular in Greece and services are provided by four companies: Cosmote (a subsidiary of OTE and the largest), Q-Telecom, TIM and Vodafone. There's intense competition so you should shop around and compare prices before buying a phone or signing a contract. Mobile phones work in most parts of Greece except for remote rural or mountainous areas, although Cosmote provides the best coverage outside urban areas. Most GSM mobile phones from European countries work in Greece, but those from North America don't. Mobile phone numbers start with 6.

Internet

Greece isn't particularly well catered for when it comes to internet facilities, although things have improved hugely over the last few years and the authorities have made a concerted effort to get the country online. Most large organisations have websites, many of which are in English. There's a good choice of internet providers and internet cafés are commonplace in large towns and cities and resort areas. The cost of connecting to the internet is generally the same as for local calls, although most companies offer discount services, which allow you to purchase a fixed number of internet access hours per month at a discount.

Broadband (ADSL) has got off to a slow start in Greece and is currently only available in selected areas of the mainland and main islands (e.g. some areas of Crete), although ADSL technology has yet to reach most islands. To find out if ADSL is available in your area, you can phone OTE (☎ 134) or type your phone number into their ADSL page on their website (🖳 www.ote.gr). If you don't have a phone number, use any local number (e.g. your neighbour's). Connection charges and monthly rates vary from one company to another. OTE currently charges €35.90 a month for 24-hour connection at the speed of 512kbps.

TELEVISION & RADIO

Greek television isn't renowned for its quality, although it has improved in recent years and it's generally no worse than the fare dished up in most European countries. Satellite TV reception is generally good in Greece and is popular among the expatriate community (not that its output is much better than Greek TV). Cable TV isn't common in Greece compared with northern European countries and the US, mainly because of the problems and expense of installation to remote areas and islands.

There are several terrestrial TV channels as well as a number of pay-TV channels available, including three state-controlled channels, ET1, ET3 and NET, and the private Antenna, Alpha, Alter, Makedonia TV, Mega and Star channels. Some remote or mountain areas have poor TV reception and only receive one or two channels. Programmes on all stations are a predictable mix of soap-operas (mainly Italian, Latin-American and Spanish), game shows, films and sports. All foreign films and series are broadcast in the original language with Greek subtitles, so you can enjoy re-runs of the soap operas you've come to love! State-controlled channels broadcast from early morning until late at night, while many private channels broadcast around the clock.

In Greece, the TV and radio licence payment is automatically included in your electricity bill. TV programmes are listed in Greek newspapers and TV guides. Some programmes are also listed in English-language newspapers and magazines, along with a selection of satellite TV programmes.

TV Standards

The standards for TV reception in Greece **aren't necessarily the same as in other countries.** Local TVs and video recorders operate on the continental PAL system so TVs operating on the North American NTSC system or the British PAL system won't function in Greece. If you want a TV that will work in Greece and other European countries, and a VCR that will play back videos, you must buy a multi-standard TV and VCR. These are widely available and contain automatic circuitry that can switch from PAL-I (Britain), to PAL-B/G (rest of Europe) to SECAM-L (France). Some multi-standard TVs also handle the North American NTSC standard and have an NTSC-in jack plug connection allowing you to play American videos. Some people opt for two TVs, one to receive local TV programmes and another (i.e. PAL-I or NTSC) to play their favourite videos. A British or US video recorder won't work with a Greek TV unless it's dual-standard or you have it modified at an electrical shop, which costs around €50.

Satellite TV

Greece is well served by satellite TV and there are a number of satellites positioned over Europe carrying over 200 stations broadcasting in a variety of languages. Satellite reception varies around the country and in some areas reception is very poor or even non-existent. You may wish to check this before buying a property, particularly if you plan to live permanently in the area. Satellite services are provided by a number of companies, but beware of those offering 'cheap' viewing cards – these are often illegal copies and can render your satellite box useless if the fake card is detected by the satellite company.

Sky Television

In order to receive Sky television in Greece you need a Sky Digital receiver and a dish. There are two ways to obtain the equipment and Skycard. You can subscribe in the UK or Ireland (either personally if you have an address there or via a friend) and then take the Sky receiver and card to Greece. Note, however, that this is illegal under Sky's terms and conditions – although many people do it! (Sky doesn't send smart cards to overseas viewers as they have the copyright for a British-based audience only.)

Alternatively you can buy the equipment privately and obtain a Sky card in Greece (a number of satellite companies in Greece supply Sky cards). Note that the equipment and Sky cards are much more expensive in Greece. A Sky digital receiver and card costs around €400 plus the monthly subscription, while the card on its own costs around €200 (plus the subscription). To receive Sky TV in Greece a dish must be at least 1.2m in size (costing from around €200).

You must subscribe to Sky to receive most English-language channels (other than Sky News, which isn't scrambled). If you subscribe to the basic (value) pack you will have access to around 100 channels including BBC1, BBC2, ITV1, CH4 and CH5. Various packages are available costing from around GB£13.50 for the basic 'value pack' to GB£41 for the 'Sky World & Family Pack'. The latter offers over 100 channels, including the Movie and Sports channels, along with many interactive services such as Sky News Active. Subscribers receive a coded card 'smart' card (like a credit card) that must be inserted in the receiver (cards are updated every few years to thwart counterfeiters).

Information about Sky installation in the UK and viewing packages can be found on Sky's website (🖳 www.sky.com).

BBC

The BBC's commercial subsidiary, BBC Worldwide Television, broadcasts two 24-hour channels: BBC Prime (general entertainment) and BBC World (24-hour news and information). BBC World is free-to-air and is transmitted via the Eutelsat Hot Bird satellite, while BBC Prime is encrypted and requires a D2-MAC decoder and a smartcard, available on subscription from BBC Prime, PO Box 5054, London W12 0ZY, UK (☎ 020-8433 2221, 🖳 www.bbcprime.co.uk). For more information and a programming guide contact BBC Worldwide Television, Woodlands, 80 Wood Lane, London W12 0TT, UK (☎ 020-8433 2221). A programme guide is also available on the Internet (🖳 www.bbc.co.uk/schedules) and both BBC World and BBC Prime have websites (🖳 www. bbcworld.com and 🖳 www.bbcprime.com).

Satellite Dishes

To receive programmes from any satellite, there must be no obstacles between the satellite and your dish, i.e. no trees, buildings or mountains must obstruct the signal, so check before renting or buying a home. Before buying or erecting a satellite dish, you must check whether you need permission from your landlord or the local authorities. Some towns and buildings (such as apartment blocks) have strict laws regarding the positioning of antennae, although generally owners can mount a dish almost anywhere without receiving complaints. Dishes can usually be mounted in a variety of unobtrusive positions and can also be painted. All new community properties must include a collective antenna to receive television, radio and telephone services, and this also applies to existing communities when one-third of the owners agree.

Video & DVD

Video and DVD films are popular in Greece and there are video and DVD rental shops in towns, large villages and resort areas. Video and DVD films are readily available in Greece; most DVDs have an English-language option and videos are usually in English with Greek subtitles. Most rental shops stock a large selection of English-language films. Latest releases cost around €2 and older films cost from €1.50 per day. If you aren't a permanent resident with proof of your address, you usually need to pay a deposit, e.g. €60 and show your passport. Rental costs can sometimes be reduced by paying a monthly membership fee or a lump sum in advance. If you have a large collection of SECAM or NTSC videotapes, you can buy a multi-standard TV and VCR, or buy a separate TV and video to play back your favourite videos.

Radio

Greece has two state-owned radio channels ET-1 and ET-2. ET-1 broadcasts a brief news programme in English at 7.30am from Mondays to Saturdays and at 9pm from Mondays to Fridays. The frequencies are 91.6 MHz and 105.8 MHz on FM and 729 kHz on the AM waveband. Athens International Radio broadcasts the BBC World Service on 107.1 FM live from 6.30 to 11pm and also has British and American news every hour on the hour.

BBC

The BBC World Service is broadcast on short wave on several frequencies simultaneously (e.g. 12095, 9760, 9410, 7325, 6195, 5975 and 3955 Khz) and you can usually receive a good signal on one of them. The signal strength varies depending on where you live, the time of day and year, the power and positioning of your receiver, and atmospheric conditions. All BBC radio stations, including the World Service, are also available via the Astra satellites. The BBC publishes a monthly magazine, *BBC On Air*, containing comprehensive information about BBC world service radio and television programmes. It's available on subscription from the BBC: On Air Magazine, Room 207 NW, Bush House, Strand, London WC2B 4PH, UK (☎ 020-7240 4899, ✉ on.air.magazine@bbc.co.uk).

Satellite Radio

If you have satellite TV you can also receive many radio stations via your satellite receiver. For example, BBC Radio 1, 2, 3, 4 and 5, BBC World Service, Sky Radio, Virgin 1215 and many foreign (i.e. non-English) stations are broadcast via the Astra satellites. Satellite radio stations are listed in British satellite TV magazines such as the *Satellite Times*. If you're interested in receiving radio stations from further afield, the *World Radio TV Handbook* (Watson-Guptill Publications) may be of interest.

TIME DIFFERENCE

Greece is two hours ahead of Greenwich Mean Time (GMT) and three hours ahead of Britain during 'daylight-saving time', which runs from the last Sunday in March to the last Sunday in October. Time changes are announced in local newspapers and on radio and TV stations. When making international telephone calls to Greece, check the time difference with your home country, which is usually shown in phone books and diaries. The time difference between Greece at noon during 'daylight-saving time' and some major international cities is shown below:

LONDON	CAPE TOWN	BOMBAY	TOKYO	NEW YORK
9am	11am	2.30pm	11pm	4am

UTILITIES

Immediately after buying or renting a property (unless utilities are included in the rent), you should arrange for the meter (if applicable) to be read, the contract (e.g. electricity, gas or water) to be registered in your name and the service switched on (e.g. mains gas).

Always check in advance that all bills have been paid by the previous owner, otherwise you will be liable for any debts outstanding.

This usually entails a visit to the company's office, although you may be able to register online or by telephone. If you visit the utility company's office, you must take some form of identification (e.g. your passport or residence permit) and the contract and bills paid by the previous owner. Note that water connection is usually arranged at the local town hall. If you've purchased a home in Greece, the estate agent may arrange for the utilities to be transferred to your name or go with you to the offices.

If you're a non-resident owner, you should also give details of your foreign address in case there are any problems requiring your attention, such as your bank failing to pay the bills. You may also need to pay a deposit.

Electricity, gas and water connections and supplies are covered in this section. See also **Heating & Air-conditioning** on page 254 and **Sewerage** on page 287.

Electricity

Electricity in Greece is mainly provided by *Dimmossia Steria Ilektrismou* (DEH or PPC in English), Greece's largest company, which in theory no longer has a monopoly (despite deregulation it's still the only provider in many parts of Greece). DEH can be contacted on ☎ 10500 and 🖳 www.dei.gr (also in English).

Power Supply

The electricity supply in Greece is 220–240 volts AC with a frequency of 50 Hertz (cycles). Power cuts are frequent in many areas of Greece (almost daily) and last from a few micro-seconds (just long enough to crash a computer) to a few hours. If you use a computer, it's sensible to fit an uninterrupted power supply (UPS – costing around €150) or use a laptop with a battery, which allows you time to save your work and shut down your computer after a power failure. If you live in an area where cuts are frequent and rely on electricity for your livelihood, you may need to install a back-up generator.

In remote rural areas of Greece you will need to install a generator if you want electricity, as there's no mains electricity, although some people make do with gas and oil lamps (and without television and other modern conveniences). Note that in some developments, water is provided by electric pump, so if your electricity supply fails, your water supply is also cut off.

Wiring Standards

Most modern properties, e.g. less than 20 years old, have good electrical installations. However, if you buy an old home you may need to rewire it or install electricity from scratch. You should ensure that the electricity installations are in good condition well in advance of moving house, as it can take some time to get a new meter installed or to be reconnected.

Plugs, Fuses & Bulbs

Plugs: Depending on where you currently live, you will usually need new plugs or a lot of adapters. Greece uses two-pin plugs, with or without earth points, as in many other European countries. Plug adapters can be purchased in Greece, although it's wise to bring some adapters with you, plus extension cords and multi-plug extensions that can be fitted with local plugs. There's often a shortage of electric points in homes, with perhaps just one per room (including the kitchen), so multi-plug adapters may be essential.

Small low-wattage electrical appliances such as table lamps, small TVs and computers, don't require an earth. However, plugs with an earth must always be used for high-wattage appliances such as fires, kettles, washing machines and refrigerators. Electrical appliances that are earthed have a three-core wire and must never be used with a two-pin plug without an earth socket.

 Always make sure that a plug is correctly and securely wired, as bad wiring can be fatal.

Fuses: In modern properties, fuses are of the circuit breaker type. When there's a short circuit or the system has been overloaded, a circuit breaker is tripped and the power supply is cut. If your electricity fails, you should suspect a fuse of tripping off, particularly if you've just switched on an electrical appliance (you may hear the power switch off). Before reconnecting the power, switch off any high-power appliances such as a stove, washing machine or dishwasher. Make sure you know where the trip switches are located and keep a torch handy so you can find them in the dark.

Bulbs: Light bulbs in Greece tend to be of the Edison type with a screw fitting, although many older properties have fittings that accept bulbs with a bayonet fitting. If you have lamps requiring bayonet bulbs you should bring some with you, as they cannot easily be purchased in Greece. You can, however, buy adapters to convert from bayonet to screw fitting (or vice versa). Bulbs for non-standard electrical appliances (i.e. appliances that aren't made for the Greek market) such as refrigerators and sewing machines may not be available locally.

Converters & Transformers

If you have electrical equipment rated at 110 volts AC (for example, from the US) you will require a converter or a step-down transformer to convert the 220 volt supply. However, some electrical appliances are fitted with a 110/220-volt switch. Check for the switch, which may be inside the casing, and make sure that it's switched to 220 volts **before** connecting it to the power supply. Converters can be used for heating appliances, but transformers are required for motorised appliances. Total the wattage of the devices you intend to connect to a transformer and make sure that its power rating **exceeds** this sum.

Generally, small, high-wattage, electrical appliances, such as kettles, toasters, heaters, and irons need large transformers. Motors in large appliances such as cookers, refrigerators, washing machines, dryers and dishwashers will need replacing or fitting with a large transformer. In most cases it's simpler to buy new appliances locally, which are of good quality and reasonably priced. Note also that the dimensions of cookers, microwave ovens, refrigerators, washing machines, dryers and dishwashers purchased abroad may differ from those in Greece, so they may not fit into a Greek kitchen.

An additional problem with some electrical equipment is the frequency rating, which, in some countries, e.g. the US, is designed to run at 60 Hertz (Hz) and not Europe's 50Hz. Electrical equipment **without** a motor is generally unaffected by the drop in frequency to 50Hz (except televisions). Equipment with a motor may run with a 20 per cent drop in speed, but automatic washing machines, cookers, electric clocks, record players and tape recorders must be converted from 60Hz to 50Hz. To find out, look at the label on the back of the equipment. If it says 50/60Hz, there shouldn't be a problem; if it says 60Hz, you can try it, **but first ensure that the voltage is correct as outlined above.** Bear in mind that the transformers and motors of electrical devices designed to run at 60Hz will run hotter at 50Hz, so make sure that apparatus has sufficient space around it for cooling.

Connection & Registration

The cost of electricity connection and the installation of a meter is usually between €100 and €600, although it varies considerably depending on the region, power supply and type of meter installed.

If you plan to buy a property with no electricity supply, bear in mind that the cost of connection can be very high. If the property is near a transformer, connection costs from €600. If there isn't a transformer nearby, the electricity company will install one and charge you for it, which can cost thousands of euros.

Registration: When you buy a property with an electricity supply already installed, you should go to the nearest DEH office to register the contract and supply in your name. DEH recommends that you (or your representative) go to the office with the previous owner so that the old contract can be cancelled and the new one signed at the same time. This ensures you aren't responsible for paying for electricity used by the previous owner.

You need to present the following documents: a previous electricity bill or the electricity service number (found on the meter); a rental contract or final purchase contract (title deeds); personal identification; your tax identity number; and the property's electrical layout (in the form of a certificate issued by an electrician). Note that if the present certificate was issued more than 14 years ago, you will need a new one.

Tariffs

Electricity in Greece is currently the cheapest in Western Europe. The tariff charged depends on your power rating, how the electricity is produced and when you use it. Power rating tariffs are €1.70 per kW per month so if your power rating is 3.3kW your monthly standing charge is 3.3 x €1.70 (€5.61). The standing charge is payable irrespective of whether you use any electricity during the billing period.

The actual consumption is charged per kW and the rate varies depending on the time of day electricity is used. Consumption is divided into three daily tariffs, known as 'loads'. 'Peak load' is from 10am to 2pm and 6 to 9pm from October to April, and from 10am to 2pm for the rest of the year. 'Low load' is from 1 to 8am from October to April, and from midnight to 8am for the rest of the year. 'Immediate load' is charged at all other times. On the mainland and interconnected islands, the charge ranges from €0.03 to €0.066. On non-interconnected islands, the charge ranges from €0.064 to €0.082. A couple living in a home with electric water heating can expect to spend around €70 every two months on electricity.

Night Tariff: To save on electricity costs, you can switch to night tariff and run high-consumption appliances overnight, e.g. storage heaters, water heater, dishwasher and washing machine, which can be operated by a timer. If you use a lot of water, it's better to have a large water heater (e.g. 150 litres) and heat water overnight. If you use electricity for your heating, you can install night-storage heaters that run on the cheaper night tariff. The night tariff rate provides substantial reductions and generally runs from 11pm to 7am, although in some areas it's from midnight to 8am. Connection to the night tariff costs €29.35. Bills are subject to VAT at 8 per cent.

Meters

All detached homes have their own electricity meters. Meters for apartment blocks or community properties may be installed in a basement or in a meter 'cupboard' under the stairs or outside a group of properties. You should have free access to your meter and should be able read it (some meters don't have a window to allow you to read the consumption).

Bills

Electricity consumption is estimated three times a year, estimates being based on the previous year's consumption. Meters in urban areas are read three times a year, whereas those in remote areas may only be read once or twice a year. You receive a bill every two months: one for estimated consumption and the following one for actual consumption. If your estimated bill is higher than your actual bill, credit is given on your next bill.

You should learn to read your electricity bill (note that it's in Greek and complicated to decipher) and check your consumption. Bills must be paid within 30 days of receipt. If you don't pay your electricity bill your electricity may be cut off. Repeated failure to pay leads to the cancellation of the contract.

Paying your bills by direct debit from a Greek bank account is advisable if you own a holiday home in Greece, as you may not be present when you need to make payments. Bills should then be paid automatically on presentation to your bank, although some banks cannot be relied on 100 per cent. Both the electricity company and your bank should notify you when they've sent or paid a bill. Alternatively, you can pay bills at post offices, participating shops (e.g. some chemists), local banks (listed on the bill), at some cash machines or at DEH offices (in cash only). Payment for your radio and TV licence is included in your electricity bill.

Gas

Mains gas is available only in Athens; in other towns and rural areas you must use gas bottles. Bottled gas costs around €15 for a 12.5kg bottle, available from supermarkets, garages and refill centres in large towns and on most islands. A 12.5kg bottle lasts an average family around a month when used just for cooking. In rural areas, many people use as many gas appliances as possible, e.g. for cooking, hot water and heating. You can have a combined gas hot water and heating system (providing background heat) installed, which is relatively inexpensive as well as being cheap to run. Bear in mind that gas bottles are heavy and have a habit of running out at the most inconvenient times, so keep a spare bottle handy and make sure you know how to change them (get the previous owner or a neighbour to show you).

Water

Water, or rather the lack of it, is a major concern in Greece and the price paid for all those sunny days. Shortages are exacerbated by poor infrastructure (much is lost from leaking pipes), wastage due to poor irrigation methods, and the huge influx of visitors to resort areas where the local population swells five to tenfold during the summer tourist season (the hottest and driest period of the year). **As in all hot countries, water is a precious resource and not something simply to pour down the drain!** Contact the local town hall for information about the local water supply and to transfer bills to your name. Water is particularly expensive in Greece, where bills increase frequently.

Quality

Water is supposedly safe to drink in all urban areas, although it can be of poor quality (possibly brown or rust coloured), full of chemicals and taste awful. Many residents prefer to drink bottled water. In rural areas, water may be extracted from mountain springs and taste excellent, although the quality standards applied in cities are usually ignored and it may be of poor quality. Water in rural areas may also be contaminated by fertilisers and nitrates used in farming, and by salt water in some coastal areas. If you're in any doubt about the quality of your water, you should have it analysed.

Note that, although boiling water will kill any bacteria, it won't remove any toxic substances contained in it.

You can install filtering, cleansing and softening equipment to improve its quality or a water purification unit to provide drinking water. Note, however, that purification systems operating on the reverse osmosis system waste three times as much water as they produce. Obtain expert advice before installing a system, as not all are effective.

Restrictions

During water shortages, local municipalities may restrict water consumption or cut off supplies altogether for days at a time. You can forget about watering the garden or washing your car unless you have a private water supply. If a water company needs to cut off your supply, e.g. to carry out maintenance work on pipes or installations, it will usually notify you in advance so that you can store water for cooking. In some areas, water shortages can create low water pressure, resulting in insufficient water to take a bath or shower and sometimes no water at all on the upper floors of apartment buildings.

Note that in some developments, water is provided by electric pump and therefore if your electricity is cut off, so is your water supply. In communal developments, the tap to turn water on or off is usually located outside properties, so if your water goes off suddenly you should check that someone hasn't switched it off by mistake. In areas where water shortages are common, water tankers deliver to homes – some properties don't have a mains supply at all, but a storage tank that's filled periodically by a tanker.

Water shortages are common in many parts of Greece, particularly in Thessaly, remote villages and on some islands, e.g. the Cyclades.

Supply

One of the most important tasks before buying a home abroad is to investigate the reliability of the local water supply (over a number of years) and the cost. Ask your prospective neighbours and other local residents for information. In most towns and cities, supplies are adequate, although there may be cuts in summer. Dowsing or divining (finding water by holding a piece of forked wood) is as accurate as anything devised by modern science (it has an 80 per cent success rate) and a good dowser can also estimate the water's yield and purity with 80 or 90 per cent accuracy. Before buying land without a water supply, engage an experienced dowser with a successful track record to try to find water.

Wells: Many rural properties rely on wells for their water supply, but bear in mind that there are numerous disadvantages. For example, most well water is undrinkable and suitable for washing only; wells often dry up in the summer after which the new water may be tainted for weeks; well water may be tainted with silt and sediment after bad weather; and if the well pump is run by electricity, you won't have a water supply during power cuts. If you have a well, make sure that you have access to an alternative supply of water, but note that you may have no rights to extract water from a channel running alongside your land.

Storage Tanks

If you have a detached house or villa, you can reduce your water costs by collecting and storing rainwater, and by having a storage tank installed. Tanks can be roof mounted or installed underground; the latter are cheaper and can be any size but require an electric pump. Check whether a property has a water storage tank or whether you can install one. Most modern properties have storage tanks and these are usually large enough to last a family of four around a week or even longer with careful use. It's also possible to use recycled water from baths, showers, kitchens and apparatus such as washing machines and dishwashers, to flush toilets or water a garden.

Hot Water

Water heating in apartments may be provided by a central heating source for the whole building, or apartments may have their own water heaters. Many holiday homes have quite small water boilers, which are inadequate for more than two people. If you install your own water heater, it should have a capacity of at least 75 litres (sufficient for two people). If you need to install a water heater (or fit a larger one), you should consider the merits of both electric and bottled gas heaters.

A 75l electric water boiler usually takes between 60 and 90 minutes to heat water to 40 degrees in winter. A gas flow-through water heater is more expensive to purchase and install than an electric water boiler but gives you unlimited hot water immediately whenever you want it and there are no standing charges. Make sure that a gas heater has a capacity of 10 to 16 litres per minute if you want it for a shower. **A gas water heater with a permanent flame may use up to 50 per cent more gas than**

one without one. A resident family with regular water consumption is better off with an electric heater operating on the night tariff, while non-residents using a property for short periods will find a self-igniting gas heater more economical. Solar energy (see page 256) can also be used to provide hot water and many modern homes have a combined solar/electric water heater.

Costs

Water is a local matter in Greece and is usually controlled by local municipalities, many of which have their own wells and springs.

Connection: The cost of connection to the local water supply varies considerably depending on the distance between the supply and the property, but you should expect to pay from €500 to €800. Connection to the supply for rural homes situated some distance from the mains supply can cost more than €1,500. Note, however, that many homes, particularly on islands and in remote areas, don't have mains supply water and have to rely on wells and springs.

Usage: In most areas there's a standing quarterly charge, e.g. €15, or a monthly charge for a minimum consumption. Water use is charged per cubic metre (m3) and the price rises the more water you use. A couple living in a small house can expect to pay around €40 a quarter for water, although the cost is considerably higher if you water the garden or have a pool. Note that water is very expensive on Hydra where all fresh water is delivered by boat daily (weather permitting). VAT is levied at 18 per cent on all tariffs.

Bills

Bills are generally sent out quarterly and can be paid by direct debit (the best option for holiday-home owners) at banks, post offices and water company offices.

Sewerage

Greece has one of the southern Mediterranean's better records for water treatment and as a consequence, most beaches have blue flag status awards and the sea around Greece is among the world's cleanest. It's illegal to dump untreated waste water into the sea or rivers and in recent years, the government has taken some highly publicised legal action against hotels for polluting the sea with untreated sewage. Most areas on the mainland and some of the larger islands have sewage treatment plants.

Rural areas and smaller islands tend to rely on cesspits or septic tanks, which when functioning properly, gradually filter the waste water into the surrounding earth. Cesspits need emptying every so often depending on the number of people using a house – usually once a year for a household occupied by four people all year-round – which costs from €100 to €200.

APPENDICES

Appendix A: USEFUL ADDRESSES

Embassies & Consulates

Embassies are located in the capital Athens; some countries also have consulates in other cities or resorts (British consulates are listed on page 295). Embassies and consulates are listed in the yellow pages. Note that some countries have more than one office; therefore before writing or calling in person you should telephone to confirm that you have the correct office.

Albania: 7 Dekialeri Street, 105 37 Filothei (☎ 210 687 6200).

Algeria: 14 Vas. Konstantinou Street, 116 35 Athens (☎ 210 756 4191).

Argentina: 59,Vas. Sofias Avenue, 115 21 Athens (☎ 210 722 4451).

Armenia: 159, Syngrou Avenue, 171 21 N. Smyrni (☎ 210 934 5727).

Australia: 37, D. Soutsou & 24, An. Tsocha Streets, 115 21 Athens (☎ 210 645 0404, 🖥 www.ausemb.gr).

Austria: 26, Alexandras Avenue, 106 83 Athens (☎ 210 825 7230).

Belgium: 3 Sekeri Street, 106 71 Athens (☎ 210 361 7886).

Brazil: 14 Platia Philikis Eterias Street, 106 73 Athens (☎ 210 721 3039).

Bulgaria: 33 Kallari Street, 154 52 P. Psychiko (☎ 210 647 8105).

Canada: 4 Gennadiou Street, 115 21 Athens (☎ 210 727 3400, 🖥 www.athens.gc.ca).

Chile: 25 Vas Sofias Avenue, 106 74 Athens (☎ 210 725 2574).

China: 2A Krinon Street, 154 52 P. Psychiko (☎ 210 672 3282).

Croatia: 4 Tzavela Street, 154 51 N. Psychiko (☎ 210 677 7059).

Cuba: 5 Sofokleous Street, 152 37 Filothei (☎ 210 685 5550).

Cyprus: 16 Irodotou Street, 106 75 Athens (☎ 210 723 7883).

Czech Republic: 6 Seferis Street, 154 52 P. Psychiko (☎ 210 671 3755, 🖥 www.mfa.cz/athens).

Denmark: 11 Vas Sofias Avenue, 106 71 Athens (☎ 210 360 8315).

Egypt: 3 Vas Sofias Avenue, 106 71 Athens (☎ 210 361 8612).

Estonia: 48-50 Patr Ioakim Street, 106 76 Athens (☎ 210 722 9803).

Finland: 1 Eratosthenou Street, 116 35 Athens (☎ 210 701 1775).

Former Yugoslav Republic of Macedonia (FYRM): 4 Papadiamandi Street, 154 52 P. Psychiko (☎ 210 674 9585).

France: 7 Vas Sofias Avenue, 106 71 Athens (☎ 210 339 1000, 💻 www.ambafrance-gr.org).

Germany: 3 Karaoli-Dimitriou Street, 106 75 Athens (☎ 210 728 5111, 💻 www.athen.diplo.de).

Hungary: 16 Kalvou Street, 154 52 P. Psychiko (☎ 210 675 2300).

India: 3 Kleanthous Street, 106 74 Athens (☎ 210 721 6227).

Indonesia: 99 Marathonodromon Street, 154 52 P. Psychiko (☎ 210 676 6418).

Iran: 16 Kallari Street, 154 52 P. Psychiko (☎ 210 674 1937).

Iraq: 4 Mazaraki Street, 154 52 P. Psychiko (☎ 210 672 2330).

Ireland: 7 Vas Konstantinou Avenue,106 74 Athens (☎ 210 723 2771).

Israel: 1 Marathonodromon Street, 154 52 P. Psychiko (☎ 210 671 9530).

Italy: 2 Sekeri Street, 106 74 Athens (☎ 210 361 7260).

Japan: 2-4 Messogion Avenue, 115 27 Athens (☎ 210 775 8101).

Jordan: 21 Papadiamandi Street, 154 52 P. Psychiko (☎ 210 674 4161).

Korea (South): 124 Kifissias Avenue, 115 26 Athens (☎ 210 698 4080).

Kuwait: 27 Marathonodromon Street, 154 52 P. Psychiko (☎ 210 647 3593).

Lebanon: 6 25th Martiou Street, 154 52 P. Psychiko (☎ 210 675 5873).

Lithuania: 49 Vas Sofias Avenue, 106 75 Athens (☎ 210 729 4356).

Luxembourg: 11-13 Skoufa Street, 106 73 Athens (☎ 210 725 6400).

Malta: 63 Vas Sofias Avenue, 115 21 Athens (☎ 210 725 8153).

Mexico: 14 Philikis Etairias Square, 106 73 Athens (☎ 210 729 4780).

Morocco: 14 Mouson Street, 154 52 P. Psychiko (☎ 210 647 4209).

The Netherlands: 5-7 Vas. Konstantinou Avenue, 106 74 Athens (☎ 210 725 4900).

New Zealand: 268 Kifissias Avenue, 152 32 Halandri (☎ 210 687 4700).

Norway: 23 Vas Sofias Avenue, 106 74 Athens (☎ 210 724 6173, 🖳 www.norway.gr).

Pakistan: 6 Loukianou Street, 106 75 Athens (☎ 210 729 0214).

Panama: 129 Praxitelous & II Merarchias Streets, 185 35 Piraeus (☎ 210 428 6441).

Paraguay: 2 Alopekis Street, 106 75 Athens (☎ 210 721 0669).

Peru: 2 Semitelou Street, 115 28 Athens (☎ 210 779 2761).

Philippines: 26 Antheon Street, 154 52 P. Psychiko (☎ 210 672 1883).

Poland: 22 Hrissanthemon Street, 154 52 P. Psychiko (☎ 210 677 8260, 🖳 www.poland-embassy.gr).

Portugal: 23 Vas Sofias Avenue, 106 74 Athens (☎ 210 729 0096).

Romania: 7 Em Benaki Street, 154 52 P. Psychiko (☎ 210 677 4035).

Russia: 28 N Lytra Street, 154 52 P Psychiko (☎ 210 672 5235).

Saudi Arabia: 71 Marathonodromon Street, 154 52 P. Psychiko (☎ 210 671 6911).

Slovakia: 4 Seferi Street, 154 52 P. Psychiko (☎ 210 677 1980).

Slovenia: 10 Mavili Street, 154 52 P. Psychiko (☎ 210 677 5683).

South Africa: 60 Kifissias Street, 151 25 Maroussi (☎ 210 610 6645, 🖳 www.southafrica.gr).

Spain: 21 Dionyslou Aeropagitou Street, 117 42 Athens (☎ 210 921 3123).

Sweden: 7 Vas Konstantinou Street, 106 74 Athens (☎ 210 726 6100).

Switzerland: 2 Iasiou Street, 115 21 Athens (☎ 210 723 0364, 🖳 www.eda.admin.ch/athens).

Syria: 61 Diamantidou Street, 154 52 P. Psychiko (☎ 210 672 5577).

Taiwan: 57 Marathonodromon Street, 154 52 P. Psychiko (☎ 210 677 6750).

Thailand: 23 Marathonodromon Street, 154 52 P. Psychiko (☎ 210 671 0155).

Tunisia: 2 Antheon & Marathonodromon Street, 154 52 P. Psychiko (☎ 210 671 7590).

Turkey: 8 Vas. Georgiou II St, 106 74 Athens (☎ 210 726 3000).

Ukraine: 2-4 Stefanou Delta Street, 152 37 Filothei (☎ 210 680 0230, 🖳 www.ukrembas.gr).

United Kingdom: 1 Ploutarhou Street, 106 75 Athens (☎ 210 727 2600, 🖳 www.british-embassy.gr).

United States of America: 91 Vas Sofias Avenue, 101 60 Athens (☎ 2107-212 951, 🖳 www.usembassy.gr).

Uruguay: 1c Lykavitou Street, 106 72 Athens (☎ 210 360 2635).

Venezuela: 19 Marathonodromon Street, 154 52 P. Psychiko (☎ 210 672 1246).

British Consulates

Corfu: British Consulate, 2 Alexandra Avenue, 491 00 Corfu (☎ 266 103 0055, ✉ corfu@british-consulate.gr).

Crete: British Consulate, 16 Papa-Alexandrou Street, 712 02 Heraklion (☎ 281 022 4012, ✉ crete@british-consulate.gr).

Kos: Honorary Vice Consulate, 8 Annetas Laoumtzi, Aghia Marina, 853 00 Kos (☎ 224 202 1549, ✉ kos@british-consulate.gr).

Patras: Honorary Vice Consulate, 2 Votsi Street, 262 21 Patras (☎ 261 027 7329).

Rhodes: Honorary Consulate, 3 Pavlou Mela Street, PO Box 47, 851 00 Rhodes (☎ 224 102 2055, ✉ rhodes@british-consulate.gr).

Syros: Honorary Vice Consulate, 8 Akti Petrou Ralli Street, 841 00 Ermoupolis (☎ 228 108 2232).

Thessaloniki: Honorary Consulate, 21 Aristotelous Street, 546 24 Salonika (☎ 231 028 3868, ✉ thessaloniki@british-consulate.gr).

Zakynothos: Honorary Vice Consulate, 5 Foskolos Street, 291 00 Zakynthos (☎ 269 502 2906, ✉ zakynthos@british-consulate.gr).

Greek Embassies Abroad

Australia: 9, Turrana Street, Yarralumla, Canberra A.C.T. 26000 (☎ 2-733158/733011, ✉ greekemb@greekembassy-au.org).

Canada: 80 MacLaren St., Ottawa, Ontario K2P 0K6 (☎ 613-238 6271-3, 💻 www.greekembassy.ca).

Ireland: 1 Upper Pembroke Street, Dublin 2 (☎ 3531-676 7254, ✉ dubgremb@eircom.net).

New Zealand: 5-7 Willeston Street, 10th Floor Wellington (☎ 4-4737775-6, ✉ info@greece.org.nz).

South Africa: 1003 Church Street, Corner Athlone, 0028 Hatfield, Pretoria (☎ 12-3427136-7, ✉ embgrsaf@global.co.za).

UK: 1A Holland Park, London W11 3TP (☎ 020-7221 6467, 💻 www.greekembassy.org.uk).

US: 2221 Massachusetts Ave NW, Washington, 20008 (☎ 202-939 5800, 💻 www.greekembassy.org).

Major Property Exhibitions

Property exhibitions are common in the UK and Ireland, and are popular with prospective property buyers who can get a good idea of what's available in a particular area and make contact with estate agents and developers. Property exhibitions tend to have a smaller choice of properties in Greece compared with some other countries and often only the main islands and resort areas are represented. Below is a list of the main exhibition organisers in the UK and Ireland. Note that you may be charged an admission fee.

A Place in the Sun Live! (☎ 0870-272 8800, 💻 www.aplace inthesunlive.com). 'A Place in the Sun Live!' exhibitions are currently held twice a year in London.

Home Buyer (☎ 020-7069 5000, 💻 www.homebuyer.co.uk). Annual exhibition held in London.

Homes Overseas (☎ 020-7002 8300, 🖥 www.homesover seas.co.uk). Homes Overseas are the largest organisers of international property exhibitions and stage over 30 exhibitions annually throughout Britain and Ireland (plus a few abroad).

International Property Show (☎ 01962-736712, 🖥 www.inter-nationalpropertyshow.com). The International Property Show is held several times a year in Dublin, London and Manchester.

World Class Homes (☎ 0800-731 4713 (UK only), 🖥 www.worldclasshomes.co.uk). Exhibitions organised by World Class Homes are held in small venues around Britain and feature mainly UK property developers.

World of Property (☎ 01323-726040, 🖥 www.outbound publishing.com). The World of Property magazine publishers (see **Appendix B**) also organise three large property exhibitions a year, two in the south of England and one in the north.

APPENDIX B: FURTHER READING

English-language Newspapers & Magazines

Aegean Times (💻 www.aegeantimes.net). Weekly newspaper with news from Greece and Turkey, and discussion forums.

A Place in the Sun (💻 www.aplaceinthesunmag.co.uk). Monthly property magazine.

Athens News, 3 Christou Lada Street, 102 37 Athens (☎ 210 333 3555, 💻 www.athensnews.gr). Weekly newspaper published on Fridays.

Greece, Merricks Media Ltd, Cambridge House South, Henry Street, Bath BA1 1JT, Uk (☎ 01225 786835, 💻 www.greece magazine.co.uk). Lifestyle magazine including Greek holidays and properties, published eight times a year.

Homes Overseas, Blendon Communications, 1st Floor, East Poultry Avenue, London EC1A 9PT, UK (☎ 020 7002 8300, 💻 www.homesoverseas.co.uk). Monthly property magazine.

Homes Worldwide, Merricks Media Ltd, Cambridge House South, Henry Street, Bath BA1 1JT, UK (☎ 01225 86800, 💻 www.homesworldwide.co.uk). Monthly property magazine.

International Homes, 3 St Johns Court, Moulsham Street, Chelmsford, Essex CM2 0JD, UK (☎ 01245-358877, 💻 www. internationalhomes.com). Bi-monthly property magazine.

Odyssey (💻 www.odyssey.gr). Bi-monthly magazine featuring political, travel and cultural articles.

Symi Visitor (💻 www.symivisitor.com). Monthly magazine with information about Symi island (Dodecanese).

World of Property, 1 Commercial Road, Eastbourne, East Sussex BN21 3XQ, UK (☎ 01323-726040, ✉ outbounduk@ aol.com). Quarterly property magazine.

Books

The books listed below are just a small selection of the many written for visitors to Greece. Note that some titles may be out of print, but may still be obtainable from book shops and libraries. Books prefixed with an asterisk (*) are recommended by the author.

General Tourist Guides

*AA Baedeker Greece (AA Publishing)

AA Essential Greece, Mike Gerrard (AA Publishing)

Athens (Insight Pocket Guide)

*Athens (Time Out)

Blue Guide: Greece, Robin Barber (A&C Black)

*Crete, Victoria Kyriakopoulos (Lonely Planet)

*DK Travel Guides: Greece, Athens & The Mainland (Dorling Kindersley)

*Eperon's Guide to the Greek Islands, Arthur Eperon (Pan)

Fodor's Greece (Fodor's)

Frommers Greece (Macmillan Travel)

*Greek Island Hopping, Frewin Poffley (Thomas Cook)

*Greece: Off the Beaten Track, Marc Dubin (Moorland)

Ionian Islands, John Gill & Nick Edwards (Rough Guides)

*Insight Guide Crete (APA Publications)

*Insight Guide Greece (APA Publications)

Landscapes of Corfu, Noel Rochford (Sunflower Books)

Landscapes of Samos, Brian & Eileen Anderson (Sunflower Books)

Landscapes of Western Crete, Johnnie Godfrey & Elizabeth Karslake (Sunflower Books)

Let's Go Greece & Turkey including Cyprus (Pan)

*Lonely Planet Greece, Caroline Bain & Others (Lonely Planet)

*Lonely Planet Greek Islands, David Willett (Lonely Planet)

Nelles Guide: Greece (Nelles Guides)

*The Rough Guide to Corfu, John Gill (Penguin)

*The Rough Guide to Crete, John Fisher & Geoff Garvey (Rough Guides)

*The Rough Guide to Greece, Mark Ellingham & Others (Rough Guides)

*The Rough Guide to the Dodecanese & the East Aegean, Marc Dubin (Rough Guides)

*The Rough Guide to the Greek Islands, Mark Ellingham & Others (Rough Guides)

Top 10 Athens (Dorling Kindersley)

A Visit to Greece, Peter & Connie Roop (Heinemann)

Visitor's Guide to Athens & Peloponnese, Brian & Eileen Anderson (Moorland)

*Which Guide to Greece & The Greek Islands (Penguin)

Travel Literature

*Ebdon's Odyssey, John Ebdon

The Greek Islands, Lawrence Durrell (Penguin)

*A House in Corfu, Emma Tennant (Vintage)

*An Island Apart, Sarah Wheeler (Abacus)

It's All Greek to Me!, John Mole (Nicolas Brealey Publishing)

A Literary Companion to Travel in Greece, Richard Stoneman (OUP)

*My Family and Other Animlas, Gerald Durrell (Penguin)

The Olive Grove: Travels in Greece, Katherine Kizilos (Lonely Planet)

Reflections on a Marine Venus, Lawrence Durrell (Penguin)

*The Summer of my Greek Taverna, Tom Stone (Simon & Schuster International)

*Stars Over Paxos, John Gill (Pavilion)

Travels in the Morea, Nikos Kazantzakis

Under Mount Ida: A Journey into Crete, Oliver Birch (Ashford)

*The Unwritten Places, Tim Salmon (Lycabettus)

Miscellaneous

Architecture of the World: Greece (Herron Books)

A Concise History of Greece, Richard Clogg (Cambridge UP)

**Buying a Home Abroad, David Hampshire (Survival Books)

The Foods of Greece, Aglaia Kremezi & Martin Brigdale (Stewart, Tabori & Chang)

Greece by Rail, Zana Katsikis (Bradt)

**Living & Working Abroad, David Hampshire (Survival Books)

*Modern Greece: A Short History, C. M. Woodhouse (Faber & Faber)

*The Most Beautiful Villages of Greece and the Greek Islands, Mark Ottway & Hugh Palmer (Thames & Hudson)

The Mountains of Greece: A Walkers' Guide, Tim Salmon (Cicerone)

Pocket Menu Reader Greece (Langenscheidt)

*A Traveller's History of Greece, Timothy Boatswain & Colin Nicholson (Windrush)

*Trekking in Greece, Marc S. Dubin (Lonely Planet)

Wild Flowers of Greece, George Sfikas (Efstathiadís)

*The Wines of Greece, Miles Lambert-Gócs (Faber & Faber)

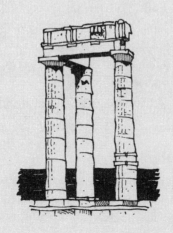

APPENDIX C: USEFUL WEBSITES

The following list contains some of the many websites dedicated to Greece as well as websites containing information about a number of countries. Websites about particular aspects of life and work in Greece are mentioned in the relevant chapters.

Greek Websites

American Women's Association (⌨ www.awog.gr). Information about the association as well as useful links and information about living in Athens.

Athens Survival Guide (⌨ www.athensguide.com). A wealth of useful information and tips about living in Athens.

Filoglossia (⌨ www.xanthi.ilsp.gr/filog). Internet guide to learning Greek.

Go Greece (⌨ http://gogreece.about.com). Useful information about Greece for visitors and residents.

Greece Magazine (⌨ www.greecemagazine.co.uk). Includes useful discussion forum on aspects of buying property and living in Greece.

Greek Islands (⌨ www.greecegreekislands.com). A wealth of useful information about the islands.

Hellas Guide (⌨ www.hellas-guide.com). Comprehensive tourist guide to Greece.

Tourist Office (⌨ www.gnto.gr). Official Greek tourist office website.

Travel Page (⌨ www.travelpage.gr). Useful information about travelling to and around Greece.

General Websites

ExpatBoards (⌨ www.expatboards.com). The mega website for expatriates, with popular discussion boards and special areas for Britons, Americans, expatriate taxes, and other important issues.

Escape Artist (💻 www.escapeartist.com). An excellent website and probably the most comprehensive, packed with resources, links and directories covering most expatriate destinations. You can also subscribe to the free monthly online expatriate magazine, Escape from America.

Expat Exchange (💻 www.expatexchange.com). Reportedly the largest online community for English-speaking expatriates, provides a series of articles on relocation and also a question and answer facility through its expatriate network.

Expat Forum (💻 www.expatforum.com): Provides interesting cost of living comparisons as well as seven European Union country-specific forums and chats (Belgium, the Czech Republic, France, Germany, the Netherlands, Spain and the UK).

Expat World (💻 www.expatworld.net). 'The newsletter of international living.' Contains a wealth of information for American and British expatriates, including a subscription newsletter.

Expatriate Experts (💻 www.expatexpert.com). A website run by expatriate expert Robin Pascoe, providing invaluable advice and support.

Expats International (💻 www.expats2000.com). The international job centre for expats and their recruiters.

Real Post Reports (💻 www.realpostreports.com). Provides relocation services, recommended reading lists and plenty of interesting 'real-life' stories containing anecdotes and impressions written by expatriates in just about every city in the world.

Travel Documents (💻 www.traveldocs.com). Useful information about travel, specific countries and the documents needed to travel.

World Travel Guide (💻 www.wtgonline.com). A general website for world travellers and expatriates.

American Websites

Americans Abroad (💻 www.aca.ch). This website offers advice, information and services to Americans abroad.

US Government Trade (🖥 www.usatrade.gov). A huge website providing a wealth of information principally for Americans planning to trade and invest abroad, but useful for anyone planning a move abroad.

Australian & New Zealand Websites

Australians Abroad (🖥 www.australiansabroad.com). Information for Australians concerning relocating, plus a forum to exchange information and advice.

Southern Cross Group (🖥 www.southern-cross-group.org). A website for Australians and New Zealanders providing information and the exchange of tips.

British Websites

British Expatriates (🖥 www.britishexpat.com). This website keeps British expatriates in touch with events and information about the UK.

Trade Partners (🖥 www.tradepartners.gov.uk). A government-sponsored website whose main aim is to provide trade and investment information on just about every country in the world. Even if you aren't planning to do business abroad, the information is comprehensive and up to date.

Worldwise Directory (🖥 www.suzylamplugh.org/worldwise). This website is run by the Suzy Lamplugh charity for personal safety and provides a useful directory of countries with practical information and special emphasis on safety, particularly for women.

Websites for Women

Family Life Abroad (🖥 www.familylifeabroad.com). A wealth of information and articles on coping with family life abroad.

Foreign Wives Club (🖥 www.foreignwivesclub.com). An online community for women in bicultural marriages.

Third Culture Kids (🖥 www.tckworld.com). A website designed for expatriate children living abroad.

Travel For Kids (🖳 www.travelforkids.com). Advice on travelling with children around the world.

Women of the World (🖳 www.wow-net.org). A website designed for female expats anywhere in the world.

Travel Information & Warnings

The websites listed below provide daily updated information about the political situation and natural disasters around the world, plus general travel and health advice and embassy addresses.

Australian Department of Foreign Affairs and Trade (🖳 www. dfat.gov.au/travel).

British Foreign and Commonwealth Office (🖳 www.fco. gov.uk).

Canadian Department of Foreign Affairs (🖳 www.dfait-maeci.gc.ca). They also publish a useful series of free booklets for Canadians moving abroad.

New Zealand Ministry of Foreign Affairs and Trade (🖳 www. mft.govt.nz).

SaveWealth Travel (🖳 www.save wealth.com/travel/warnings).

The Travel Doctor (🖳 www.tmvc.com.au). Contains a country by country vaccination guide.

US State Government (🖳 www.state.gov/travel). US Government Website.

World Health Organization (🖳 www.who.int).

Appendix D: WEIGHTS & MEASURES

Greece uses the metric system of measurement. Those who are more familiar with the imperial system of measurement will find the tables on the following pages useful. Some comparisons shown are only approximate, but are close enough for most everyday uses. In addition to the variety of measurement systems used, clothes sizes often vary considerably with the manufacturer. The following websites allow you to make instant conversions between different measurement systems: 💻 www.omnis.demon.co.uk and 💻 www.unit-conversion.info.

Women's Clothes

Continental	34	36	38	40	42	44	46	48	50	52
UK	8	10	12	14	16	18	20	22	24	26
US	6	8	10	12	14	16	18	20	22	24

Pullovers

	Women's						Men's					
Continental	40	42	44	46	48	50	44	46	48	50	52	54
UK	34	36	38	40	42	44	34	36	38	40	42	44
US	34	36	38	40	42	44	sm	med		lar	xl	

Men's Shirts

Continental	36	37	38	39	40	41	42	43	44	46
UK/US	14	14	15	15	16	16	17	17	18	-

Men's Underwear

Continental	5	6	7	8	9	10
UK	34	36	38	40	42	44
US	sm		med		lar	xl

Note: sm = small, med = medium, lar = large, xl = extra large

Children's Clothes

Continental	92	104	116	128	140	152
UK	16/18	20/22	24/26	28/30	32/34	36/38
US	2	4	6	8	10	12

Children's Shoes

Continental	18 19 20 21 22 23 24 25 26 27 28 29 30 31 32
UK/US	2 3 4 4 5 6 7 7 8 9 10 11 11 12 13
Continental	33 34 35 36 37 38
UK/US	1 2 2 3 4 5

Shoes (Women's and Men's)

Continental	35 36 37 37 38 39 40 41 42 42 43 44
UK	2 3 3 4 4 5 6 7 7 8 9 9
US	4 5 5 6 6 7 8 9 9 10 10 11

Weight

Imperial	Metric	Metric	Imperial
1oz	28.35g	1g	0.035oz
1lb*	454g	100g	3.5oz
1cwt	50.8kg	250g	9oz
1 ton	1,016kg	500g	18oz
2,205lb	1 tonne	1kg	2.2lb

Length

Imperial	Metric	Metric	Imperial
1in	2.54cm	1cm	0.39in
1ft	30.48cm	1m	3ft 3.25in
1yd	91.44cm	1km	0.62mi
1mi	1.6km	8km	5mi

Capacity

Imperial	Metric	Metric	Imperial
1 UK pint	0.57 litre	1 litre	1.75 UK pints
1 US pint	0.47 litre	1 litre	2.13 US pints
1 UK gallon	4.54 litres	1 litre	0.22 UK gallon
1 US gallon	3.78 litres	1 litre	0.26 US gallon

Note: An American 'cup' = around 250ml or 0.25 litre.

Area

Imperial	Metric	Metric	Imperial
1 sq. in	0.45 sq. cm	1 sq. cm	0.15 sq. in
1 sq. ft	0.09 sq. m	1 sq. m	10.76 sq. ft
1 sq. yd	0.84 sq. m	1 sq. m	1.2 sq. yds
1 acre	0.4 hectares	1 hectare	2.47 acres
1 sq. mile	2.56 sq. km	1 sq. km	0.39 sq. mile

Temperature

°Celsius	°Fahrenheit	
0	32	(freezing point of water)
5	41	
10	50	
15	59	
20	68	
25	77	
30	86	
35	95	
40	104	
50	122	

Notes: The boiling point of water is 100°C / 212°F.

Normal body temperature (if you're alive and well) is 37°C / 98.6°F.

Temperature Conversion

Celsius to Fahrenheit: multiply by 9, divide by 5 and add 32. (For a quick and approximate conversion, double the Celsius temperature and add 30.)

Fahrenheit to Celsius: subtract 32, multiply by 5 and divide by 9. (For a quick and approximate conversion, subtract 30 from the Fahrenheit temperature and divide by 2.)

Oven Temperatures

Gas	Electric	
	°F	°C
-	225–250	110–120
1	275	140
2	300	150
3	325	160
4	350	180
5	375	190
6	400	200
7	425	220
8	450	230
9	475	240

Air Pressure

PSI	Bar
10	0.5
20	1.4
30	2
40	2.8

Power

Kilowatts	Horsepower	Horsepower	Kilowatts
1	1.34	1	0.75

APPENDIX E: MAPS

The map of Greece opposite shows the regions of Greece (listed below). A map showing major towns and geographical features is on page 6. The maps on the following pages show ferry routes, the road and rail networks, and airports with scheduled services from the UK (see **Appendix F**).

Attica (including Athens)
Central Greece (Stereá Ellhada and Thessaly)
Crete
Cyclades Islands
Dodecanese Islands
Epirus and the West
Evia and the Sporades
Ionian Islands
North-Eastern Aegean Islands
Northern Greece (Macedonia and Thrace)
Peloponnese
Saronic Gulf Islands

REGIONS

FERRIES

Road & Rail Network

AIRPORTS

APPENDIX F: AIRLINE SERVICES

The tables on the following pages indicate flights operating from UK airports to Greece in January 2005. Airlines are coded as shown below (note that these aren't all official airline codes). All telephone number are UK numbers. **Note that Air2000, Excel Airways and Thomas Cook flights are charter flights that generally operate only from April/May to October.**

Code	Airline	Telephone	Website
A2	Air2000	0870-850 3999	www.firstchoice.co.uk
AS	Air Scotland	0141-222 2363	www-air-scotland.com
BA	British Airways	0870-850 9850	ww.britishairways.com
EJ	EasyJet	0871-750 0100	www.easyjet.com
EX	Excel Airways	0870-169 0169	www.excelairways.co.uk
GB	GB Airways	0870-850 9850	www.gbairways.com
HJ	Hellas Jet	0870-750 8202	www.hellas-jet.com
OA	Olympic Airways	0870-606 0460	www.olympicairways.co.uk
TC	Thomas Cook	0870-752 0918	www.flythomascook.com

	Belfast International	Birmingham	Bristol	Cardiff	Exeter	Glasgow Prestwick	Leeds/Bradford	Liverpool
Athens						AS		
Corfu		A2 TC	A2	A2		A2 EX TC	A2	A2
Heraklion	A2 EX	A2 TC	A2			A2 EX TC		
Kefallonia		A2	A2			A2 TC		
Kos		A2	A2			A2 TC		
Rhodes		A2 TC	A2	A2	A2	A2 EX		
Thessaloniki		A2 TC				EX		
Zakynthos		A2 TC	A2			A2 EX TC		

	London Gatwick	London Heathrow	London Luton	London Stansted	Manchester	Newcastle	Norwich	Nottingham/East Midlands
Athens	EJ EX HJ OA	BA HJ OA	EJ		EX HJ OA			
Corfu	A2 EX TC		A2 TC	A2	A2 EX TC	A2 TC	A2	A2 TC
Heraklion	A2 EX GB TC		TC	A2 TC	A2 EX TC	A2 TC		A2
Kalamata	A2				A2	A2		
Kefallonia	A2 EX TC		A2		A2 EX TC			
Kos	A2 EX TC			TC	A2 EX TC	A2		A2
Mykonos	EX				EX			
Preveza	A2 EX				A2 EX			
Rhodes	A2 EX TC				A2 EX TC	EX TC		A2
Samos	EX TC				EX TC			
Santorini	A2 EX				A2 EX	EX		
Skiathos	A2 EX TC				A2 EX TC			
Thessaloniki	A2 EX TC				A2 EX TC	EX		
Zakynthos	A2 EX TC		TC	A2 TC	A2 EX TC	A2 EX TC		A2 TC

INDEX

M

LIVING AND WORKING SERIES

Living and Working books are essential reading for anyone planning to spend time abroad, including holiday-home owners, retirees, visitors, business people, migrants, students and even extra-terrestrials! They're packed with important and useful information designed to help you **avoid costly mistakes and save both time and money.** Topics covered include how to:

- Find a job with a good salary & conditions
- Obtain a residence permit
- Avoid and overcome problems
- Find your dream home
- Get the best education for your family
- Make the best use of public transport
- Endure local motoring habits
- Obtain the best health treatment
- Stretch your money further
- Make the most of your leisure time
- Enjoy the local sporting life
- Find the best shopping bargains
- Insure yourself against most eventualities
- Use post office and telephone services
- Do numerous other things not listed above

Living and Working books are the most comprehensive and up-to-date source of practical information available about everyday life abroad. They aren't, however, boring text books, but interesting and entertaining guides written in a highly readable style.

Discover what it's really like to live and work abroad!

Order your copies today by phone, fax, post or email from: Survival Books, PO Box 3780, YEOVIL, BA21 5WX, United Kingdom (☎/🖩 +44 (0)1935-700060, ✉ sales@survivalbooks.net, 🖥 www.survivalbooks.net).

BUYING A HOME SERIES

Buying a Home books, including *Buying, Selling & Letting Property*, are essential reading for anyone planning to purchase property abroad. They're packed with vital information to guide you through the property purchase jungle and help you **avoid the sort of disasters that can turn your dream home into a nightmare!** Topics covered include:

- Avoiding problems
- Choosing the region
- Finding the right home and location
- Estate agents
- Finance, mortgages and taxes
- Home security
- Utilities, heating and air-conditioning
- Moving house and settling in
- Renting and letting
- Permits and visas
- Travelling and communications
- Health and insurance
- Renting a car and driving
- Retirement and starting a business
- And much, much more!

Buying a Home books are the most comprehensive and up-to-date source of information available about buying property abroad. Whether you want a detached house, townhouse or apartment, a holiday or a permanent home, these books will help make your dreams come true.

Save yourself time, trouble and money!

Order your copies today by phone, fax, post or email from: Survival Books, PO Box 3780, YEOVIL, BA21 5WX, United Kingdom (☎/▤ +44 (0)1935-700060, ✉ sales@survivalbooks.net, 💻 www.survivalbooks.net).

OTHER SURVIVAL BOOKS

The Alien's Guides: *The Alien's Guides to Britain and France* provide an 'alternative' look at life in these popular countries and will help you to appreciate the peculiarities (in both senses) of the British and French.

The Best Places to Buy a Home in France/Spain: The most comprehensive homebuying guides to France or Spain, containing detailed profiles of the most popular regions, with guides to property prices, amenities and services, employment and planned developments.

Buying, Selling and Letting Property: The most comprehensive and up-to-date source of information available for those intending to buy, sell or let a property in the UK.

Foreigners in France/Spain: Triumphs & Disasters: Real-life experiences of people who have emigrated to France and Spain, recounted in their own words – warts and all!

Lifelines: Essential guides to specific regions of France and Spain, containing everything you need to know about local life. Titles in the series currently include the Costa Blanca, Costa del Sol, Dordogne/Lot, Normandy and Poitou-Charentes; Brittany Lifeline is to be published in summer 2005.

Renovating & Maintaining Your French Home: The ultimate guide to renovating and maintaining your dream home in France: what to do and what not to do, how to do it and, most importantly, how much it will cost.

Retiring Abroad: The most comprehensive and up-to-date source of practical information available about retiring to a foreign country, containing profiles of the 20 most popular retirement destinations.

Broaden your horizons with Survival Books!

Order your copies today by phone, fax, post or email from: Survival Books, PO Box 3780, YEOVIL, BA21 5WX, United Kingdom (☎/▤ +44 (0)1935-700060, ✉ sales@survivalbooks.net, 🖥 www.survivalbooks.net).

ORDER FORM

Qty.	Title	UK	Europe	World	Total
	The Alien's Guide to Britain	£6.95	£8.95	£12.45	
	The Alien's Guide to France	£6.95	£8.95	£12.45	
	The Best Places to Buy a Home in France	£13.95	£15.95	£19.45	
	The Best Places to Buy a Home in Spain	£13.95	£15.95	£19.45	
	Buying a Home Abroad	£13.95	£15.95	£19.45	
	Buying a Home in Florida	£13.95	£15.95	£19.45	
	Buying a Home in France	£13.95	£15.95	£19.45	
	Buying a Home in Greece & Cyprus	£13.95	£15.95	£19.45	
	Buying a Home in Ireland	£11.95	£13.95	£17.45	
	Buying a Home in Italy	£13.95	£15.95	£19.45	
	Buying a Home in Portugal	£13.95	£15.95	£19.45	
	Buying a Home in South Africa	£13.95	£15.95	£19.45	
	Buying a Home in Spain	£13.95	£15.95	£19.45	
	Buying, Letting & Selling Property	£11.95	£13.95	£17.45	
	Foreigners in France: Triumphs & Disasters	£11.95	£13.95	£17.45	
	Foreigners in Spain: Triumphs & Disasters	£11.95	£13.95	£17.45	
	Costa Blanca Lifeline	£11.95	£13.95	£17.45	
	Costa del Sol Lifeline	£11.95	£13.95	£17.45	
	Dordogne/Lot Lifeline	£11.95	£13.95	£17.45	
	Poitou-Charentes Lifeline	£11.95	£13.95	£17.45	
	Living & Working Abroad	£14.95	£16.95	£20.45	
	Living & Working in America	£14.95	£16.95	£20.45	
	Living & Working in Australia	£14.95	£16.95	£20.45	
	Living & Working in Britain	£14.95	£16.95	£20.45	
	Living & Working in Canada	£16.95	£18.95	£22.45	
	Living & Working in the European Union	£16.95	£18.95	£22.45	
	Living & Working in the Far East	£16.95	£18.95	£22.45	
	Living & Working in France	£14.95	£16.95	£20.45	
	Living & Working in Germany	£16.95	£18.95	£22.45	
Total carried forward (see over)					

ORDER FORM

Qty.	Title	Price (incl. p&p) UK	Europe	World	Total
			Total brought forward		
	L&W in the Gulf States & Saudi Arabia	£16.95	£18.95	£22.45	
	L&W in Holland, Belgium & Luxembourg	£14.95	£16.95	£20.45	
	Living & Working in Ireland	£14.95	£16.95	£20.45	
	Living & Working in Italy	£16.95	£18.95	£22.45	
	Living & Working in London	£13.95	£15.95	£19.45	
	Living & Working in New Zealand	£14.95	£16.95	£20.45	
	Living & Working in Spain	£14.95	£16.95	£20.45	
	Living & Working in Switzerland	£16.95	£18.95	£22.45	
	Normandy Lifeline	£11.95	£13.95	£17.45	
	Renovating & Maintaining Your French Home	£16.95	£18.95	£22.45	
	Retiring Abroad	£14.95	£16.95	£20.45	
	Grand Total				

Order your copies today by phone, fax, post or email from: Survival Books, PO Box 3780, YEOVIL, BA21 5WX, United Kingdom (☎/▤ +44 (0)1935-700060, ✉ sales@ survivalbooks.net, 🖥 www.survivalbooks.net). If you aren't entirely satisfied, simply return them to us within 14 days for a full and unconditional refund.

I enclose a cheque for the grand total/Please charge my Amex/Delta/Maestro (Switch)/MasterCard/Visa card as follows. (delete as applicable)

Card No. _ _ _ _   _ _ _ _   _ _ _ _   _ _ _ _   Security Code* _ _ _

Expiry date _____ Issue number (Maestro/Switch only) _____

Signature _____ Tel. No. _____

NAME _____

ADDRESS _____

_____

_____

* The security code is the last three digits on the signature strip.

NOTES

NOTES